INOUE PRESENTS

THE DUKE OF DEATH ... D

4

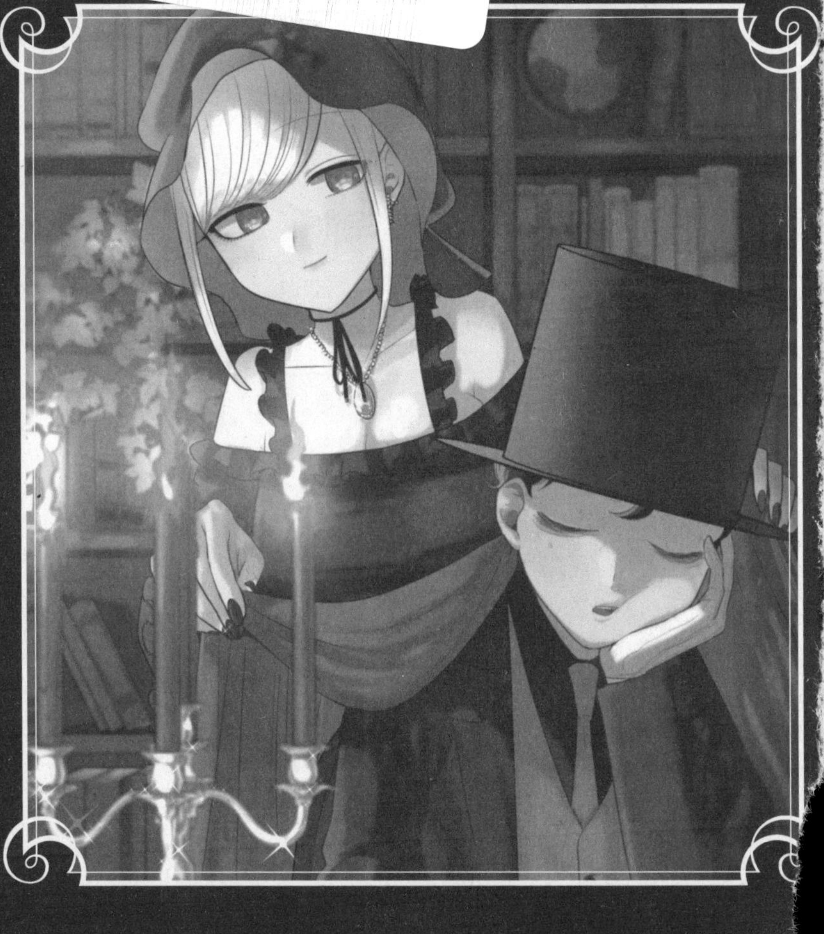

CONTENTS

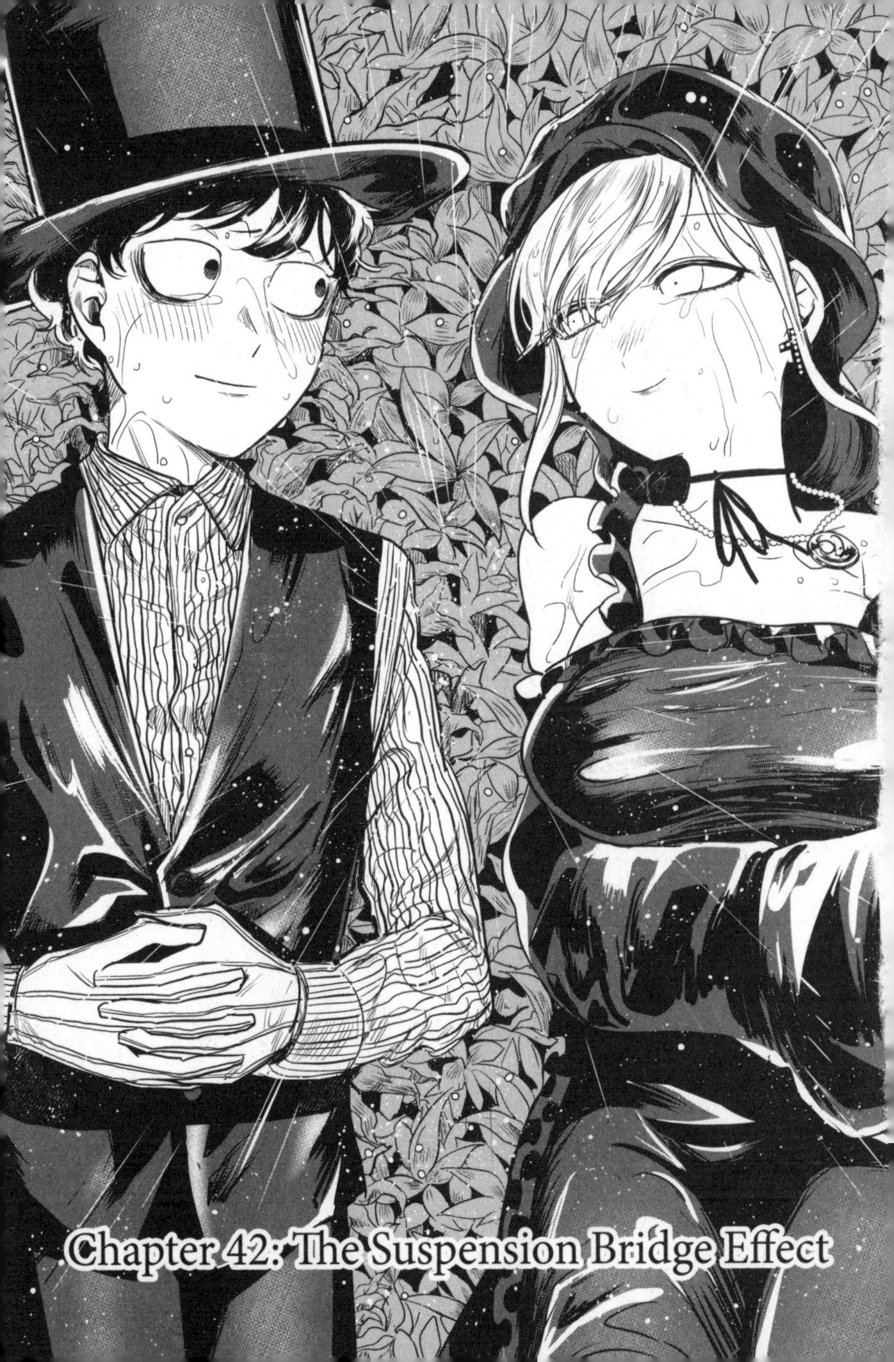
Chapter 42: The Suspension Bridge Effect

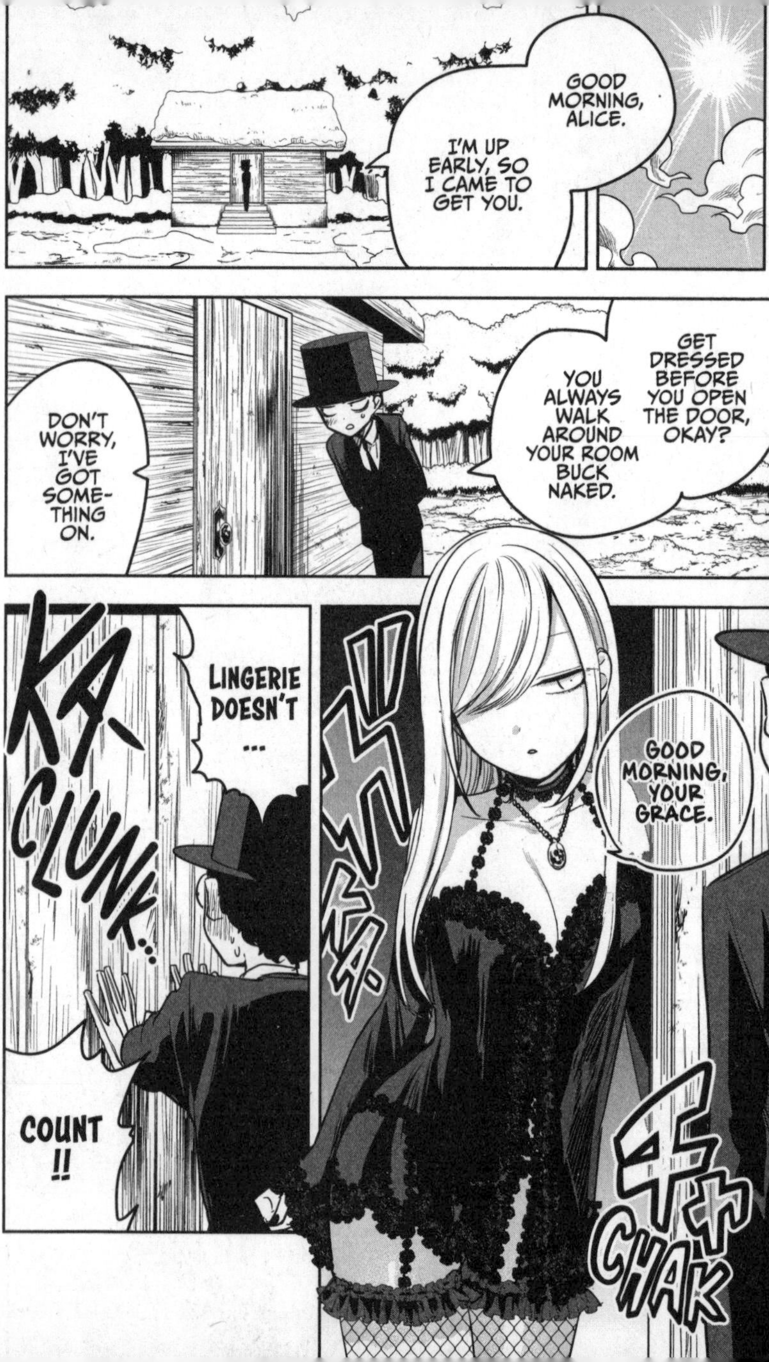
GOOD MORNING, ALICE.
I'M UP EARLY, SO I CAME TO GET YOU.
GET DRESSED BEFORE YOU OPEN THE DOOR, OKAY?
YOU ALWAYS WALK AROUND YOUR ROOM BUCK NAKED.
DON'T WORRY, I'VE GOT SOME-THING ON.
CHAK
GOOD MORNING, YOUR GRACE.
KA-CLUNK...
LINGERIE DOESN'T ...
COUNT !!

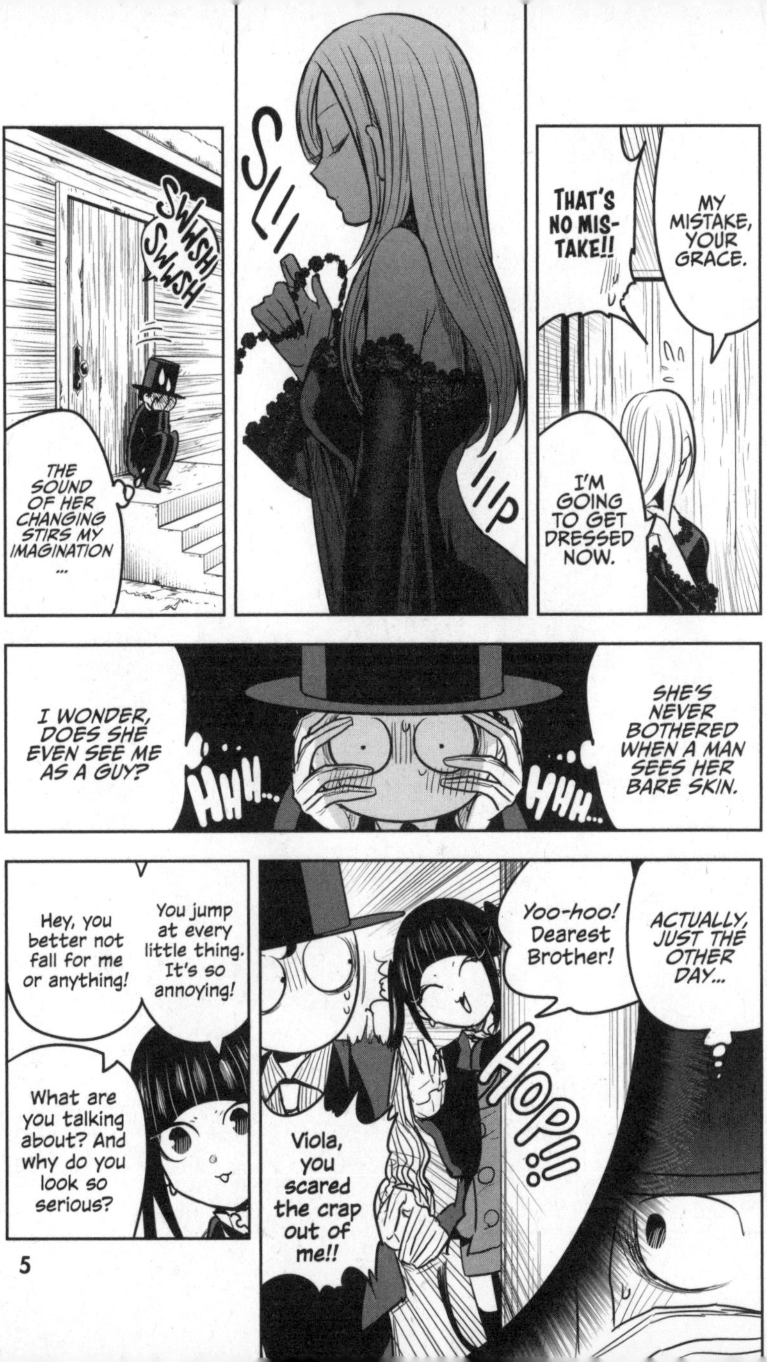
MY MISTAKE, YOUR GRACE.
THAT'S NO MIS-TAKE!!
I'M GOING TO GET DRESSED NOW.
SLIIIP
SWWSH SWWSH
THE SOUND OF HER CHANGING STIRS MY IMAGINATION...
SHE'S NEVER BOTHERED WHEN A MAN SEES HER BARE SKIN.
HHH...
I WONDER, DOES SHE EVEN SEE ME AS A GUY?
HHH...
ACTUALLY, JUST THE OTHER DAY...
Yoo-hoo! Dearest Brother!
HOP!!!
Viola, you scared the crap out of me!!
You jump at every little thing. It's so annoying!
Hey, you better not fall for me or anything!
What are you talking about? And why do you look so serious?

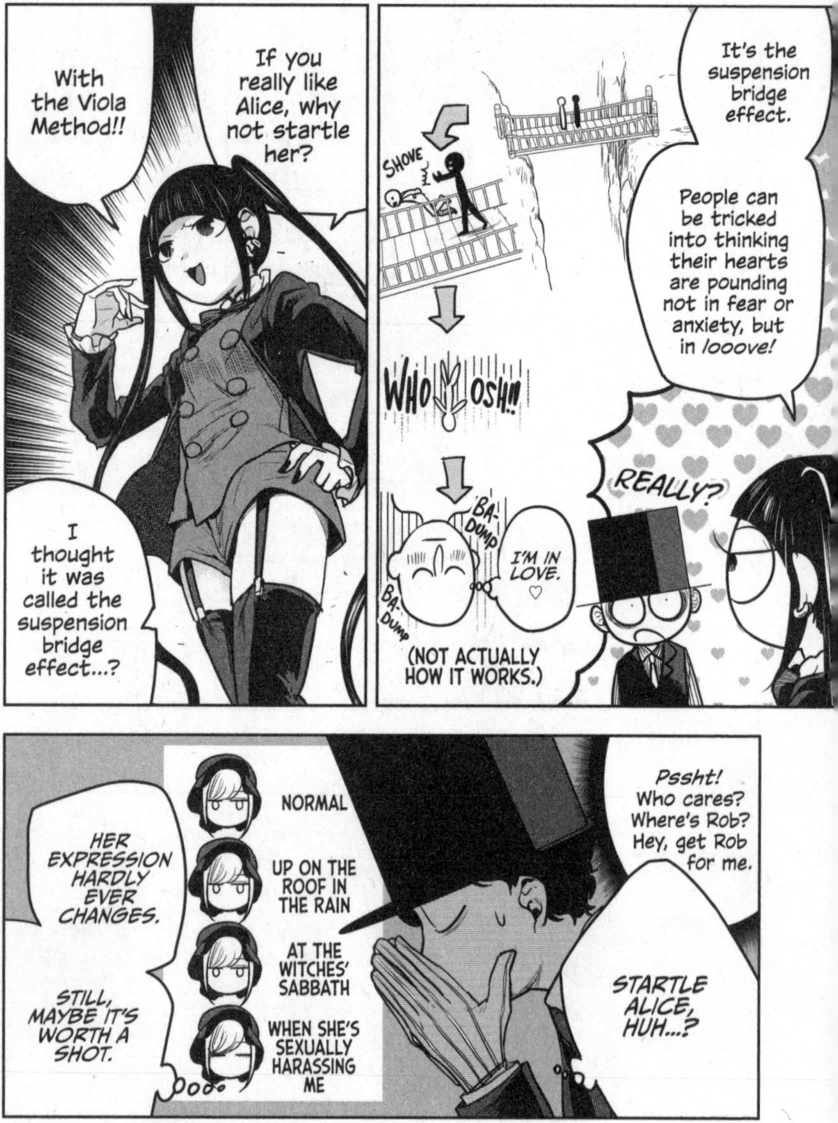
It's the suspension bridge effect.
People can be tricked into thinking their hearts are pounding not in fear or anxiety, but in *looove!*
SHOVE
WHOOSH!!
BA-DUMP
I'M IN LOVE. ♡
BA-DUMP
(NOT ACTUALLY HOW IT WORKS.)
REALLY?
If you really like Alice, why not startle her?
With the Viola Method!!
I thought it was called the suspension bridge effect...?
Psssht! Who cares? Where's Rob? Hey, get Rob for me.
STARTLE ALICE, HUH...?
HER EXPRESSION HARDLY EVER CHANGES.
NORMAL
UP ON THE ROOF IN THE RAIN
AT THE WITCHES' SABBATH
WHEN SHE'S SEXUALLY HARASSING ME
STILL, MAYBE IT'S WORTH A SHOT.

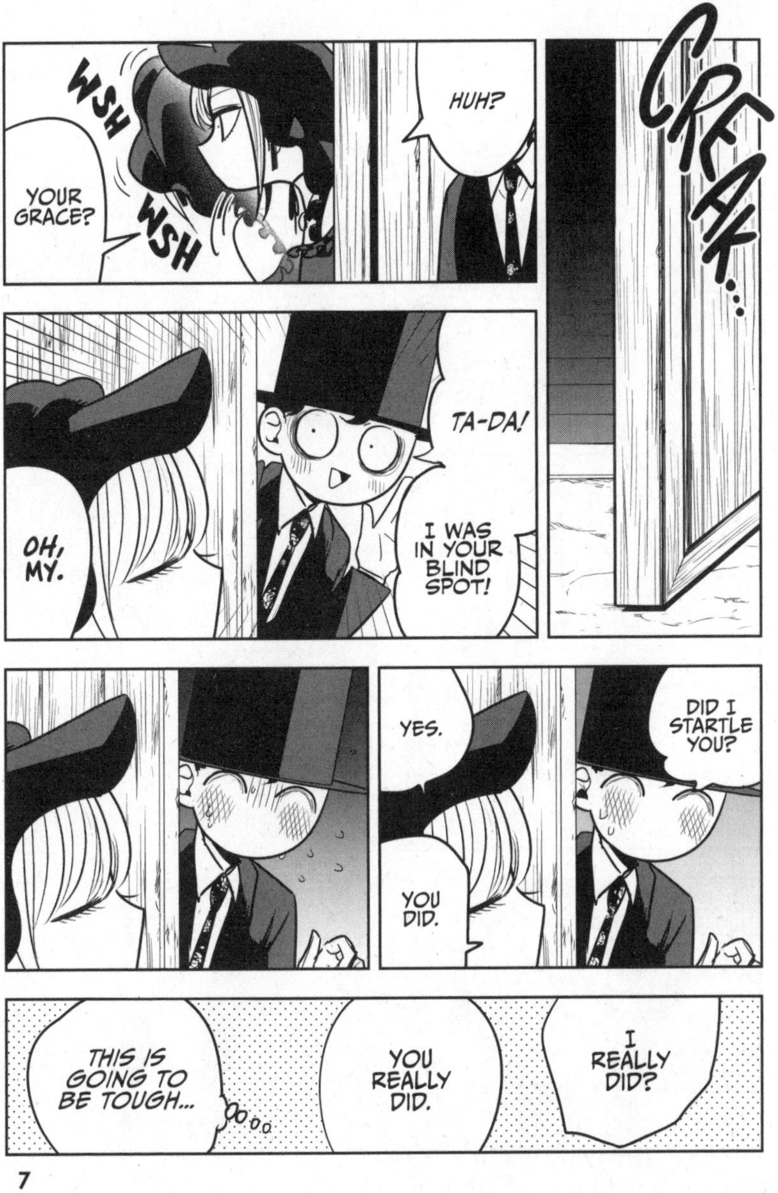
CREAK...
HUH?
WSH
WSH
YOUR GRACE?
TA-DA!
I WAS IN YOUR BLIND SPOT!
OH, MY.
DID I STARTLE YOU?
YES.
YOU DID.
I REALLY DID?
YOU REALLY DID.
THIS IS GOING TO BE TOUGH...

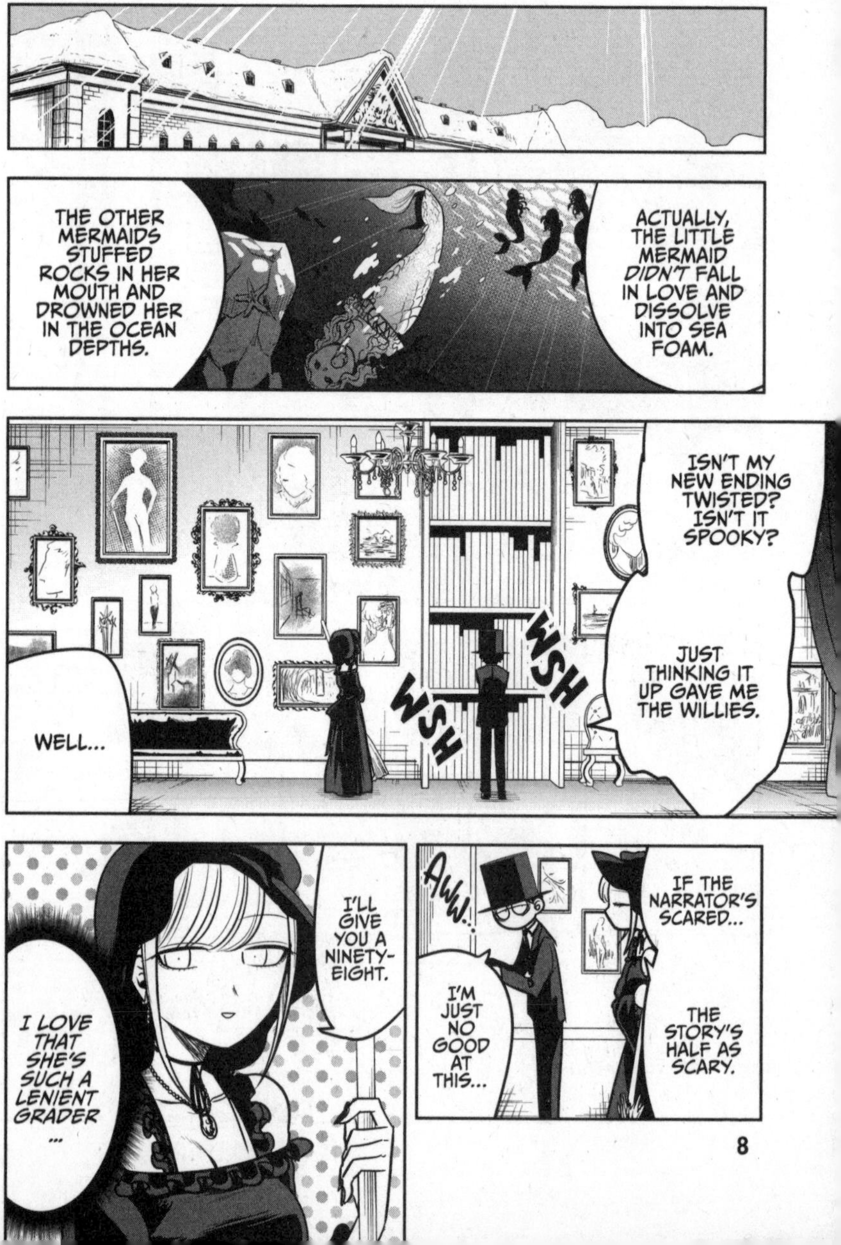
ACTUALLY, THE LITTLE MERMAID DIDN'T FALL IN LOVE AND DISSOLVE INTO SEA FOAM.
THE OTHER MERMAIDS STUFFED ROCKS IN HER MOUTH AND DROWNED HER IN THE OCEAN DEPTHS.
ISN'T MY NEW ENDING TWISTED? ISN'T IT SPOOKY?
JUST THINKING IT UP GAVE ME THE WILLIES.
WSH
WSH
WELL...
IF THE NARRATOR'S SCARED...
THE STORY'S HALF AS SCARY.
AWW...
I'M JUST NO GOOD AT THIS...
I'LL GIVE YOU A NINETY-EIGHT.
I LOVE THAT SHE'S SUCH A LENIENT GRADER...

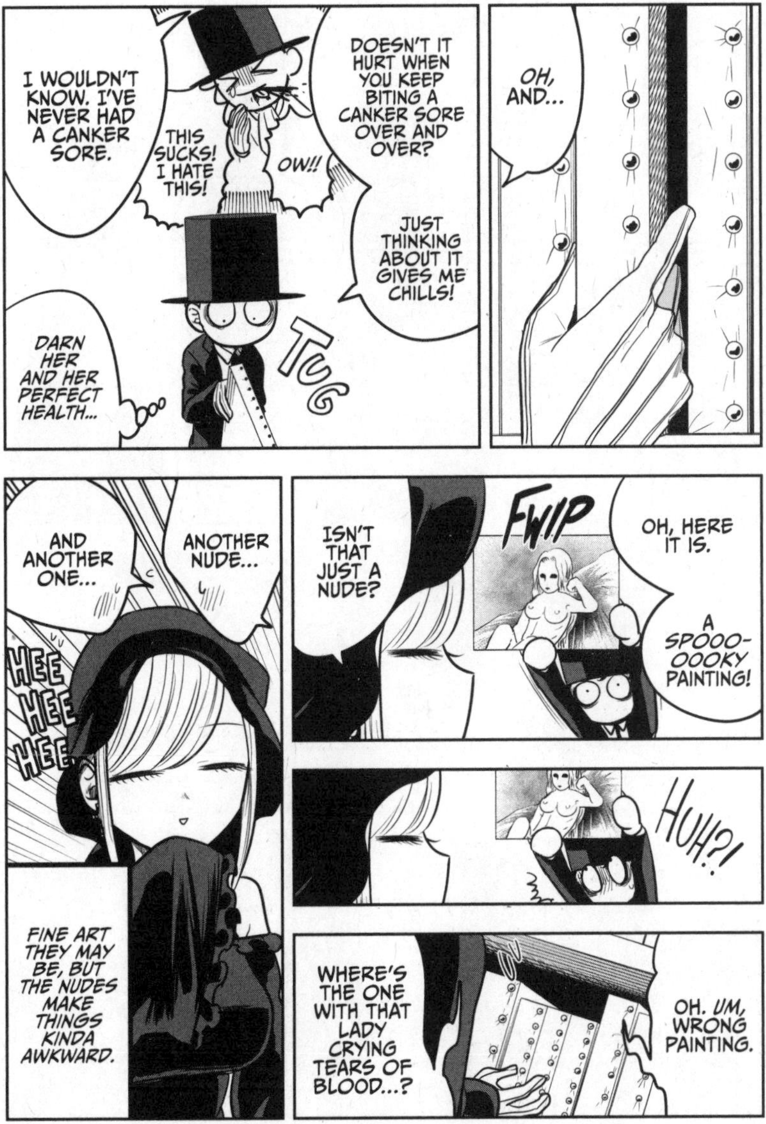
OH, AND...
DOESN'T IT HURT WHEN YOU KEEP BITING A CANKER SORE OVER AND OVER?
OW!!
THIS SUCKS! I HATE THIS!
I WOULDN'T KNOW. I'VE NEVER HAD A CANKER SORE.
JUST THINKING ABOUT IT GIVES ME CHILLS!
TUG
DARN HER AND HER PERFECT HEALTH...
OH, HERE IT IS.
FWIP
A SPOOO-OOOKY PAINTING!
ISN'T THAT JUST A NUDE?
HUH?!
OH. UM, WRONG PAINTING.
WHERE'S THE ONE WITH THAT LADY CRYING TEARS OF BLOOD...?
ANOTHER NUDE...
AND ANOTHER ONE...
HEE HEE HEE
FINE ART THEY MAY BE, BUT THE NUDES MAKE THINGS KINDA AWKWARD.

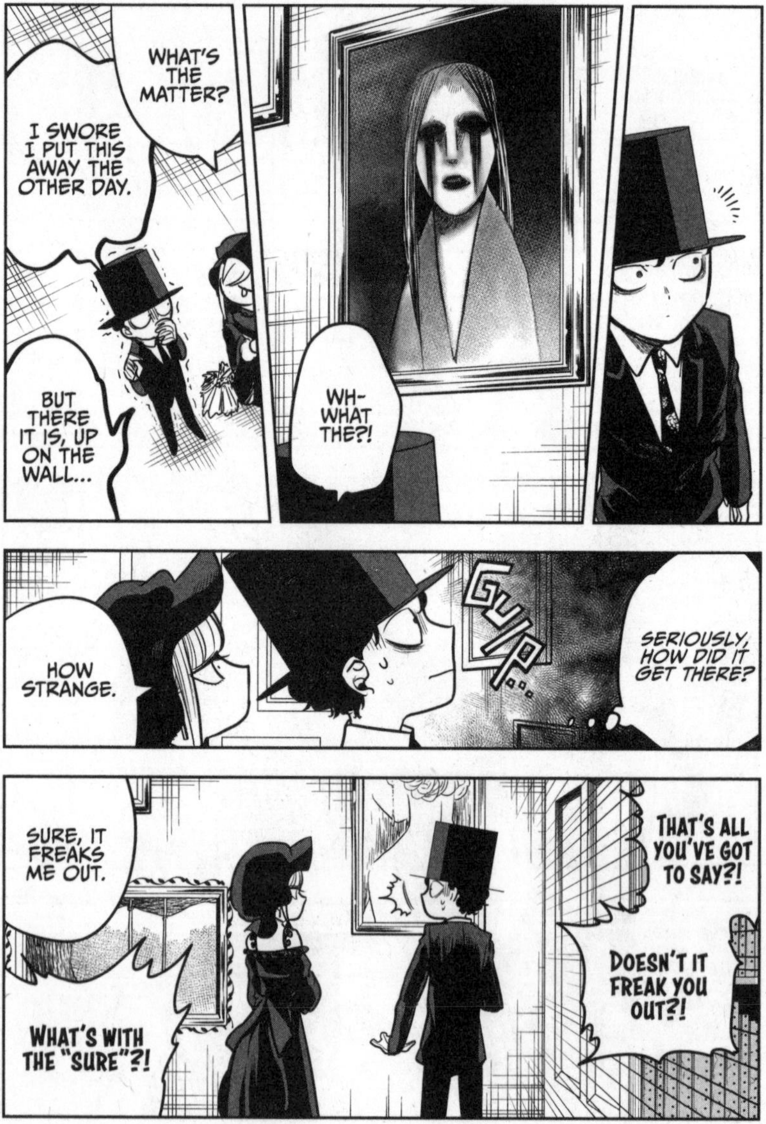
WH-WHAT THE?!
WHAT'S THE MATTER?
I SWORE I PUT THIS AWAY THE OTHER DAY.
BUT THERE IT IS, UP ON THE WALL...
SERIOUSLY, HOW DID IT GET THERE?
GULP...
HOW STRANGE.
THAT'S ALL YOU'VE GOT TO SAY?!
DOESN'T IT FREAK YOU OUT?!
SURE, IT FREAKS ME OUT.
WHAT'S WITH THE "SURE"?!

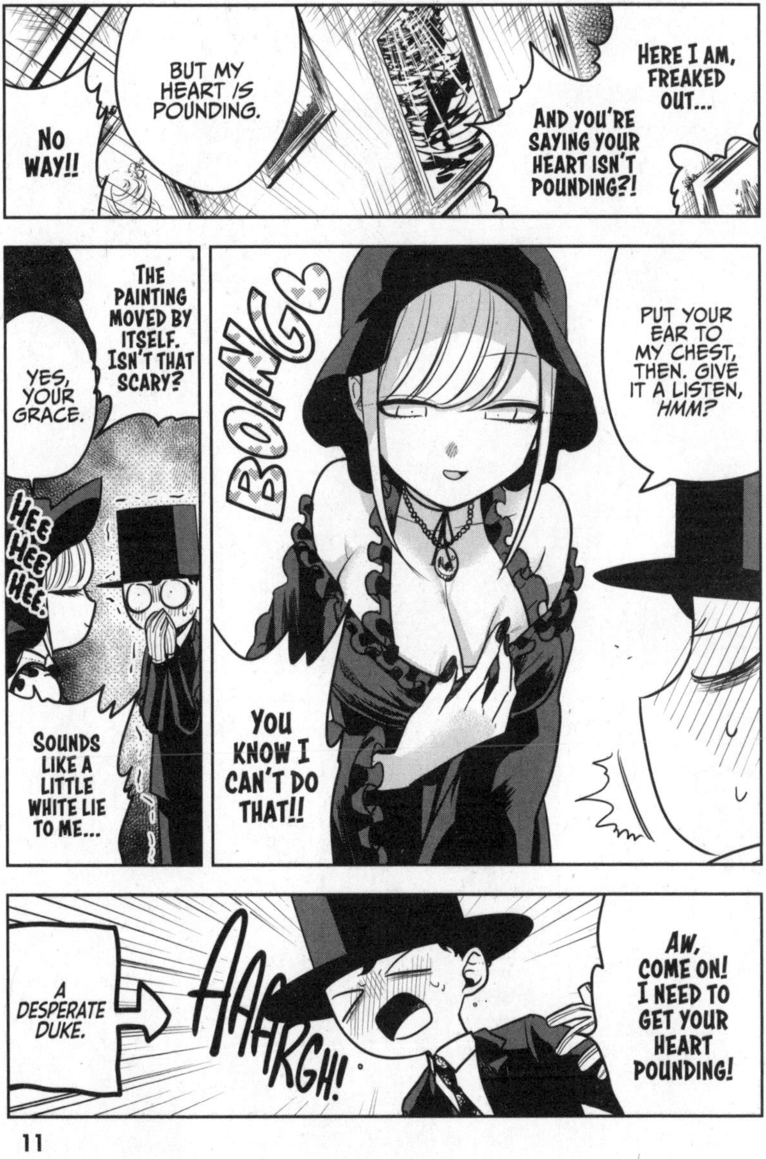
HERE I AM, FREAKED OUT...
AND YOU'RE SAYING YOUR HEART ISN'T POUNDING?!
BUT MY HEART IS POUNDING.
NO WAY!!
PUT YOUR EAR TO MY CHEST, THEN. GIVE IT A LISTEN, HMM?
BOING
YOU KNOW I CAN'T DO THAT!!
THE PAINTING MOVED BY ITSELF. ISN'T THAT SCARY?
YES, YOUR GRACE.
HEE HEE HEE.
SOUNDS LIKE A LITTLE WHITE LIE TO ME...
AW, COME ON! I NEED TO GET YOUR HEART POUNDING!
AAHRGH!
A DESPERATE DUKE.

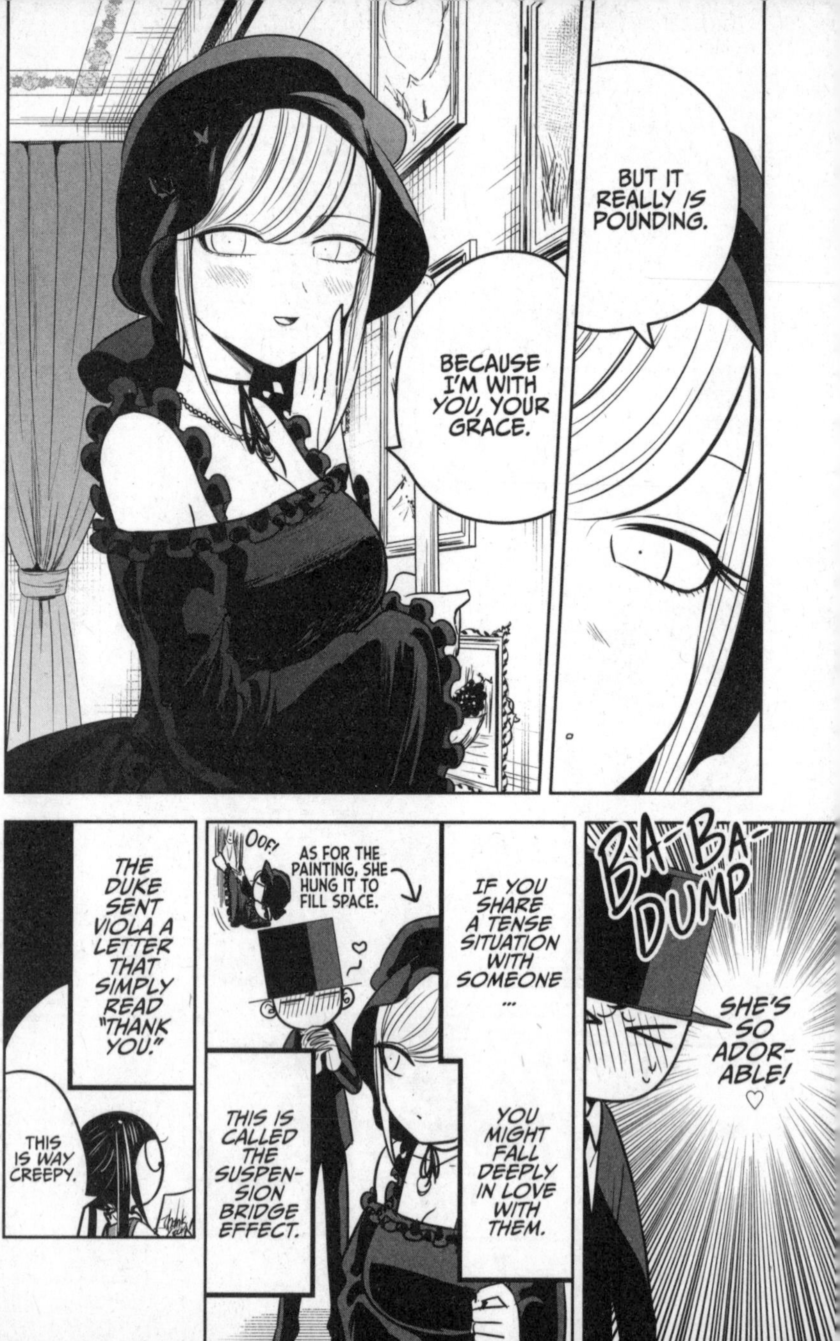
BUT IT REALLY IS POUNDING.
BECAUSE I'M WITH YOU, YOUR GRACE.
BA-BA-DUMP
SHE'S SO ADORABLE! ♡
IF YOU SHARE A TENSE SITUATION WITH SOMEONE ...
YOU MIGHT FALL DEEPLY IN LOVE WITH THEM.
OOF!
AS FOR THE PAINTING, SHE HUNG IT TO FILL SPACE.
THIS IS CALLED THE SUSPENSION BRIDGE EFFECT.
THE DUKE SENT VIOLA A LETTER THAT SIMPLY READ "THANK YOU."
THIS IS WAY CREEPY.

THE DUKE OF DEATH
AND HIS MAID

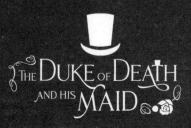

THE DUKE OF DEATH AND HIS MAID

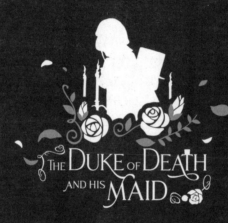

Chapter 43: Recollections Pt. 1

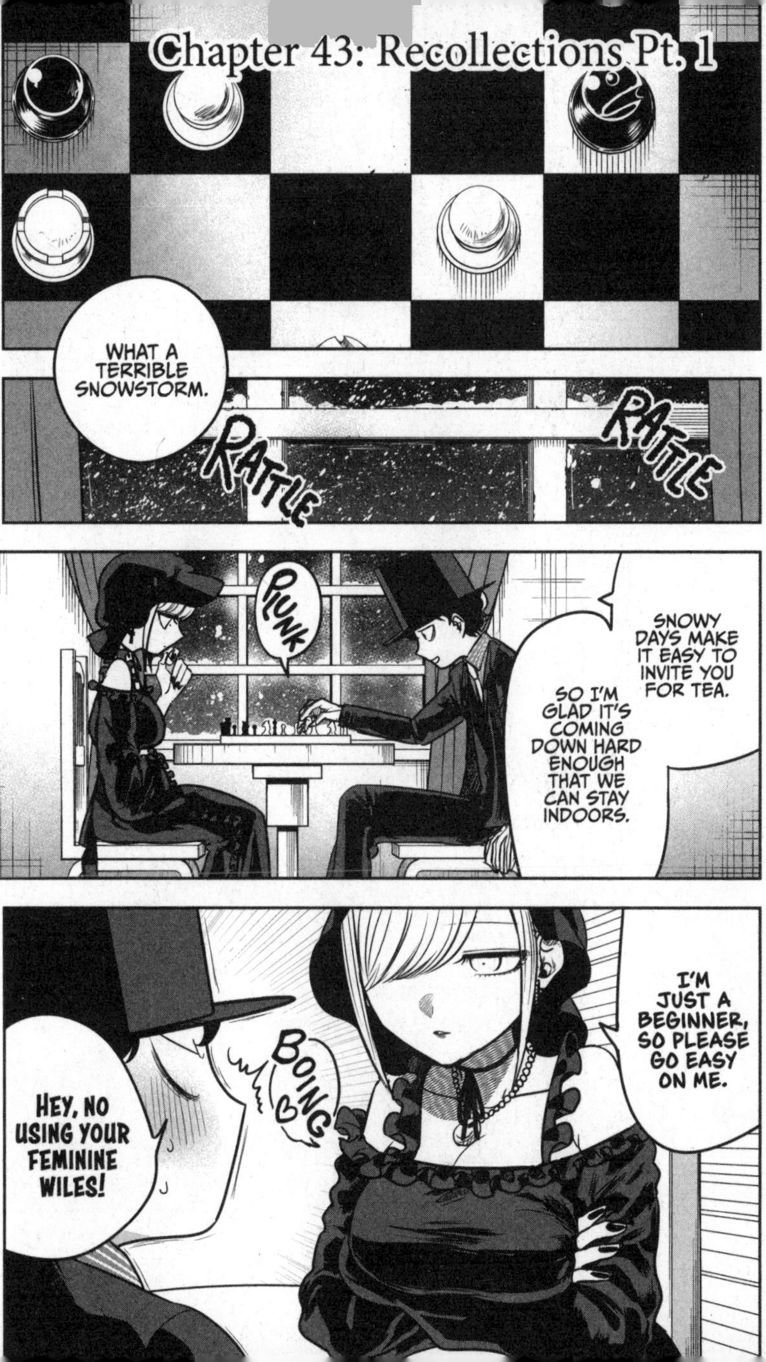
RATTLE
WHAT A TERRIBLE SNOWSTORM.
RATTLE
SNOWY DAYS MAKE IT EASY TO INVITE YOU FOR TEA.
SO I'M GLAD IT'S COMING DOWN HARD ENOUGH THAT WE CAN STAY INDOORS.
PLUNK
I'M JUST A BEGINNER, SO PLEASE GO EASY ON ME.
BOING
HEY, NO USING YOUR FEMININE WILES!

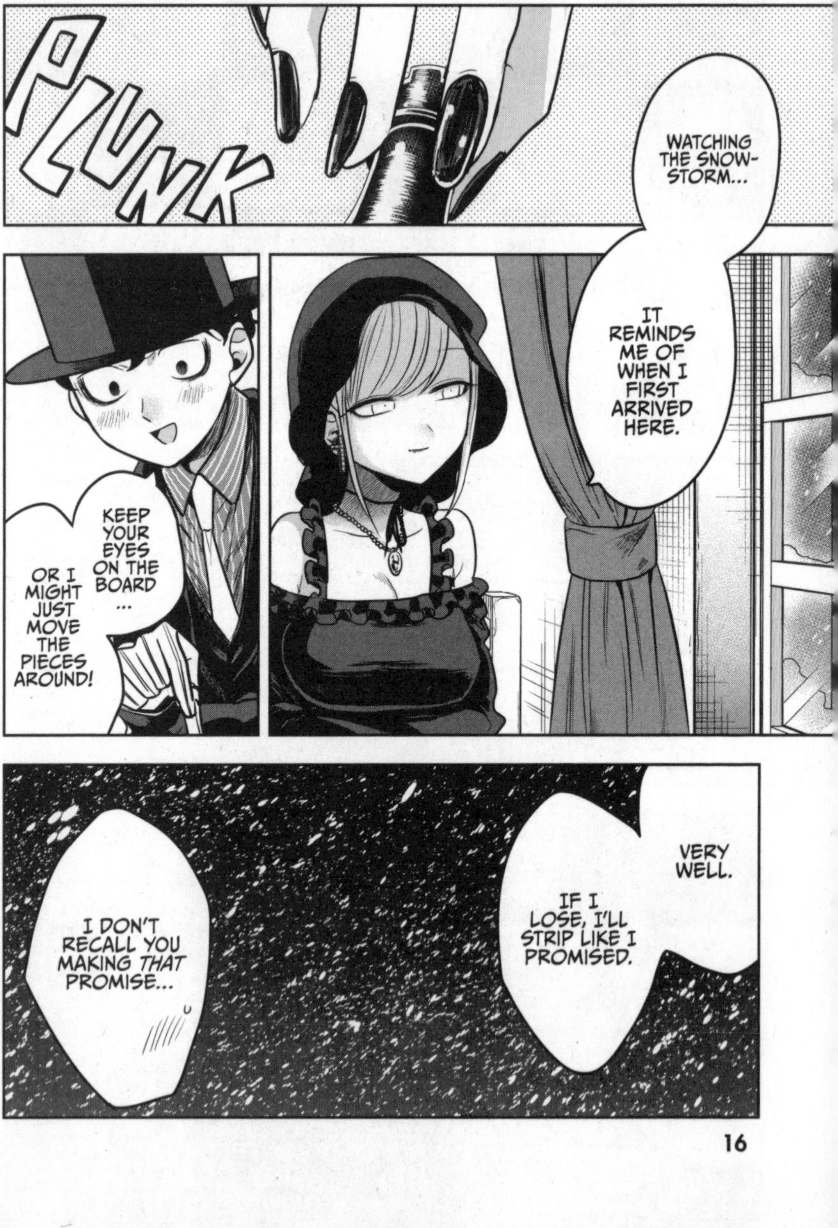
WATCHING THE SNOW-STORM...
PLUNK
IT REMINDS ME OF WHEN I FIRST ARRIVED HERE.
KEEP YOUR EYES ON THE BOARD ...
OR I MIGHT JUST MOVE THE PIECES AROUND!
VERY WELL.
IF I LOSE, I'LL STRIP LIKE I PROMISED.
I DON'T RECALL YOU MAKING *THAT* PROMISE...

Chapter 43:
Recollections Pt. 1

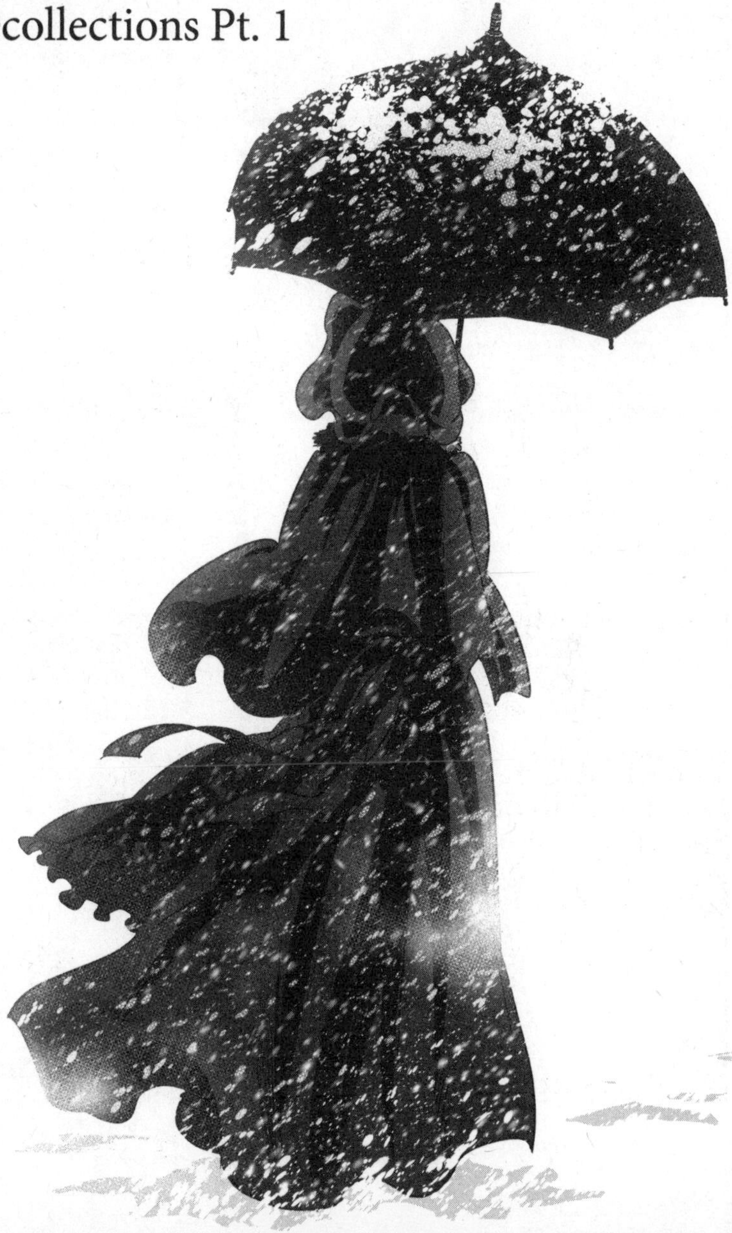

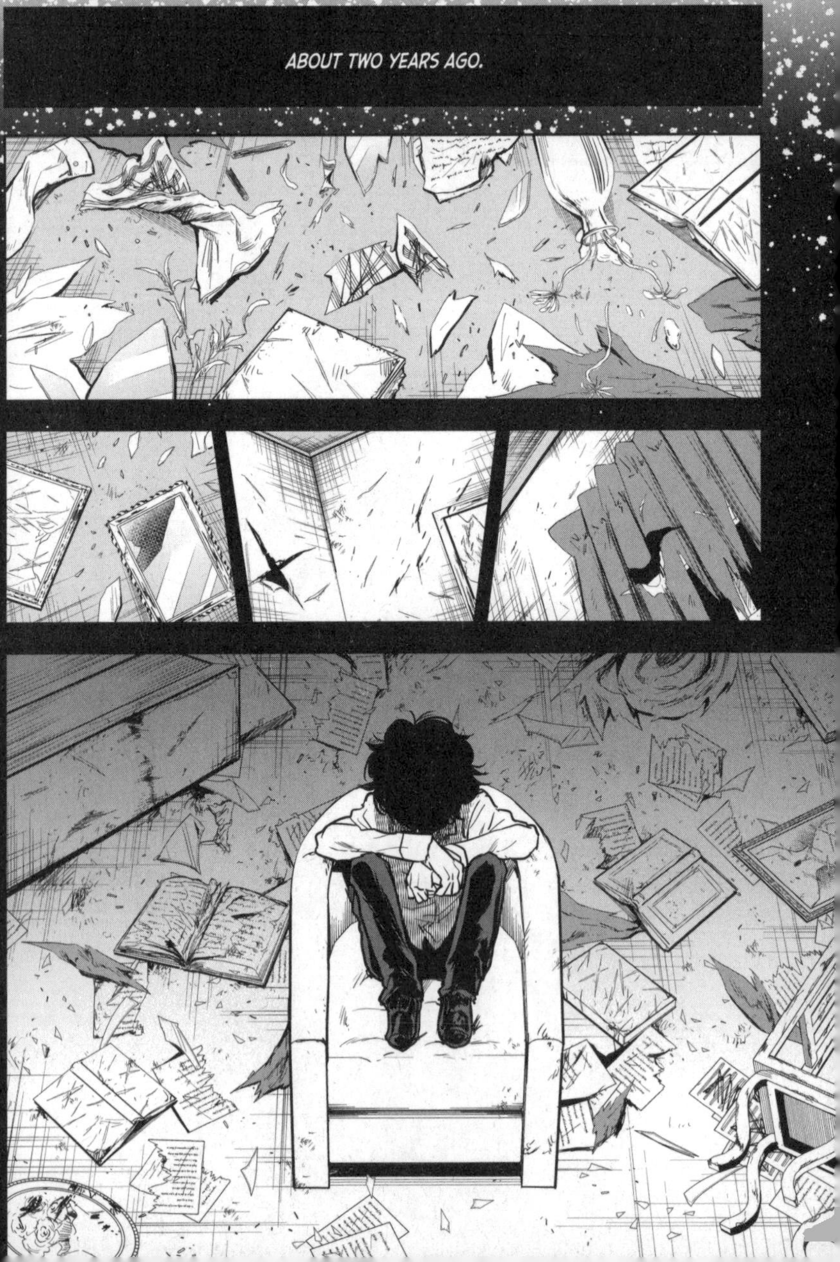
ABOUT TWO YEARS AGO.

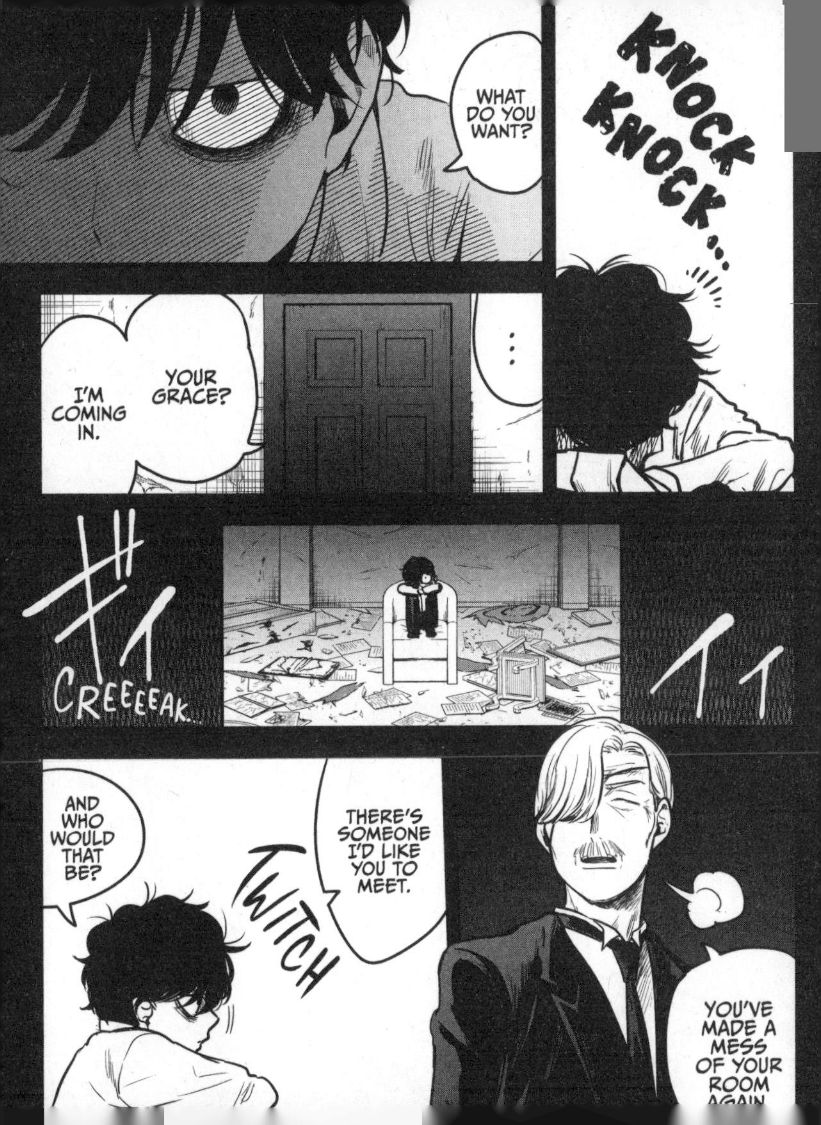

KNOCK KNOCK...
WHAT DO YOU WANT?
...
YOUR GRACE?
I'M COMING IN.
CREEEEAK...
YOU'VE MADE A MESS OF YOUR ROOM AGAIN
THERE'S SOMEONE I'D LIKE YOU TO MEET.
TWITCH
AND WHO WOULD THAT BE?

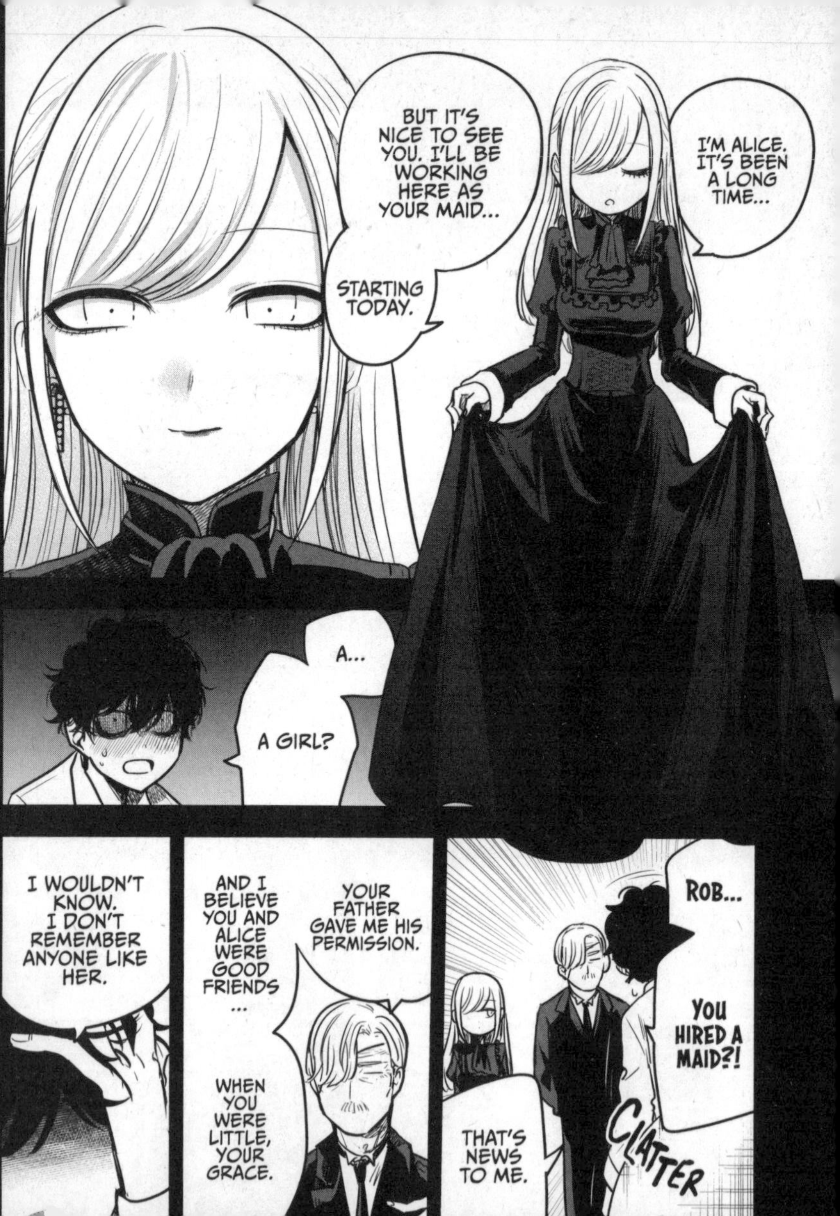
I'M ALICE. IT'S BEEN A LONG TIME...
BUT IT'S NICE TO SEE YOU. I'LL BE WORKING HERE AS YOUR MAID...
STARTING TODAY.
A...
A GIRL?
ROB...
YOU HIRED A MAID?!
CLATTER
THAT'S NEWS TO ME.
YOUR FATHER GAVE ME HIS PERMISSION.
AND I BELIEVE YOU AND ALICE WERE GOOD FRIENDS...
WHEN YOU WERE LITTLE, YOUR GRACE.
I WOULDN'T KNOW. I DON'T REMEMBER ANYONE LIKE HER.

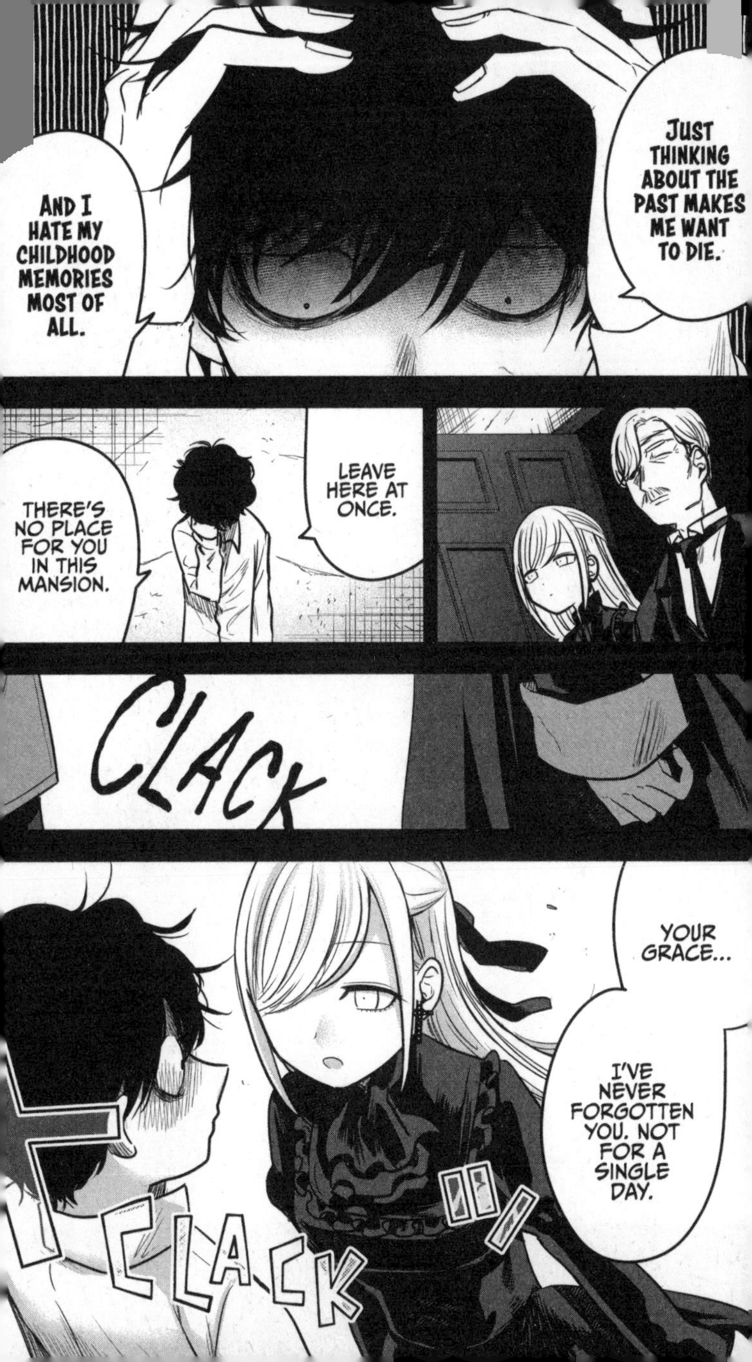
JUST THINKING ABOUT THE PAST MAKES ME WANT TO DIE.
AND I HATE MY CHILDHOOD MEMORIES MOST OF ALL.
LEAVE HERE AT ONCE.
THERE'S NO PLACE FOR YOU IN THIS MANSION.
CLACK
YOUR GRACE...
I'VE NEVER FORGOTTEN YOU. NOT FOR A SINGLE DAY.
CLACK

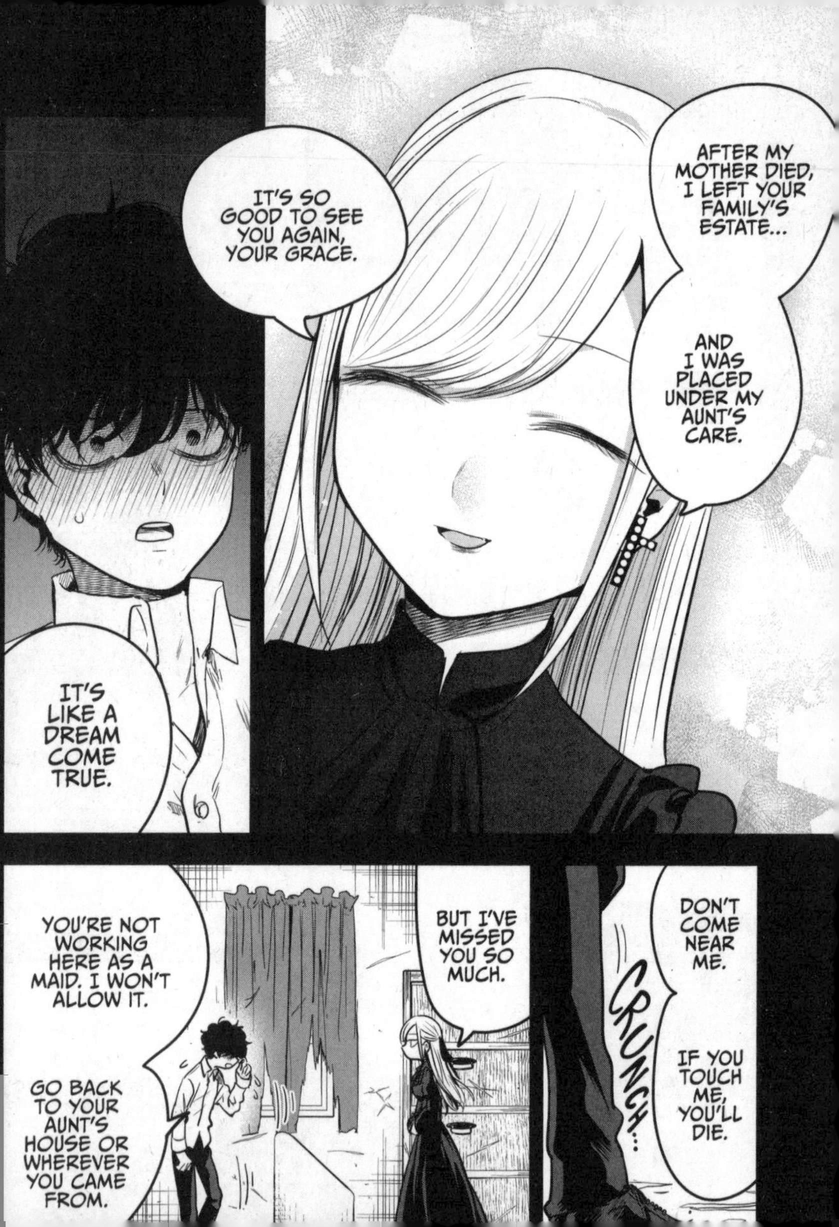
AFTER MY MOTHER DIED, I LEFT YOUR FAMILY'S ESTATE...
AND I WAS PLACED UNDER MY AUNT'S CARE.
IT'S SO GOOD TO SEE YOU AGAIN, YOUR GRACE.
IT'S LIKE A DREAM COME TRUE.
DON'T COME NEAR ME.
CRUNCH...
IF YOU TOUCH ME, YOU'LL DIE.
BUT I'VE MISSED YOU SO MUCH.
YOU'RE NOT WORKING HERE AS A MAID. I WON'T ALLOW IT.
GO BACK TO YOUR AUNT'S HOUSE OR WHEREVER YOU CAME FROM.

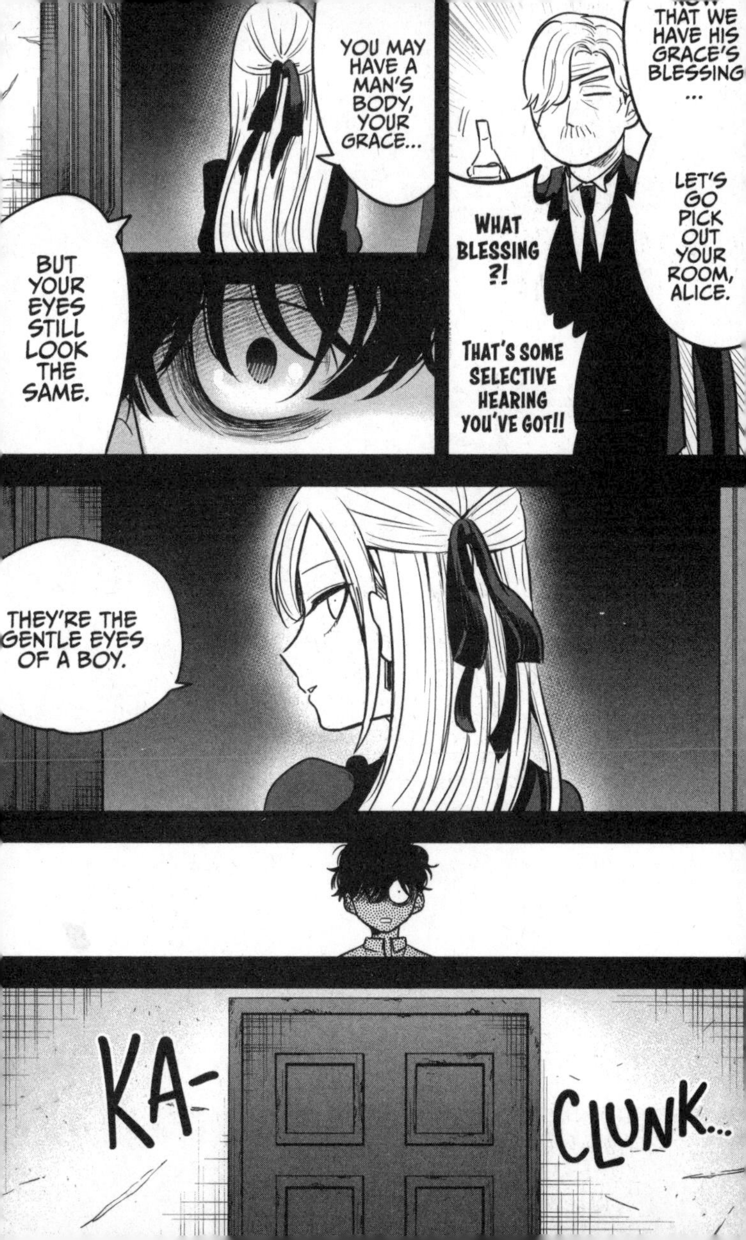
THAT WE HAVE HIS GRACE'S BLESSING ...
LET'S GO PICK OUT YOUR ROOM, ALICE.
WHAT BLESSING ?!
THAT'S SOME SELECTIVE HEARING YOU'VE GOT!!
YOU MAY HAVE A MAN'S BODY, YOUR GRACE...
BUT YOUR EYES STILL LOOK THE SAME.
THEY'RE THE GENTLE EYES OF A BOY.
KA-
CLUNK...

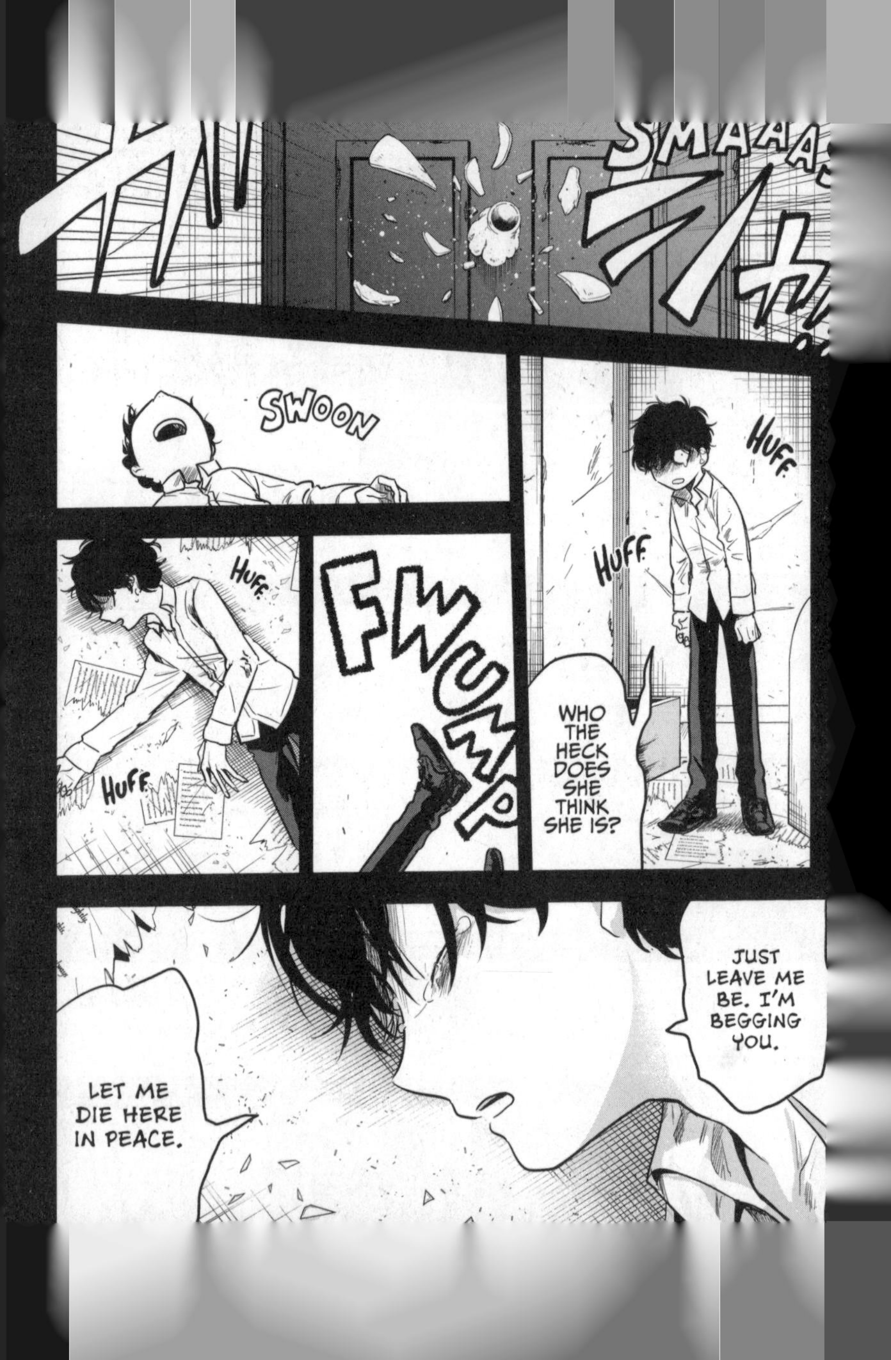
SMAAAS
HUFF
HUFF
WHO THE HECK DOES SHE THINK SHE IS?
SWOON
FWUMP
HUFF
HUFF
JUST LEAVE ME BE. I'M BEGGING YOU.
LET ME DIE HERE IN PEACE.

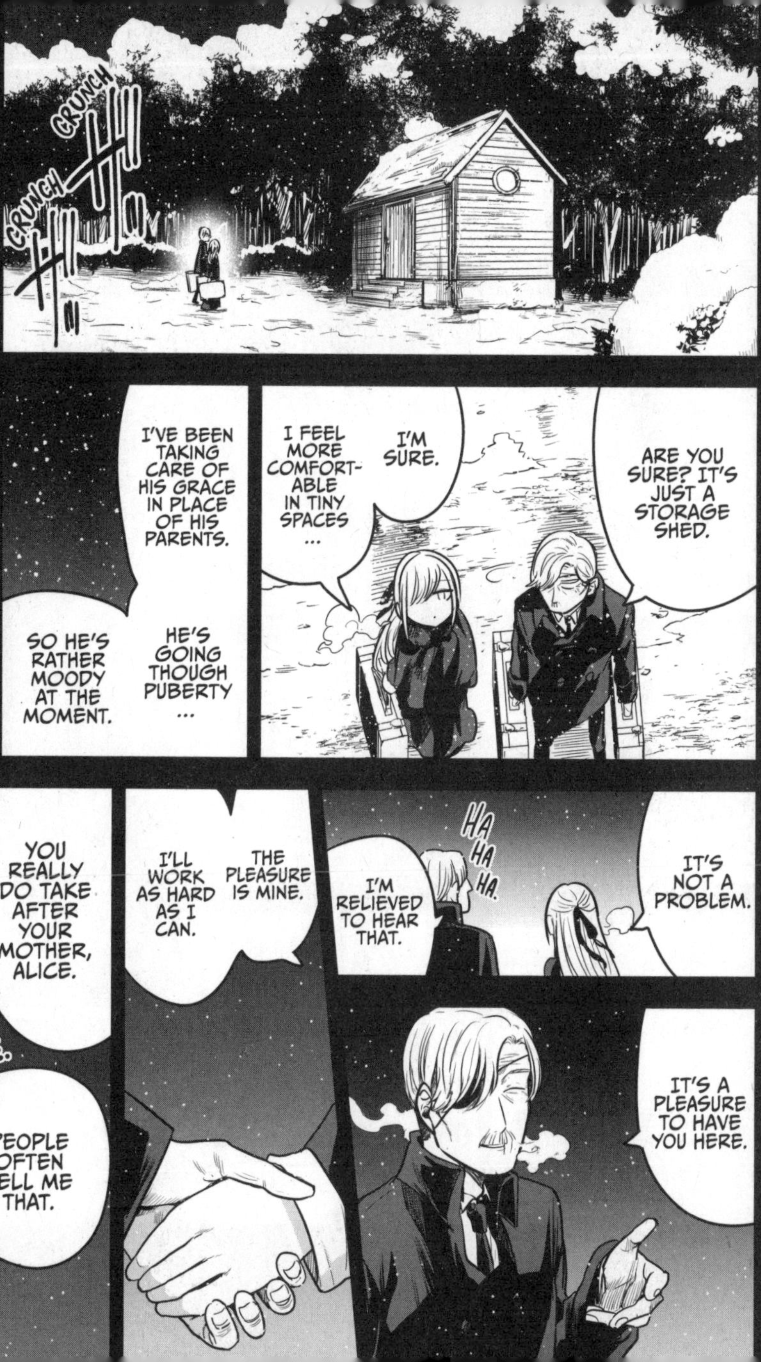
CRUNCH
CRUNCH
ARE YOU SURE? IT'S JUST A STORAGE SHED.
I'M SURE.
I FEEL MORE COMFORTABLE IN TINY SPACES ...
I'VE BEEN TAKING CARE OF HIS GRACE IN PLACE OF HIS PARENTS.
HE'S GOING THOUGH PUBERTY ...
SO HE'S RATHER MOODY AT THE MOMENT.
IT'S NOT A PROBLEM.
HA HA HA.
I'M RELIEVED TO HEAR THAT.
THE PLEASURE IS MINE.
I'LL WORK AS HARD AS I CAN.
YOU REALLY DO TAKE AFTER YOUR MOTHER, ALICE.
IT'S A PLEASURE TO HAVE YOU HERE.
HEE HEE.
PEOPLE OFTEN TELL ME THAT.

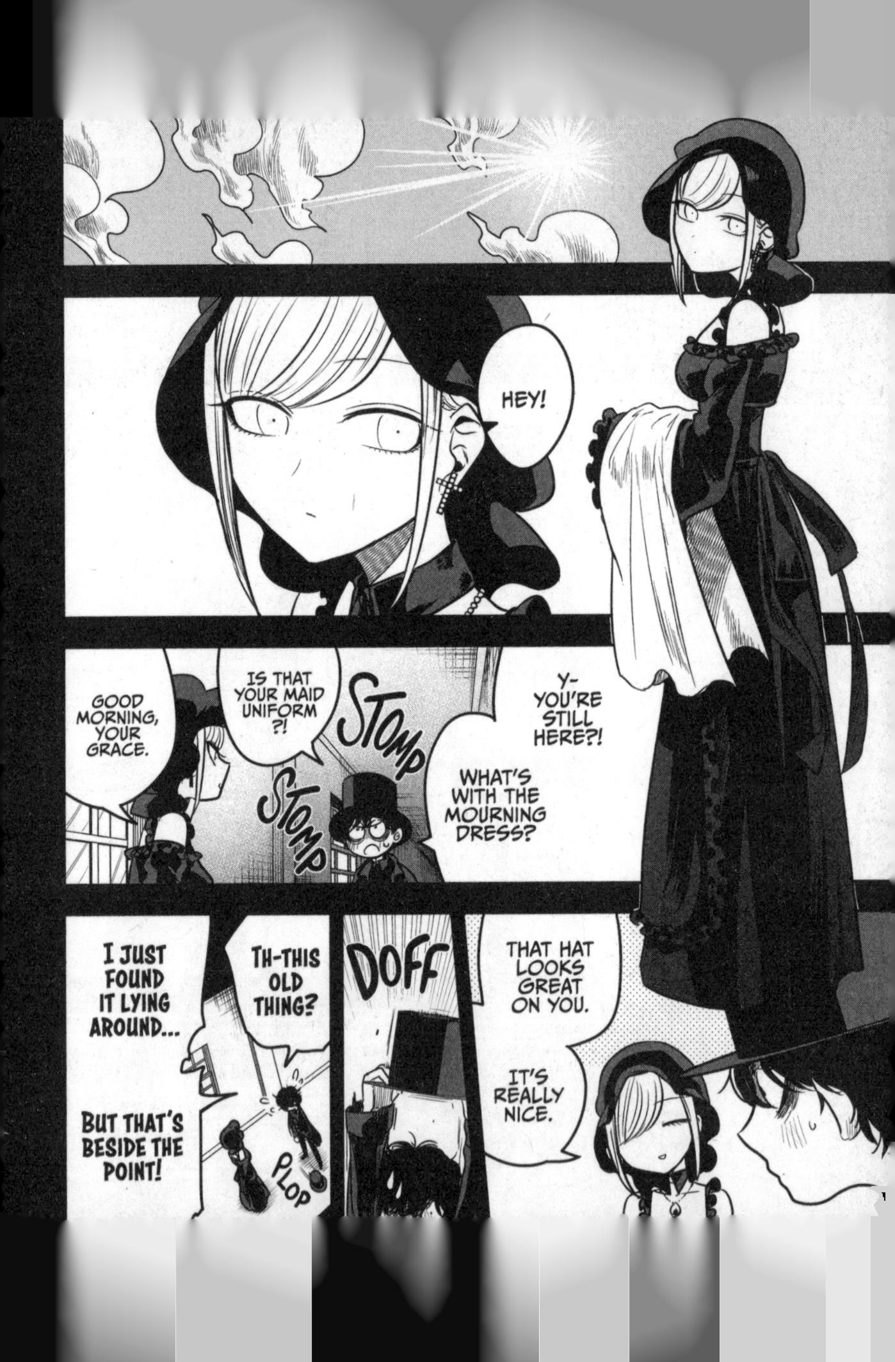
HEY!
Y- YOU'RE STILL HERE?!
WHAT'S WITH THE MOURNING DRESS?
STOMP
STOMP
IS THAT YOUR MAID UNIFORM ?!
GOOD MORNING, YOUR GRACE.
THAT HAT LOOKS GREAT ON YOU.
IT'S REALLY NICE.
DOFF
TH-THIS OLD THING?
PLOP
I JUST FOUND IT LYING AROUND...
BUT THAT'S BESIDE THE POINT!

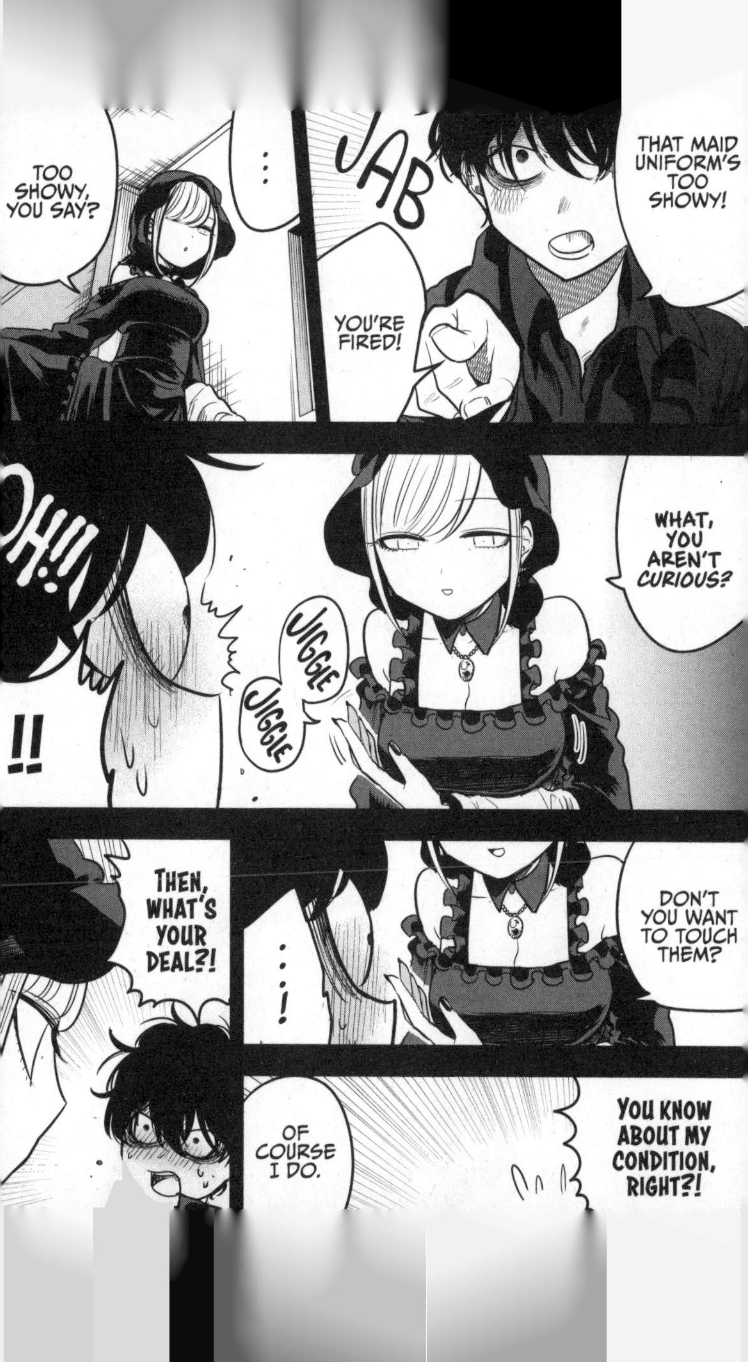
THAT MAID UNIFORM'S TOO SHOWY!
JAB
YOU'RE FIRED!
...
TOO SHOWY, YOU SAY?
WHAT, YOU AREN'T CURIOUS?
JIGGLE
JIGGLE
OH!!
!!
DON'T YOU WANT TO TOUCH THEM?
...!
THEN, WHAT'S YOUR DEAL?!
YOU KNOW ABOUT MY CONDITION, RIGHT?!
OF COURSE I DO.

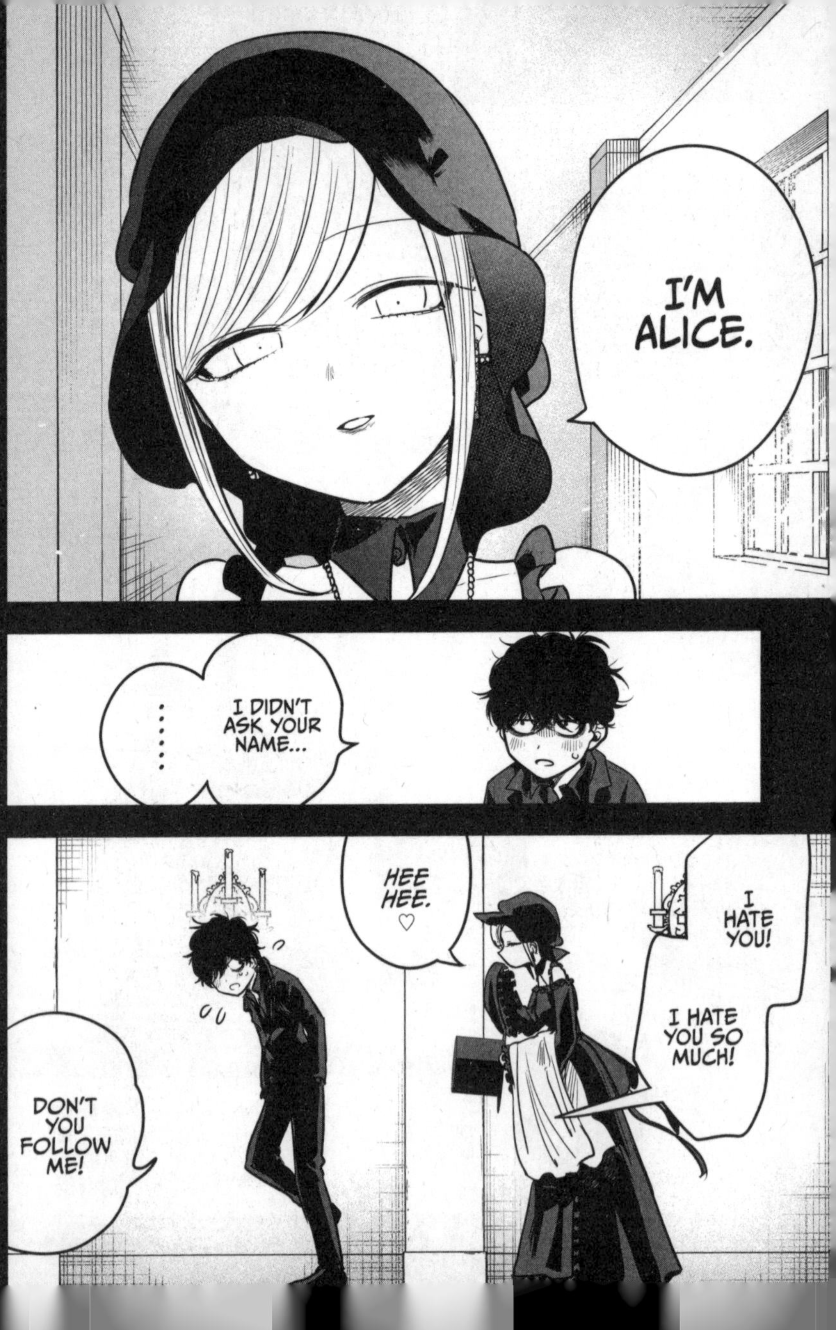
I'M ALICE.
...... I DIDN'T ASK YOUR NAME...
I HATE YOU!
I HATE YOU SO MUCH!
HEE HEE. ♡
DON'T YOU FOLLOW ME!

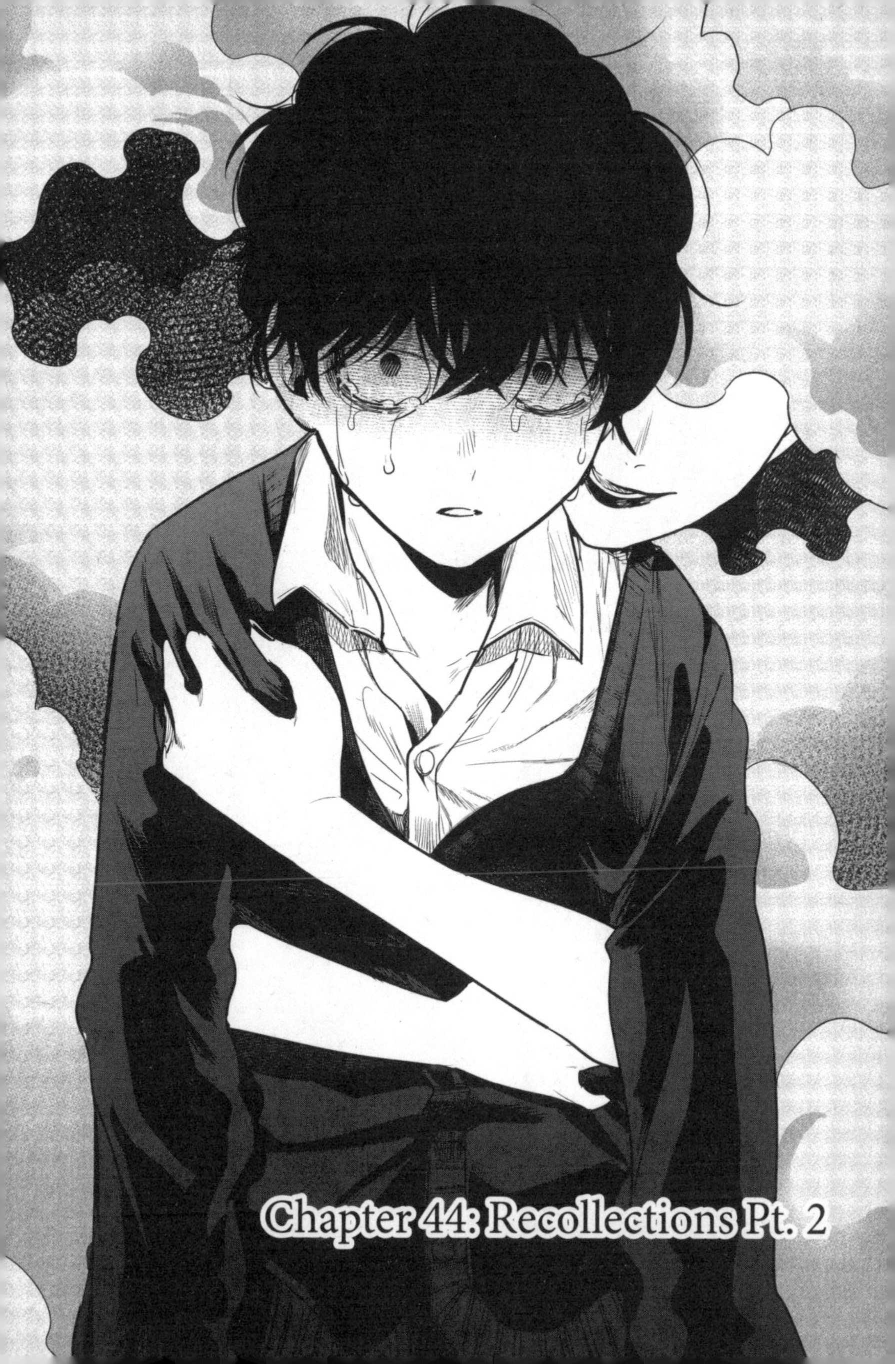
Chapter 44: Recollections Pt. 2

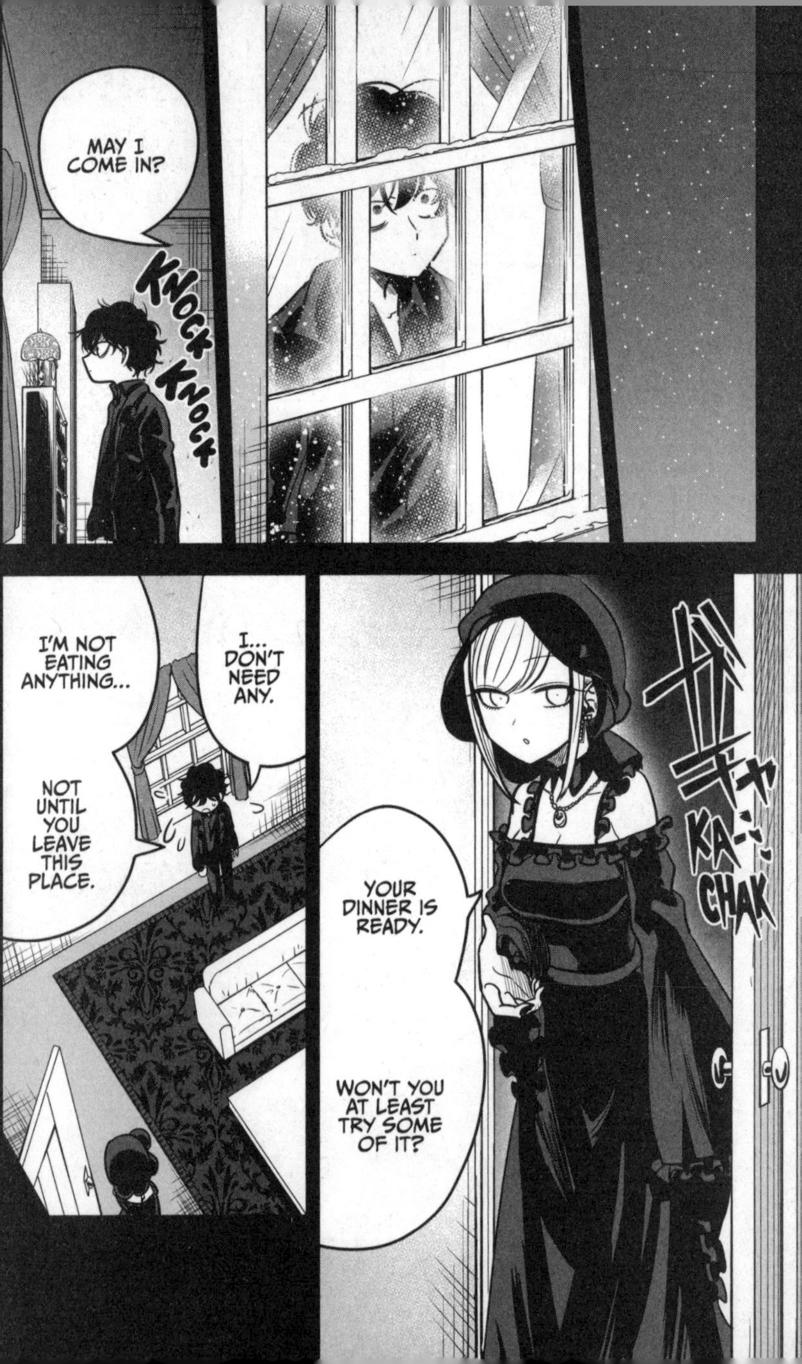
MAY I COME IN?
KNOCK KNOCK
KA-CHAK
YOUR DINNER IS READY.
WON'T YOU AT LEAST TRY SOME OF IT?
I... DON'T NEED ANY.
I'M NOT EATING ANYTHING...
NOT UNTIL YOU LEAVE THIS PLACE.

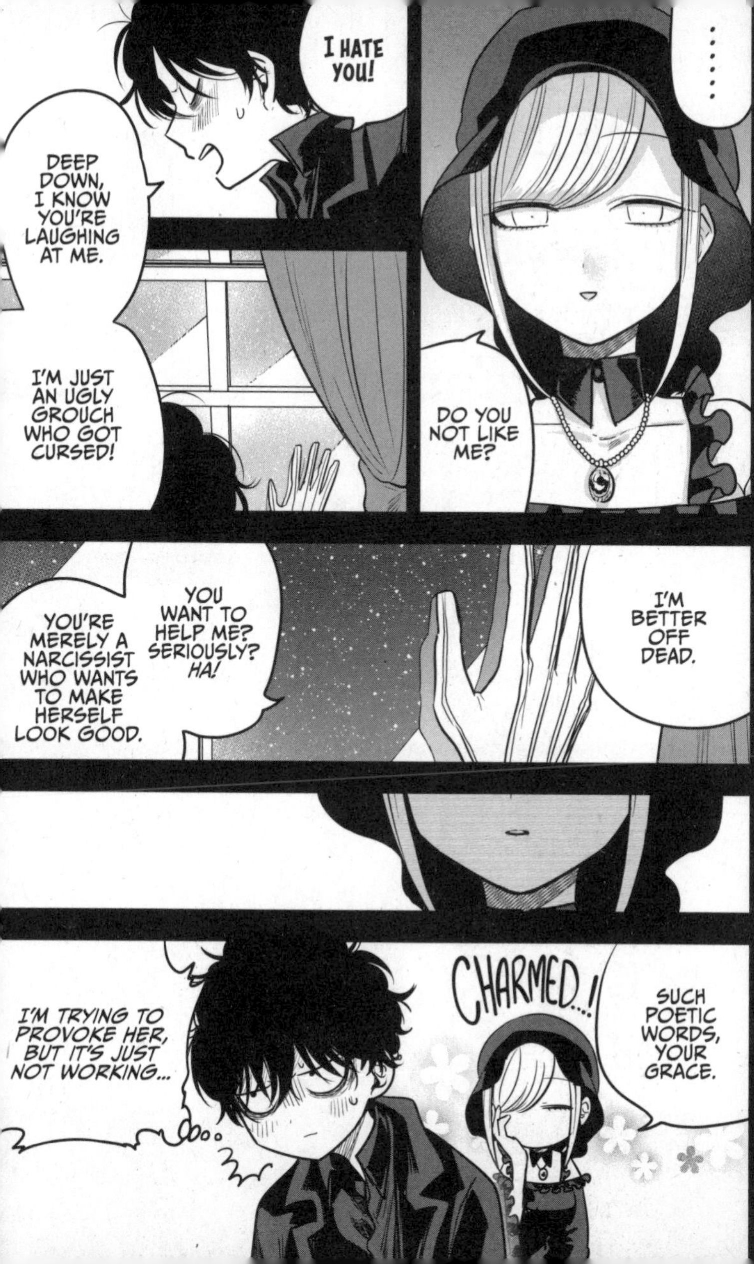
......
DO YOU NOT LIKE ME?
I HATE YOU!
DEEP DOWN, I KNOW YOU'RE LAUGHING AT ME.
I'M JUST AN UGLY GROUCH WHO GOT CURSED!
I'M BETTER OFF DEAD.
YOU WANT TO HELP ME? SERIOUSLY? HA!
YOU'RE MERELY A NARCISSIST WHO WANTS TO MAKE HERSELF LOOK GOOD.
SUCH POETIC WORDS, YOUR GRACE.
CHARMED...!
I'M TRYING TO PROVOKE HER, BUT IT'S JUST NOT WORKING...

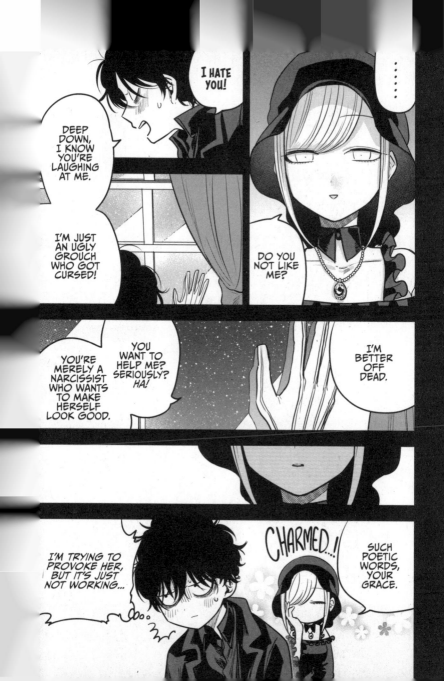

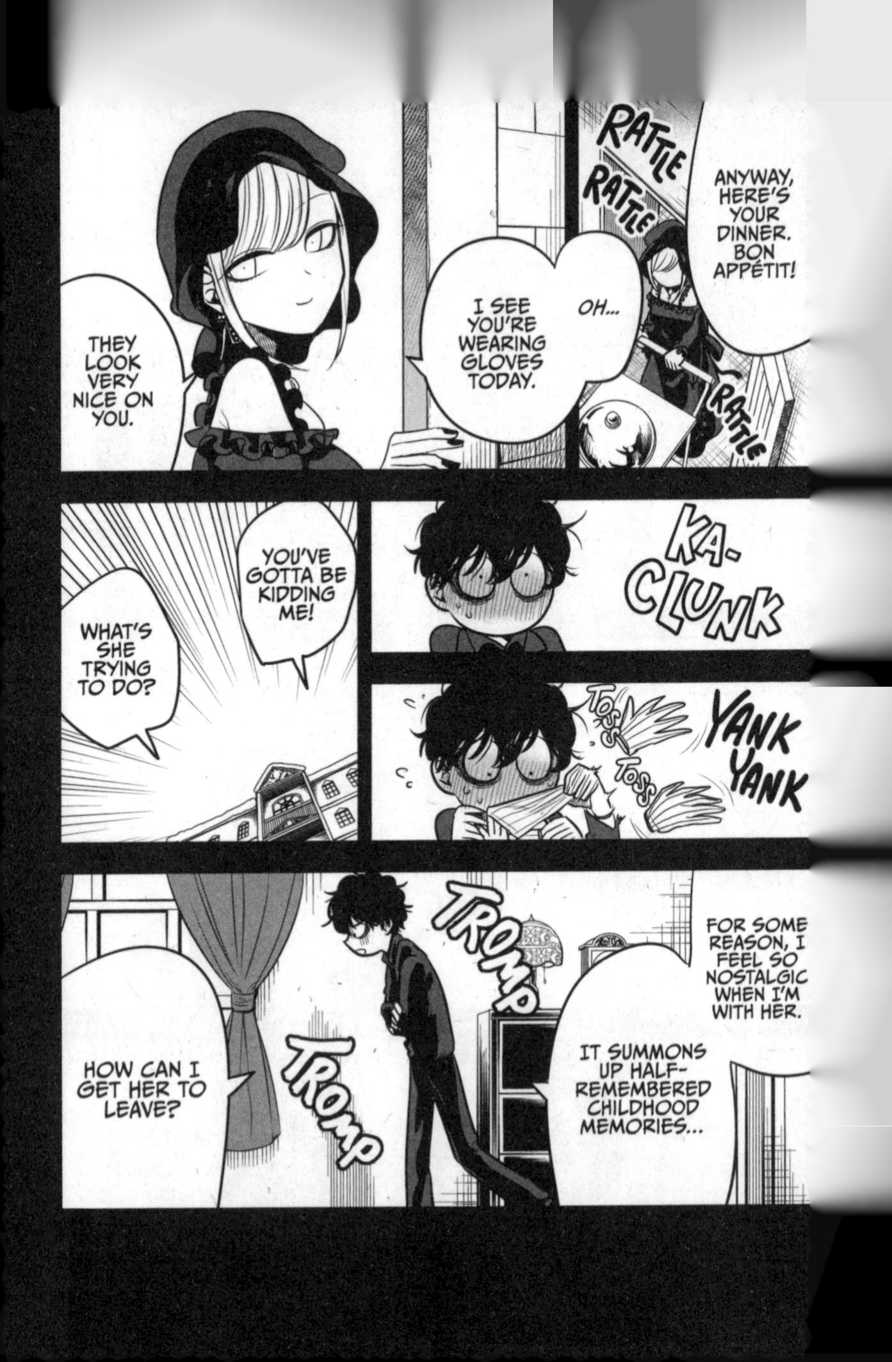
RATTLE RATTLE
ANYWAY, HERE'S YOUR DINNER. BON APPÉTIT!
RATTLE
OH...
I SEE YOU'RE WEARING GLOVES TODAY.
THEY LOOK VERY NICE ON YOU.
KA-CLUNK
YANK YANK
TOSS TOSS
YOU'VE GOTTA BE KIDDING ME!
WHAT'S SHE TRYING TO DO?
FOR SOME REASON, I FEEL SO NOSTALGIC WHEN I'M WITH HER.
IT SUMMONS UP HALF-REMEMBERED CHILDHOOD MEMORIES...
TROMP
TROMP
HOW CAN I GET HER TO LEAVE?

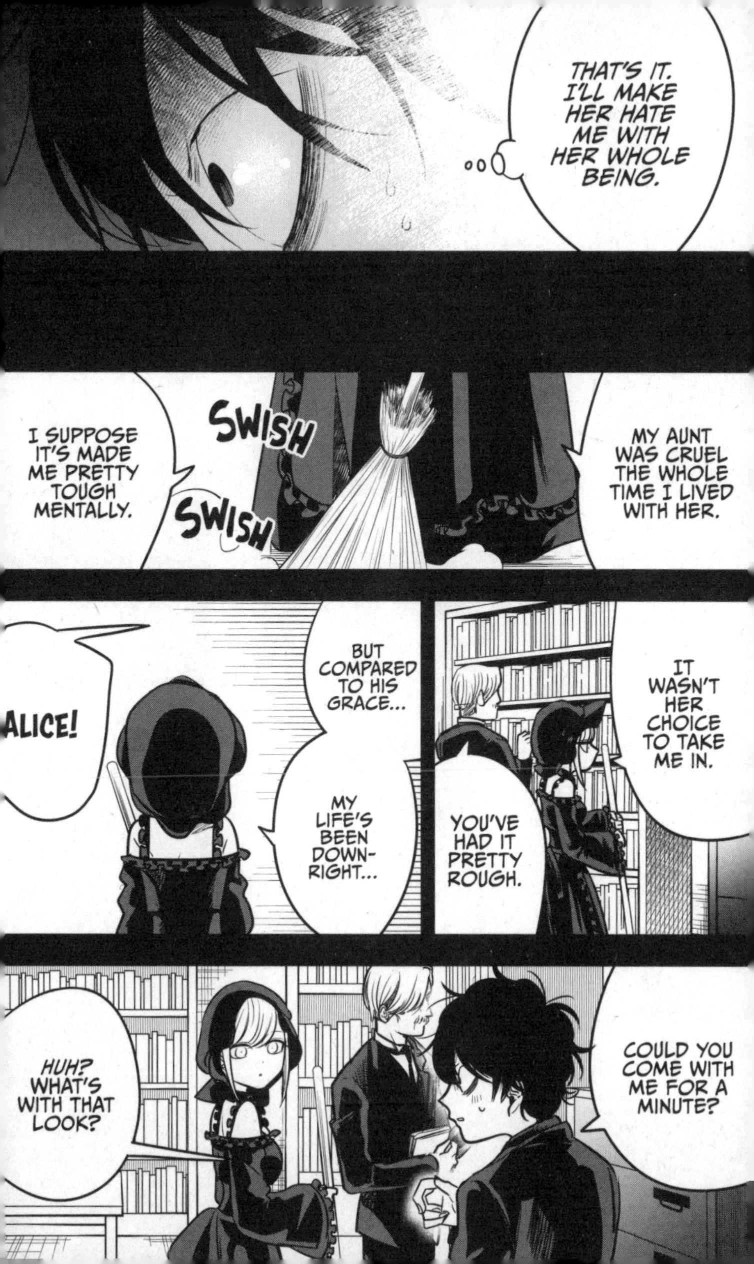
THAT'S IT. I'LL MAKE HER HATE ME WITH HER WHOLE BEING.
MY AUNT WAS CRUEL THE WHOLE TIME I LIVED WITH HER.
SWISH
SWISH
I SUPPOSE IT'S MADE ME PRETTY TOUGH MENTALLY.
IT WASN'T HER CHOICE TO TAKE ME IN.
YOU'VE HAD IT PRETTY ROUGH.
BUT COMPARED TO HIS GRACE...
MY LIFE'S BEEN DOWN-RIGHT...
ALICE!
COULD YOU COME WITH ME FOR A MINUTE?
HUH? WHAT'S WITH THAT LOOK?

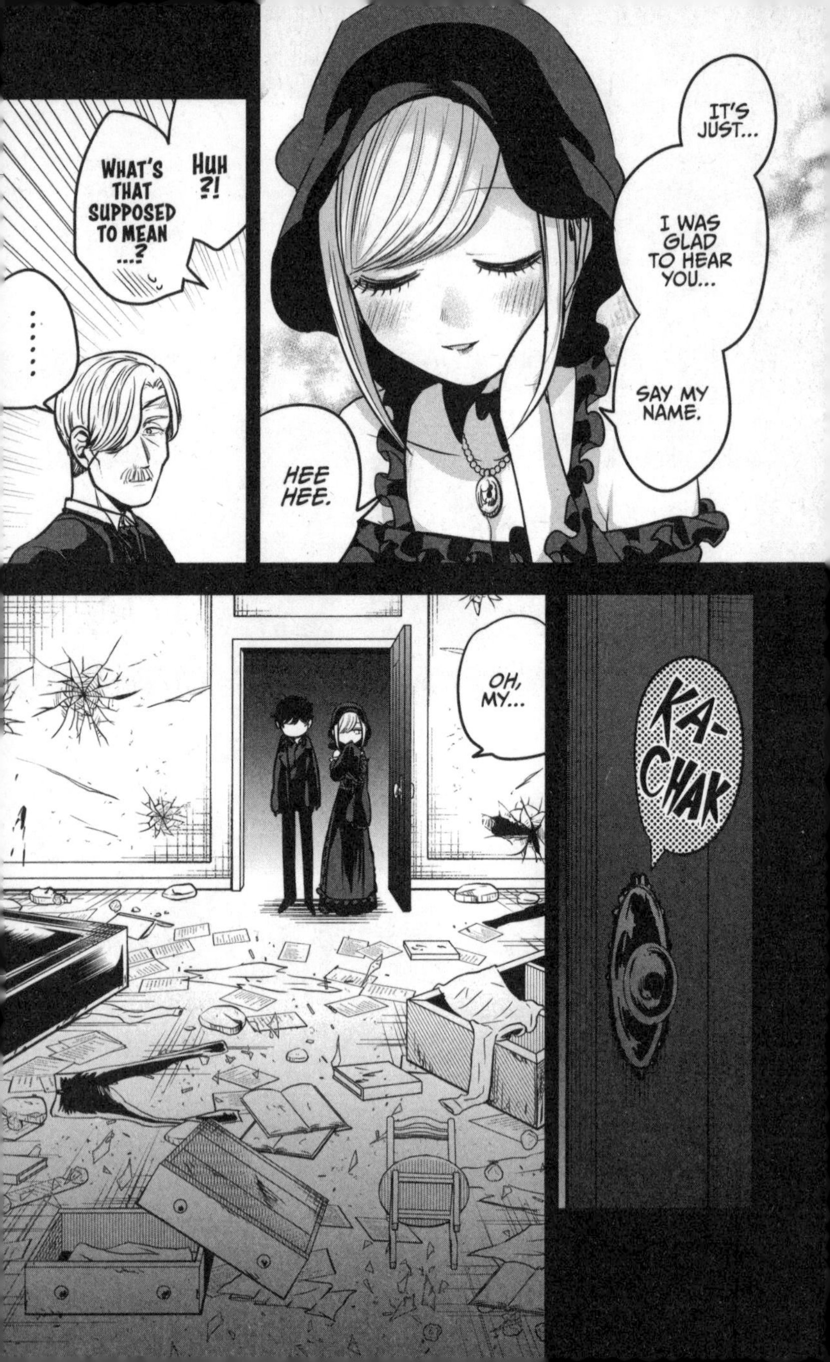
IT'S JUST...
I WAS GLAD TO HEAR YOU...
SAY MY NAME.
HEE HEE.
HUH ?!
WHAT'S THAT SUPPOSED TO MEAN ...?
......
KA-CHAK
OH, MY...

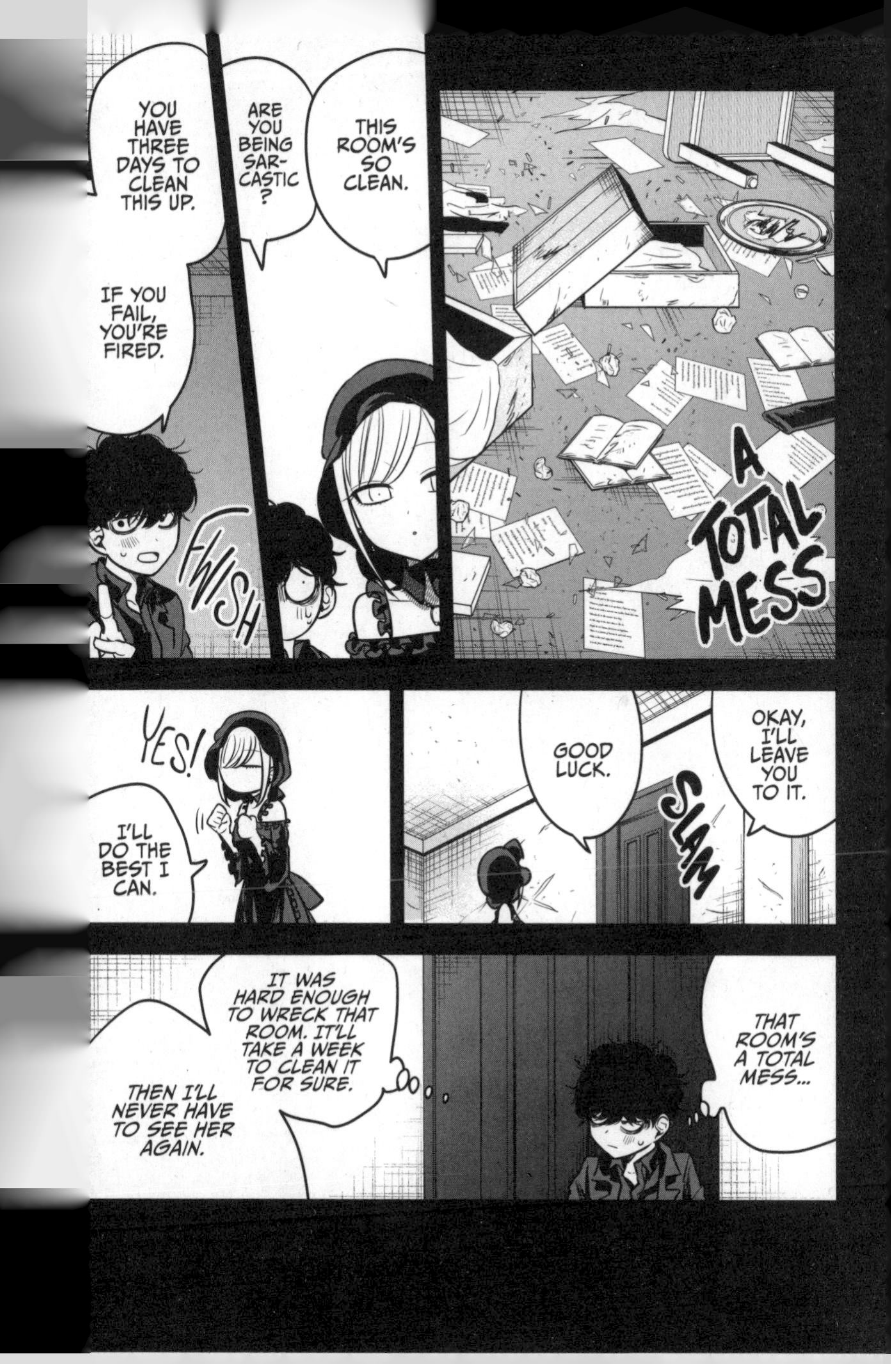
A TOTAL MESS
THIS ROOM'S SO CLEAN.
ARE YOU BEING SAR-CASTIC?
YOU HAVE THREE DAYS TO CLEAN THIS UP.
IF YOU FAIL, YOU'RE FIRED.
FWISH
OKAY, I'LL LEAVE YOU TO IT.
SLAM
GOOD LUCK.
YES!
I'LL DO THE BEST I CAN.
THAT ROOM'S A TOTAL MESS...
IT WAS HARD ENOUGH TO WRECK THAT ROOM. IT'LL TAKE A WEEK TO CLEAN IT FOR SURE.
THEN I'LL NEVER HAVE TO SEE HER AGAIN.

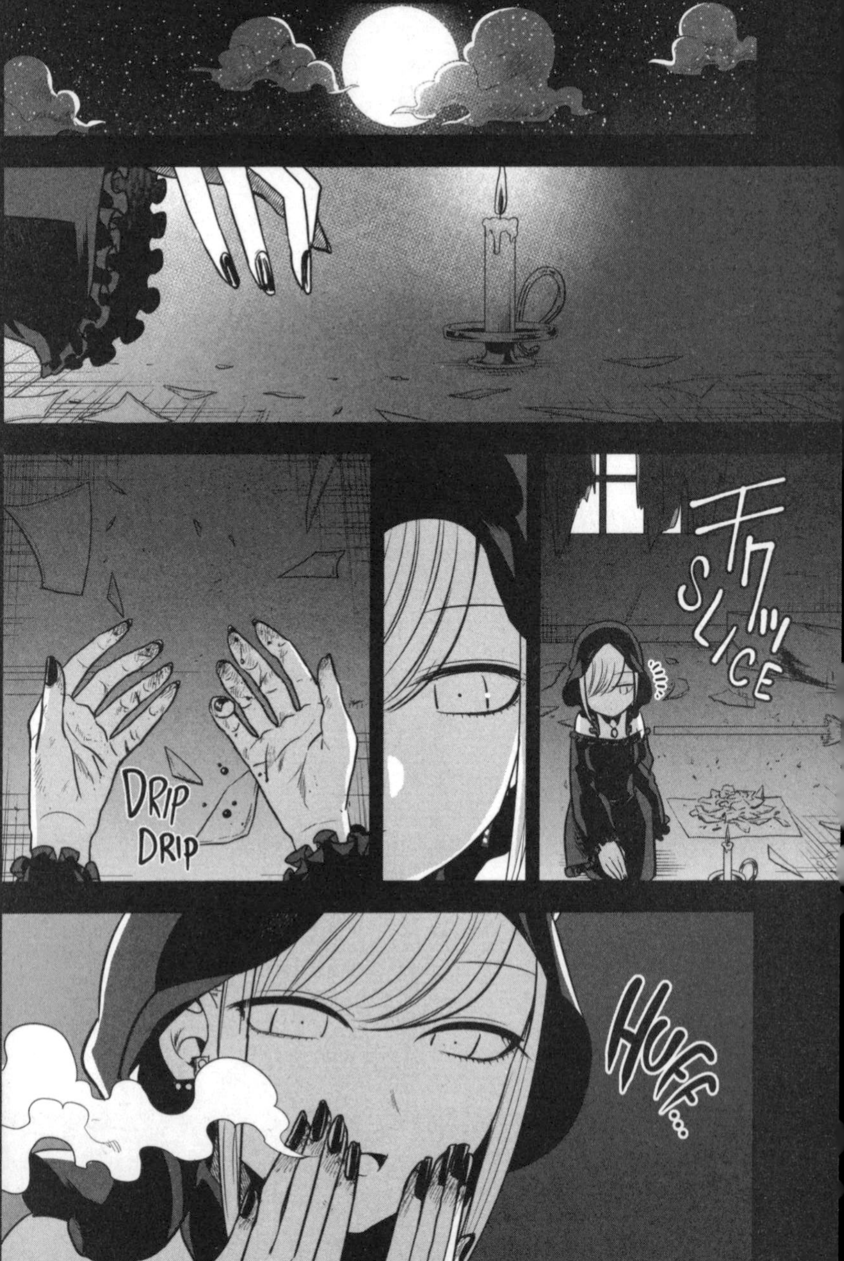
チクッ
SLICE
DRIP
DRIP
HUFF...

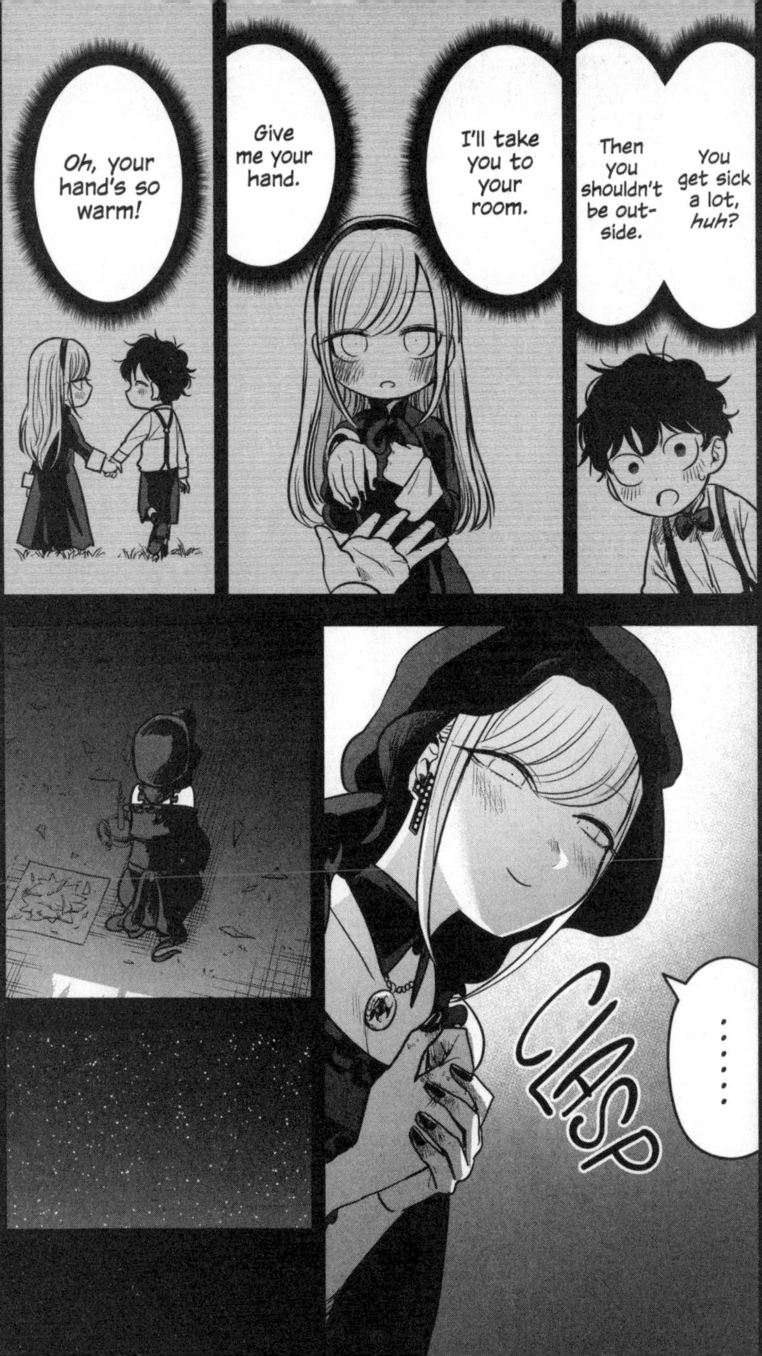
You get sick a lot, *huh?*
Then you shouldn't be out-side.
I'll take you to your room.
Give me your hand.
Oh, your hand's so warm!
CLASP
......

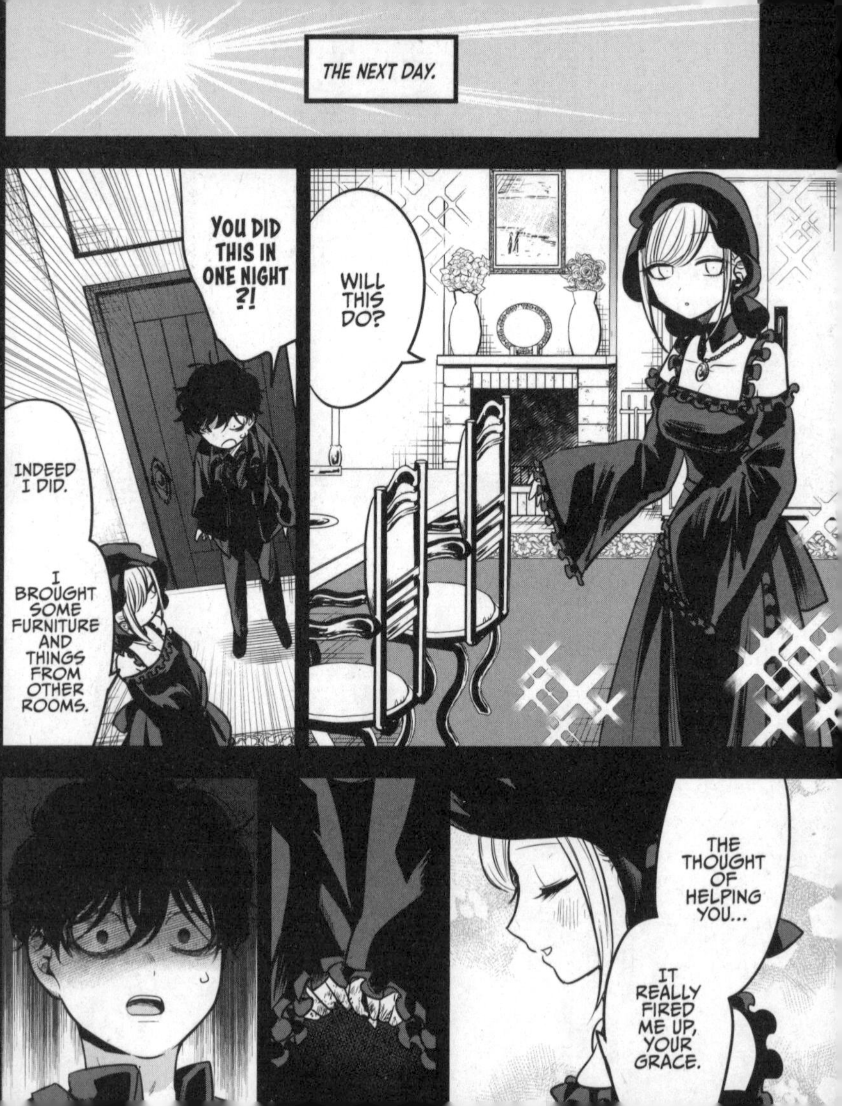
THE NEXT DAY.
WILL THIS DO?
YOU DID THIS IN ONE NIGHT ?!
INDEED I DID.
I BROUGHT SOME FURNITURE AND THINGS FROM OTHER ROOMS.
THE THOUGHT OF HELPING YOU...
IT REALLY FIRED ME UP, YOUR GRACE.

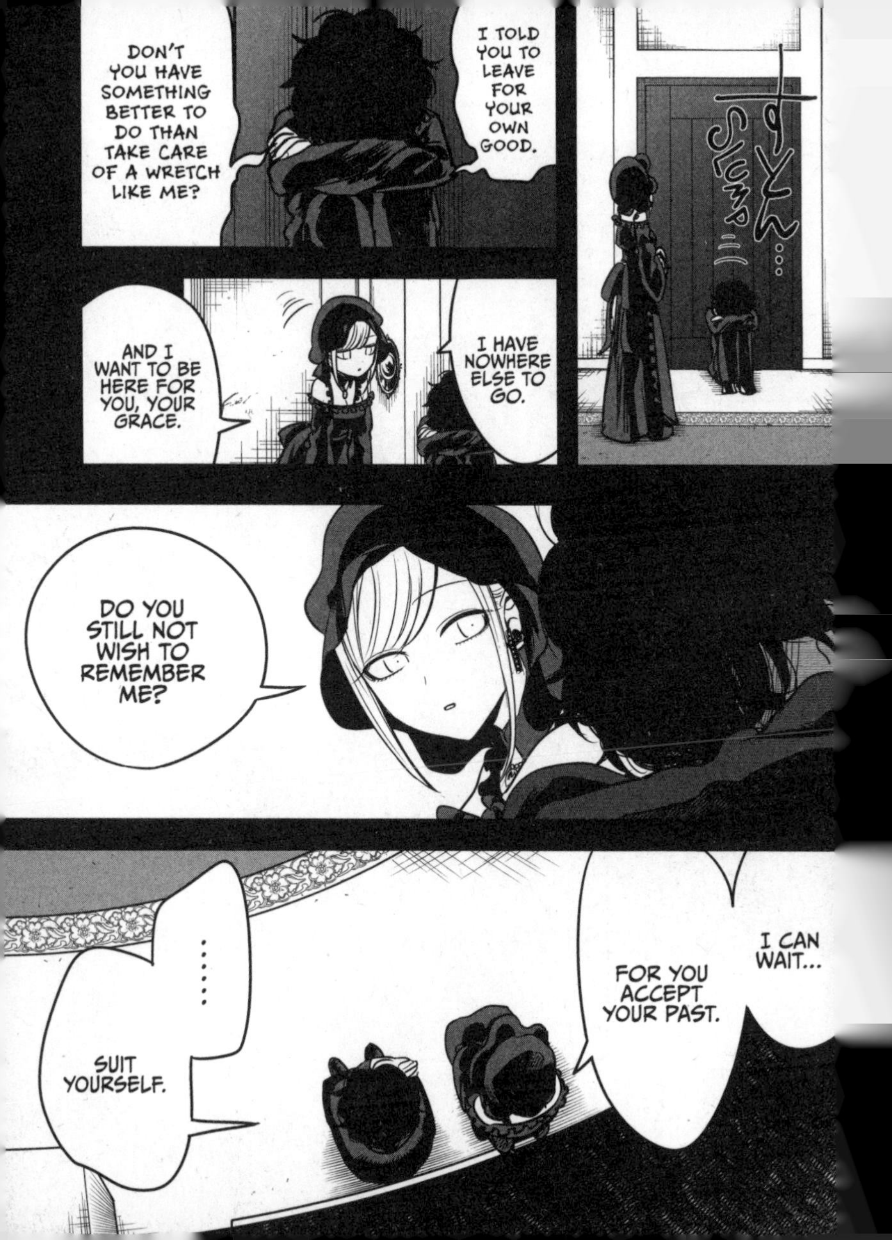
すとん…
SLUMP
I TOLD YOU TO LEAVE FOR YOUR OWN GOOD.
DON'T YOU HAVE SOMETHING BETTER TO DO THAN TAKE CARE OF A WRETCH LIKE ME?
I HAVE NOWHERE ELSE TO GO.
AND I WANT TO BE HERE FOR YOU, YOUR GRACE.
DO YOU STILL NOT WISH TO REMEMBER ME?
I CAN WAIT...
FOR YOU ACCEPT YOUR PAST.
......
SUIT YOURSELF.

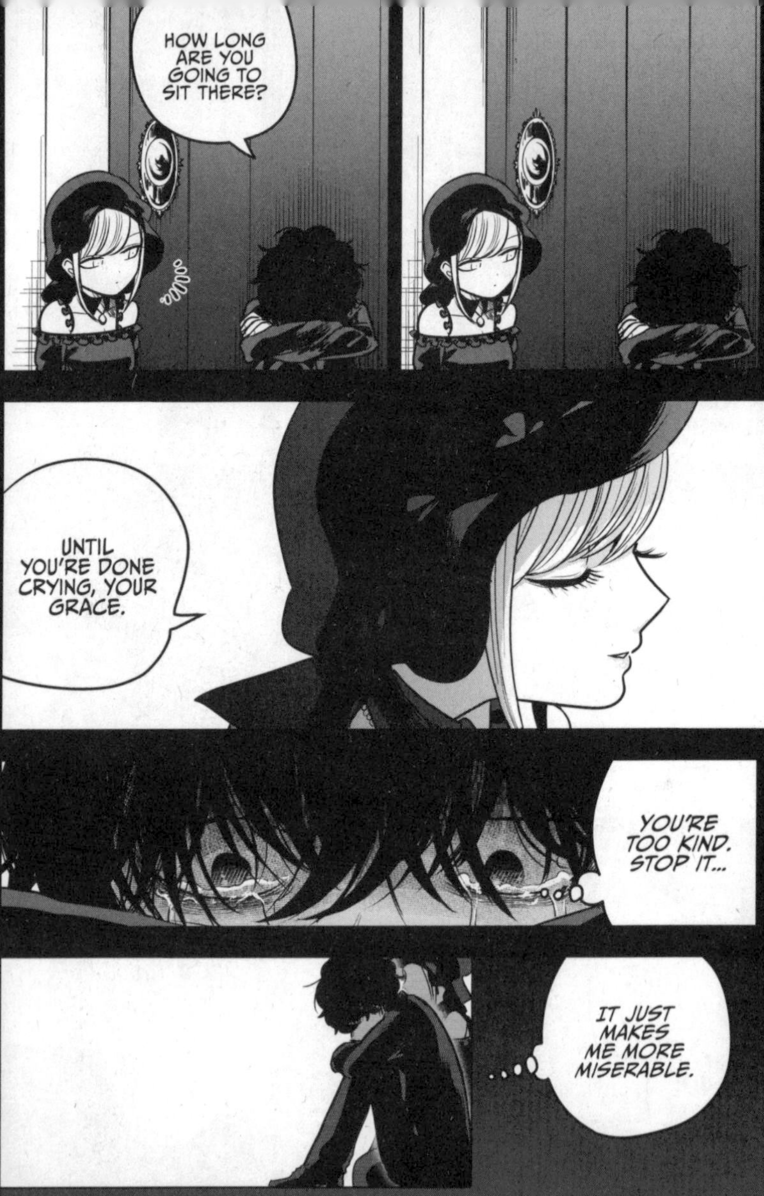
HOW LONG ARE YOU GOING TO SIT THERE?
UNTIL YOU'RE DONE CRYING, YOUR GRACE.
YOU'RE TOO KIND. STOP IT...
IT JUST MAKES ME MORE MISERABLE.

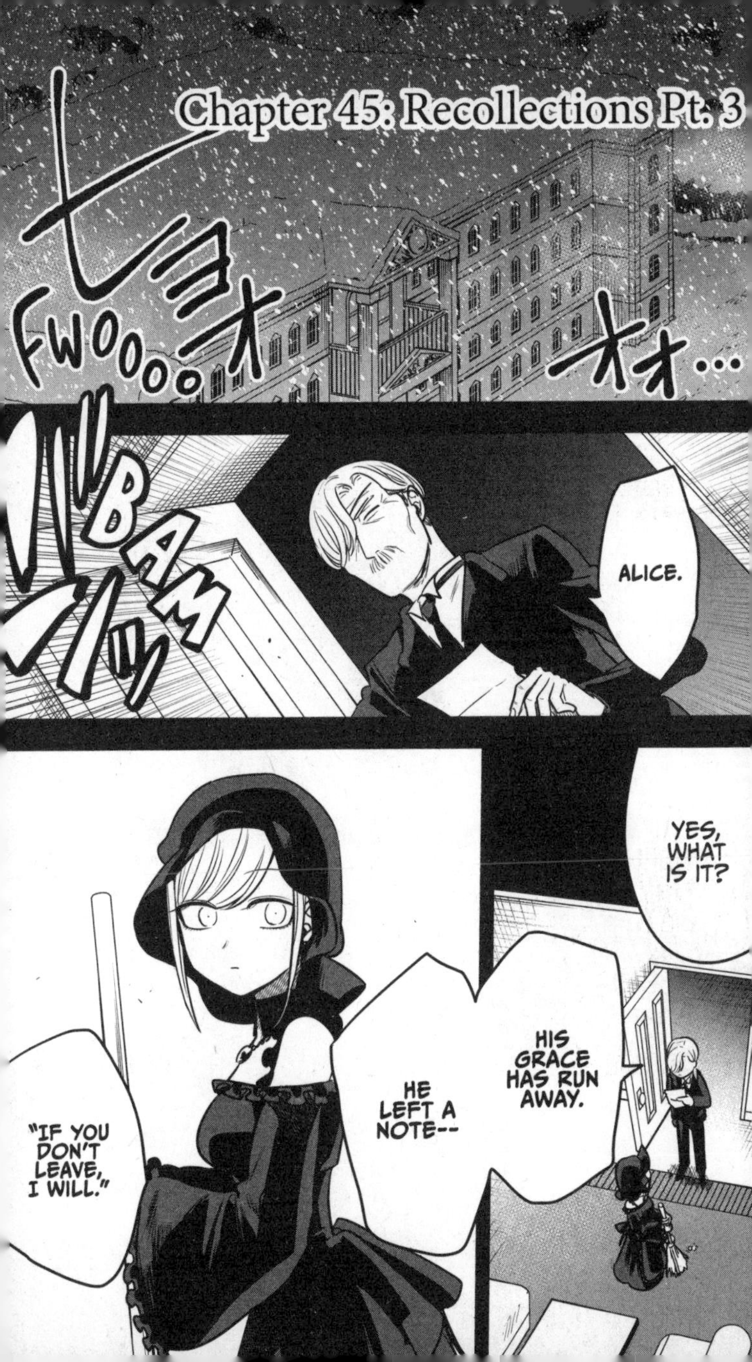

Chapter 45: Recollections Pt. 3
FWOOOO
ヒョオオオオ…
ALICE.
BAM
バンッ
YES, WHAT IS IT?
HIS GRACE HAS RUN AWAY.
HE LEFT A NOTE--
"IF YOU DON'T LEAVE, I WILL."

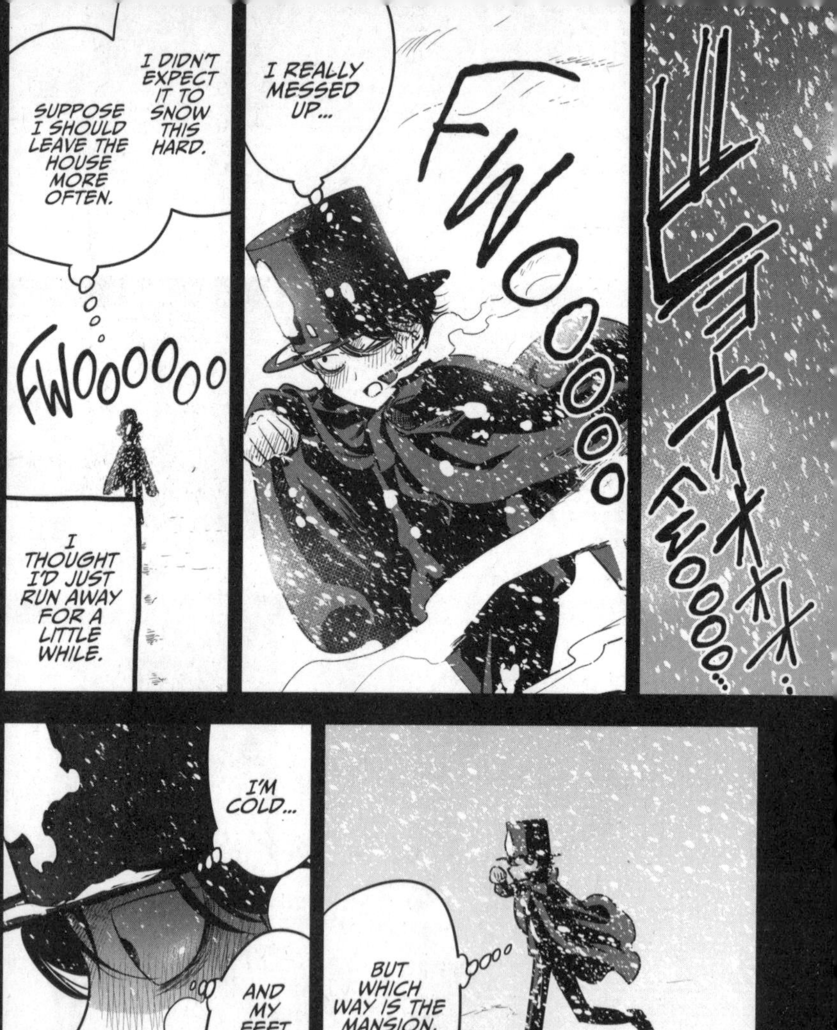
FWOOOO...
I REALLY MESSED UP...
FWOOOOOOOO
I DIDN'T EXPECT IT TO SNOW THIS HARD.
SUPPOSE I SHOULD LEAVE THE HOUSE MORE OFTEN.
FWOOOOOOO
I THOUGHT I'D JUST RUN AWAY FOR A LITTLE WHILE.
BUT WHICH WAY IS THE MANSION, ANYWAY?
I'M COLD...
AND MY FEET ARE SORE.

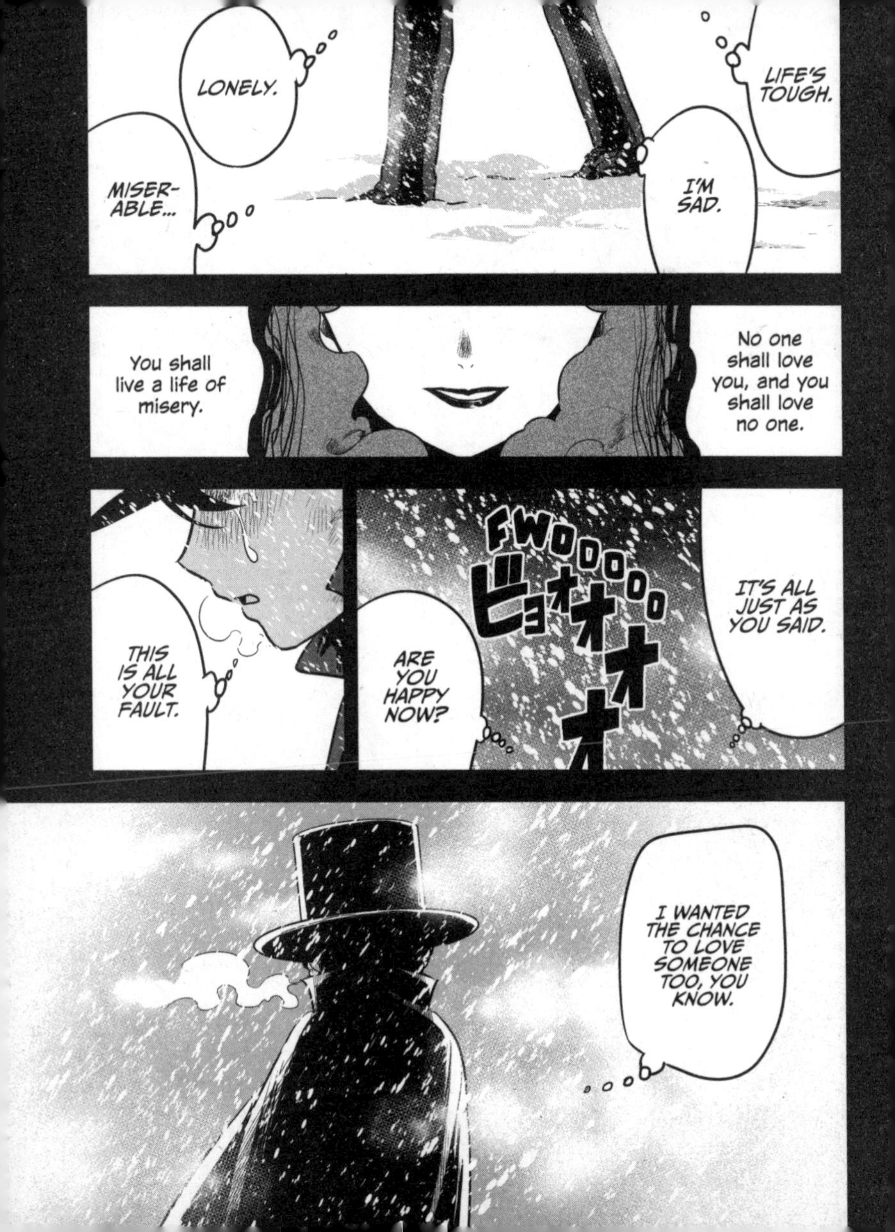

LIFE'S TOUGH.
I'M SAD.
LONELY.
MISER-ABLE...
No one shall love you, and you shall love no one.
You shall live a life of misery.
IT'S ALL JUST AS YOU SAID.
FWOOOOOOO
ビョオオオオ
ARE YOU HAPPY NOW?
THIS IS ALL YOUR FAULT.
I WANTED THE CHANCE TO LOVE SOMEONE TOO, YOU KNOW.

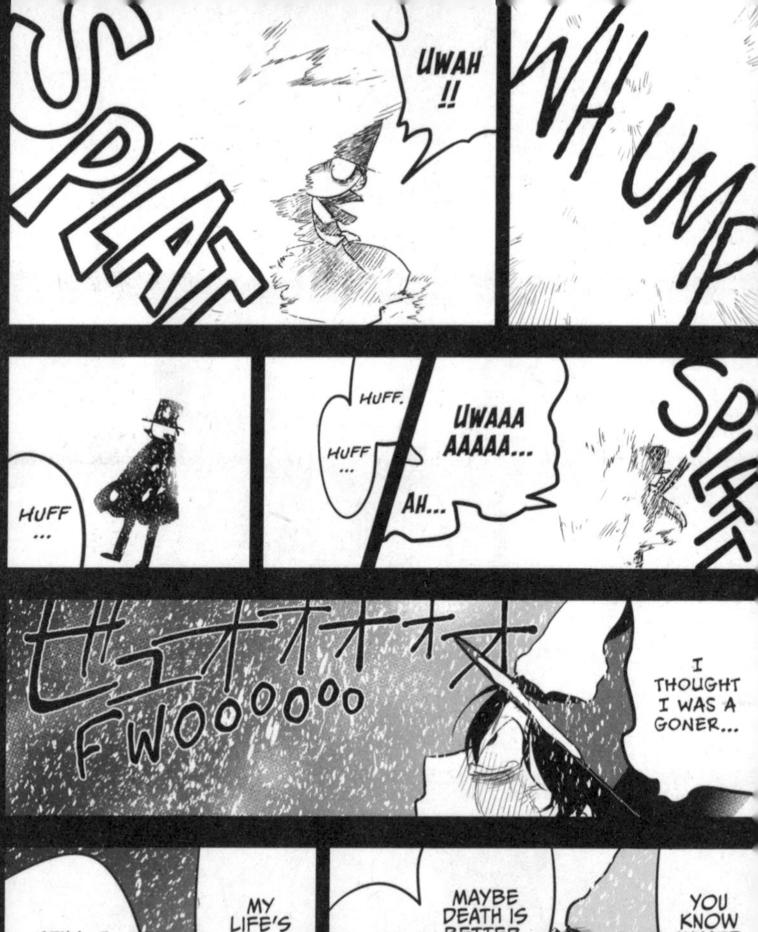

WHUMP
UWAH !!
SPLAT
SPLATT
UWAAA AAAAA...
AH...
HUFF.
HUFF ...
HUFF ...
I THOUGHT I WAS A GONER...
ゼュオオオオオ
FWOOOOOO
YOU KNOW WHAT?
MAYBE DEATH IS BETTER.
RESIGNING MYSELF TO FATE...
MY LIFE'S BEEN A MISERABLE JOKE.
STILL, I WISH I COULD'VE HAD AT LEAST ONE FRIEND.

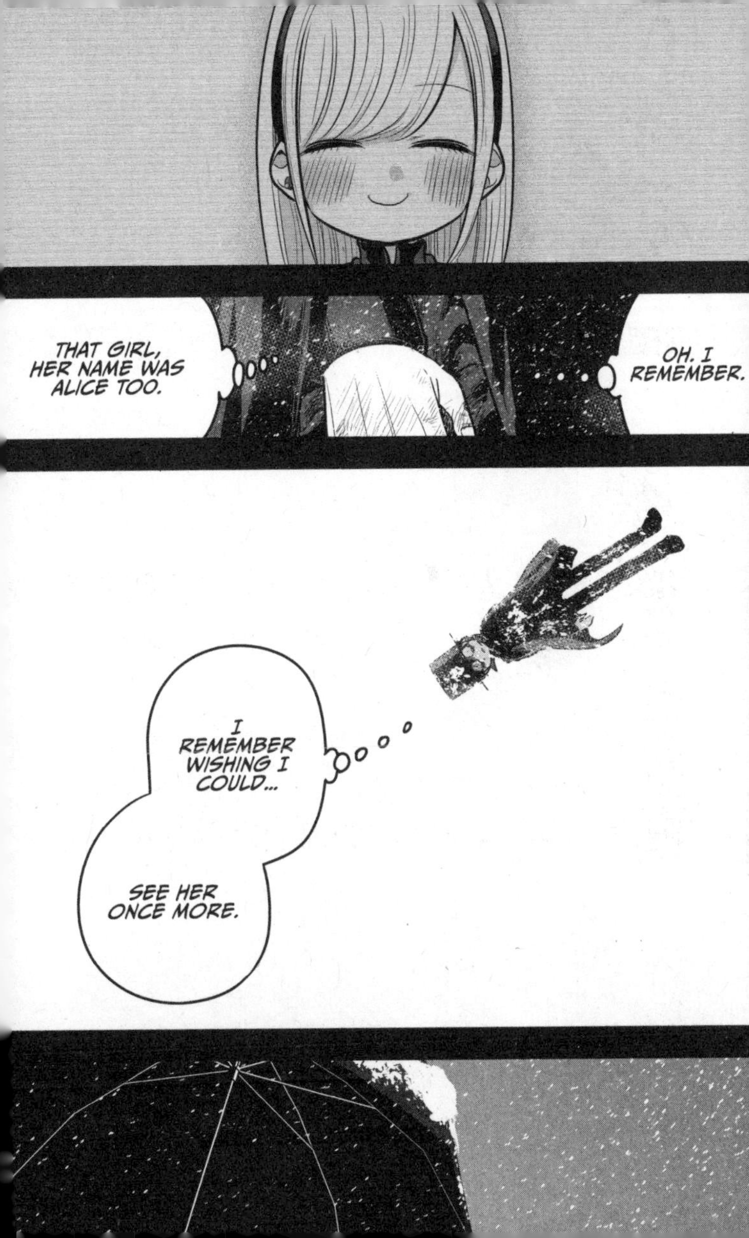
OH. I REMEMBER.
THAT GIRL, HER NAME WAS ALICE TOO.
I REMEMBER WISHING I COULD...
SEE HER ONCE MORE.

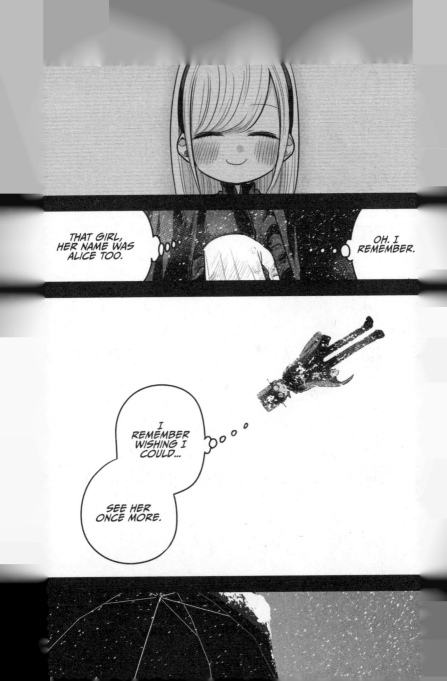

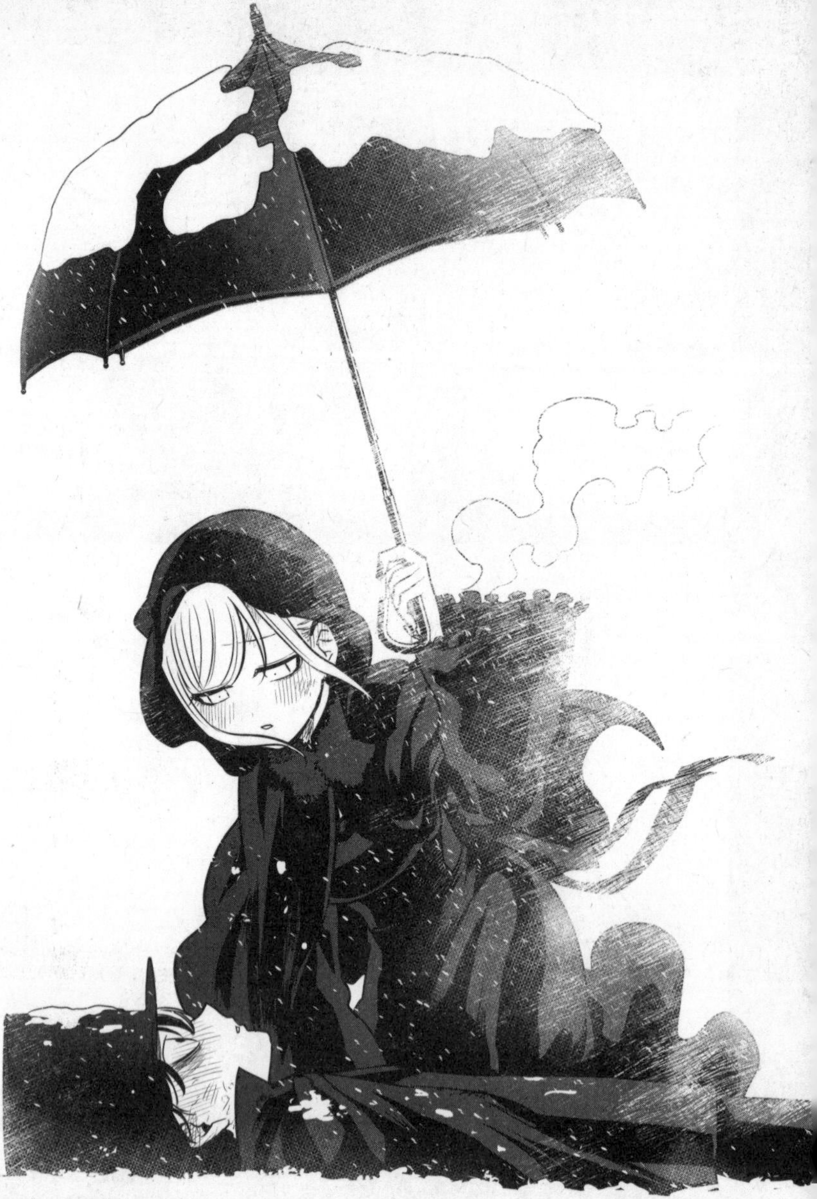

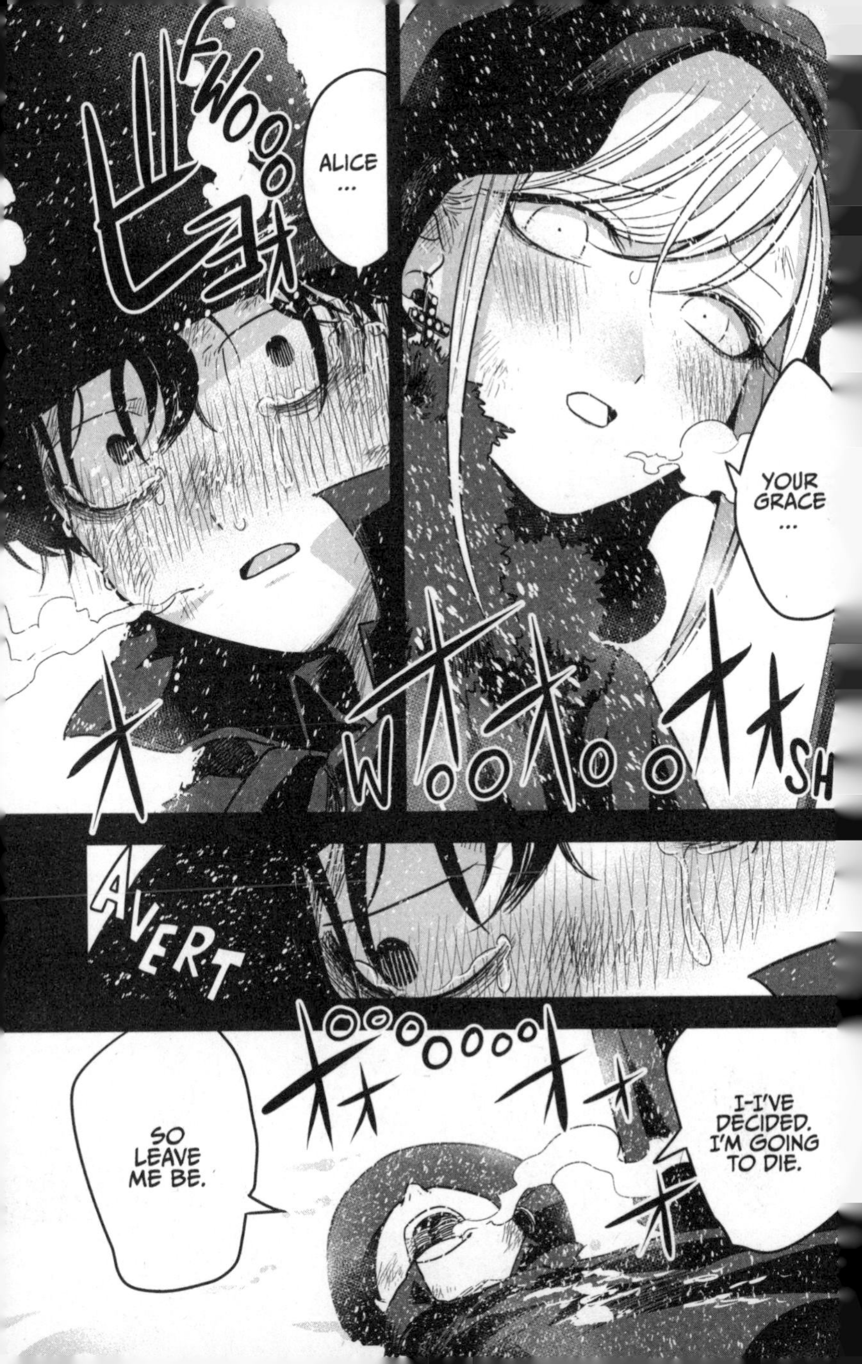
YOUR GRACE ...
ALICE ...
KWOOO
WOOOOOOSH
AVERT
I-I'VE DECIDED. I'M GOING TO DIE.
SO LEAVE ME BE.

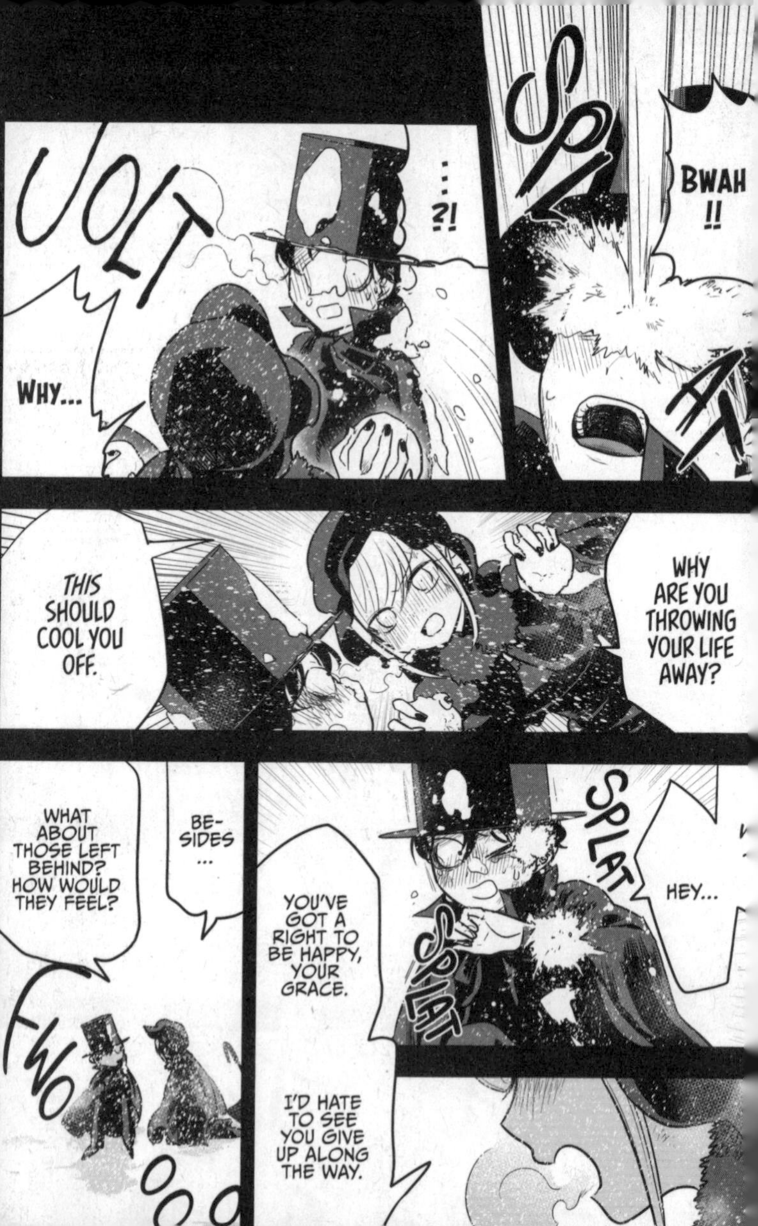
SPL
BWAH !!
AA
JOLT
...?!
WHY...
WHY ARE YOU THROWING YOUR LIFE AWAY?
THIS SHOULD COOL YOU OFF.
SPLAT
HEY...
SPLAT
YOU'VE GOT A RIGHT TO BE HAPPY, YOUR GRACE.
I'D HATE TO SEE YOU GIVE UP ALONG THE WAY.
BE-SIDES...
WHAT ABOUT THOSE LEFT BEHIND? HOW WOULD THEY FEEL?
FWOOO

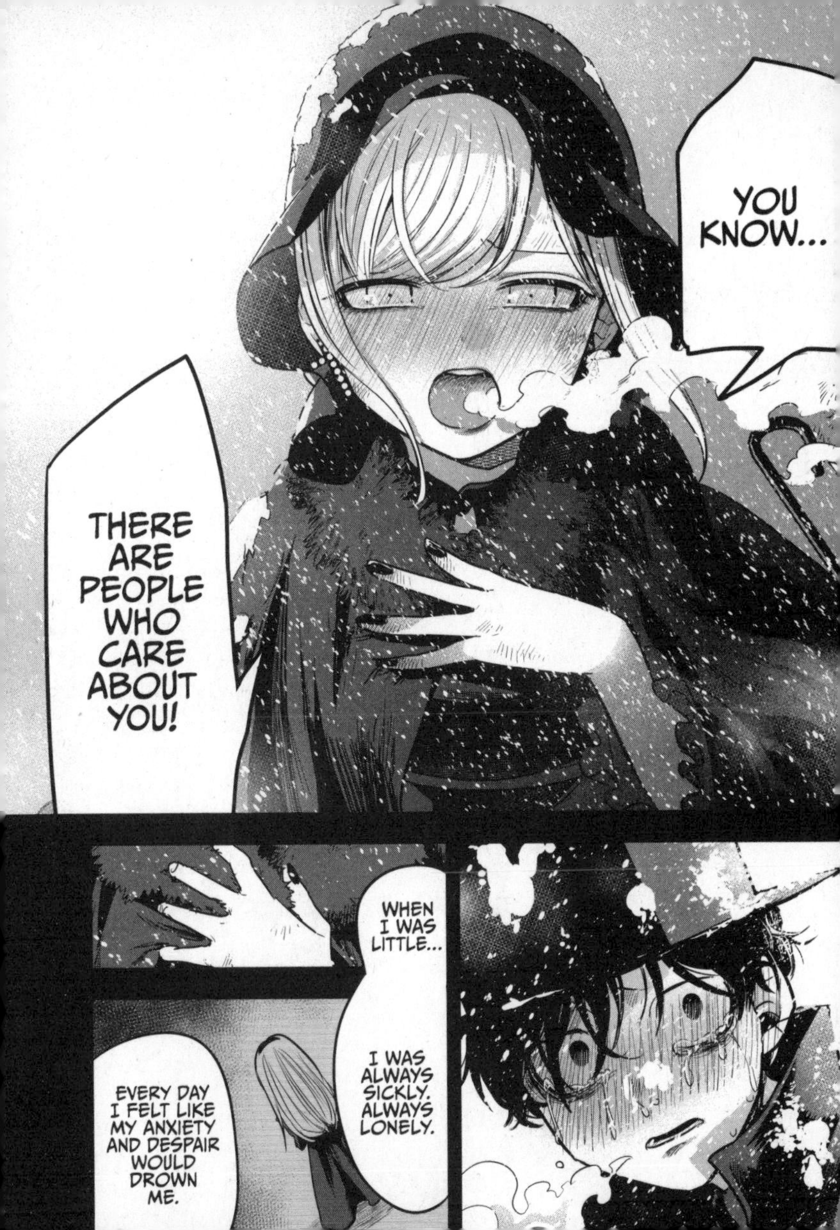
YOU KNOW...
THERE ARE PEOPLE WHO CARE ABOUT YOU!
WHEN I WAS LITTLE...
I WAS ALWAYS SICKLY. ALWAYS LONELY.
EVERY DAY I FELT LIKE MY ANXIETY AND DESPAIR WOULD DROWN ME.

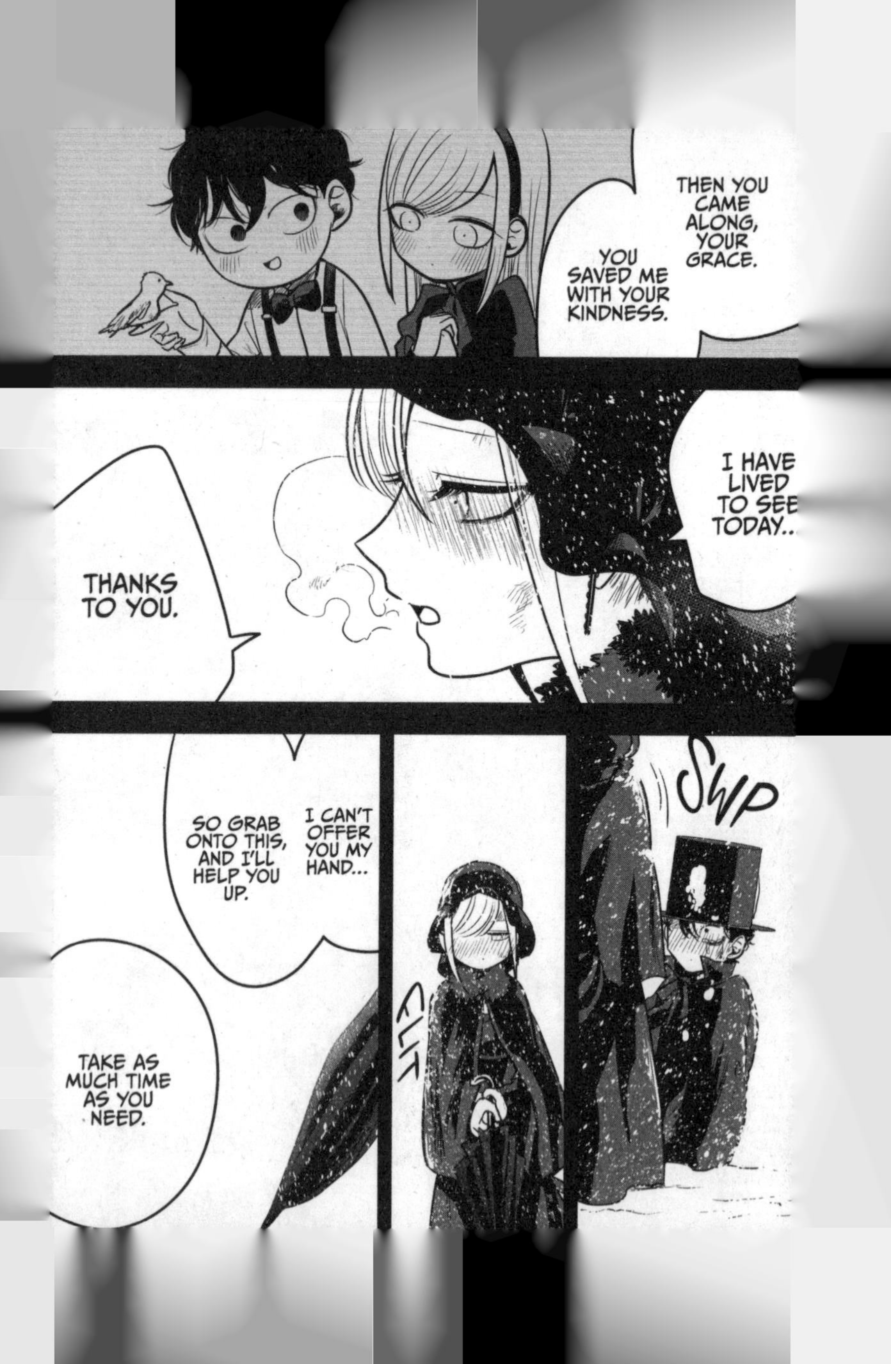
THEN YOU CAME ALONG, YOUR GRACE.
YOU SAVED ME WITH YOUR KINDNESS.
I HAVE LIVED TO SEE TODAY...
THANKS TO YOU.
SWP
FLIT
I CAN'T OFFER YOU MY HAND...
SO GRAB ONTO THIS, AND I'LL HELP YOU UP.
TAKE AS MUCH TIME AS YOU NEED.

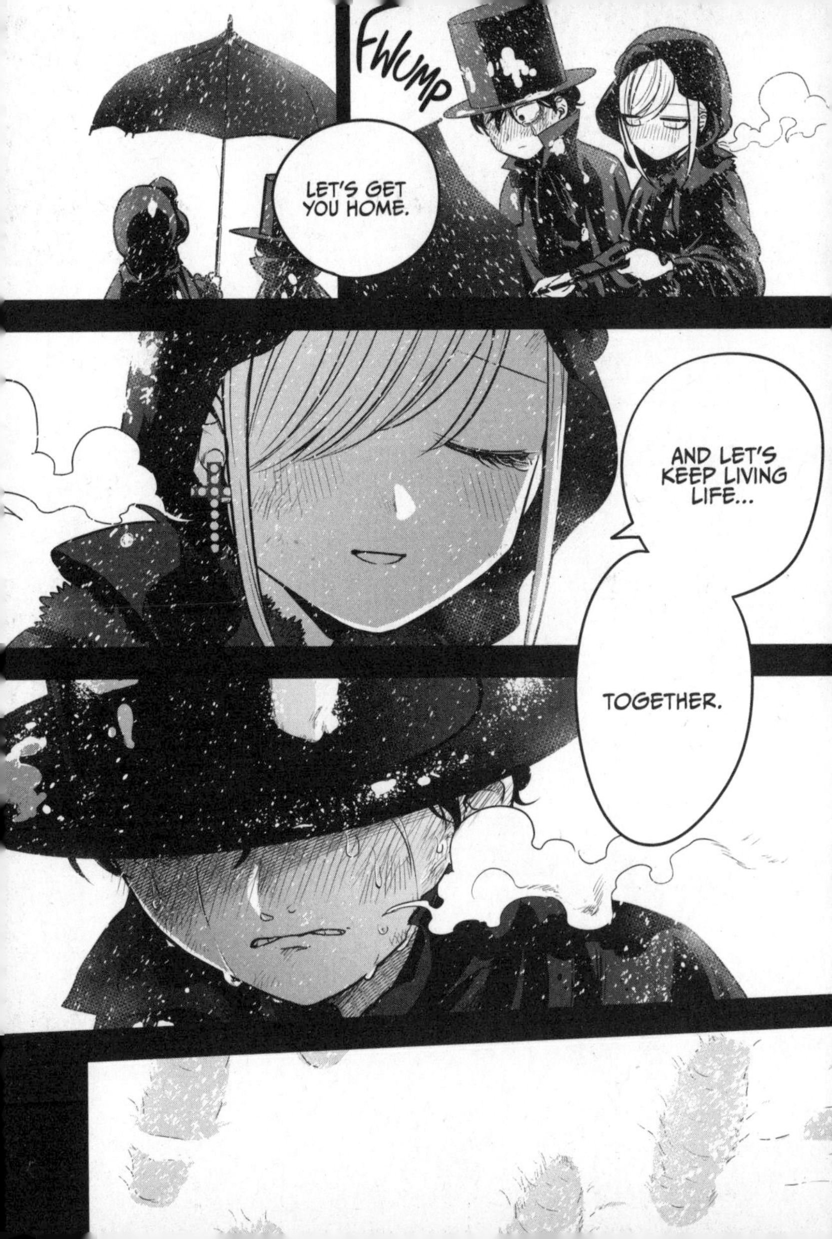
FWUMP
LET'S GET YOU HOME.
AND LET'S KEEP LIVING LIFE...
TOGETHER.

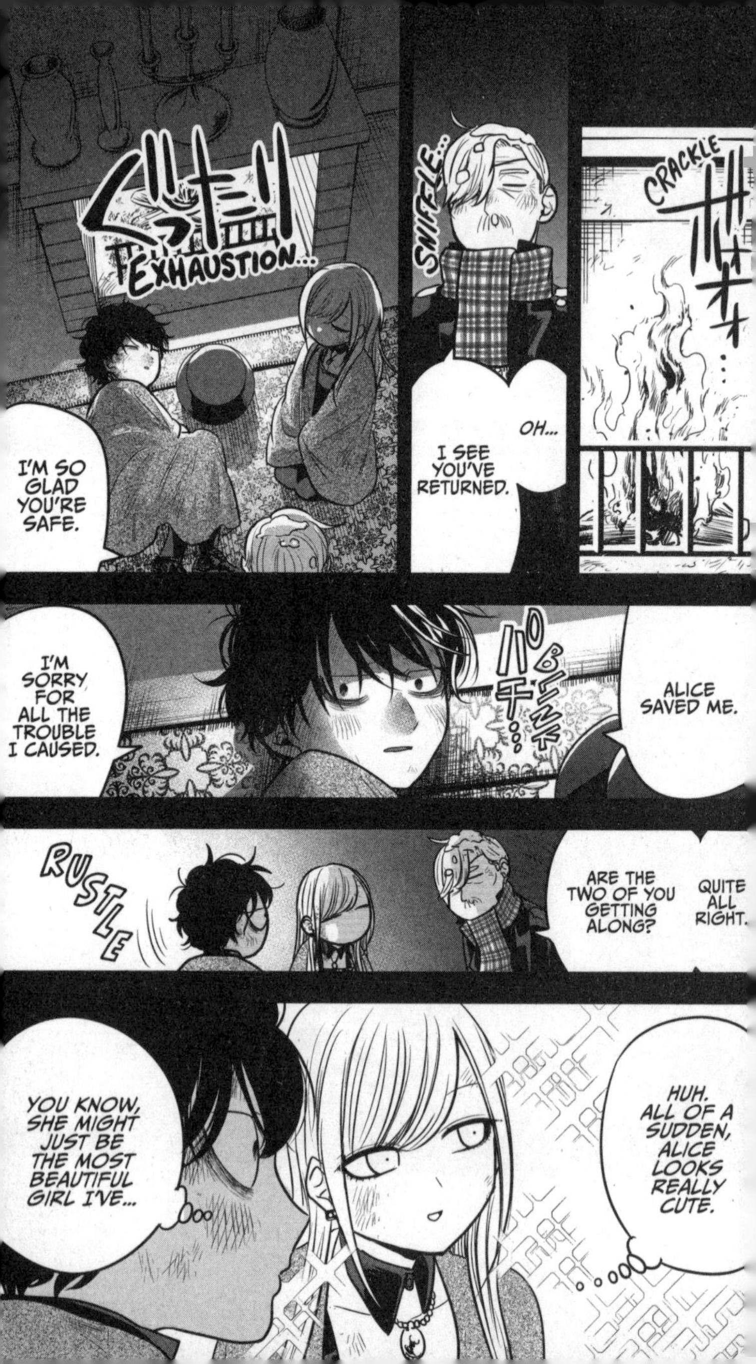
CRACKLE
SNIFFLE...
OH...
I SEE YOU'VE RETURNED.
EXHAUSTION...
I'M SO GLAD YOU'RE SAFE.
ALICE SAVED ME.
BLINK...
I'M SORRY FOR ALL THE TROUBLE I CAUSED.
QUITE ALL RIGHT.
ARE THE TWO OF YOU GETTING ALONG?
RUSTLE
HUH. ALL OF A SUDDEN, ALICE LOOKS REALLY CUTE.
YOU KNOW, SHE MIGHT JUST BE THE MOST BEAUTIFUL GIRL I'VE...

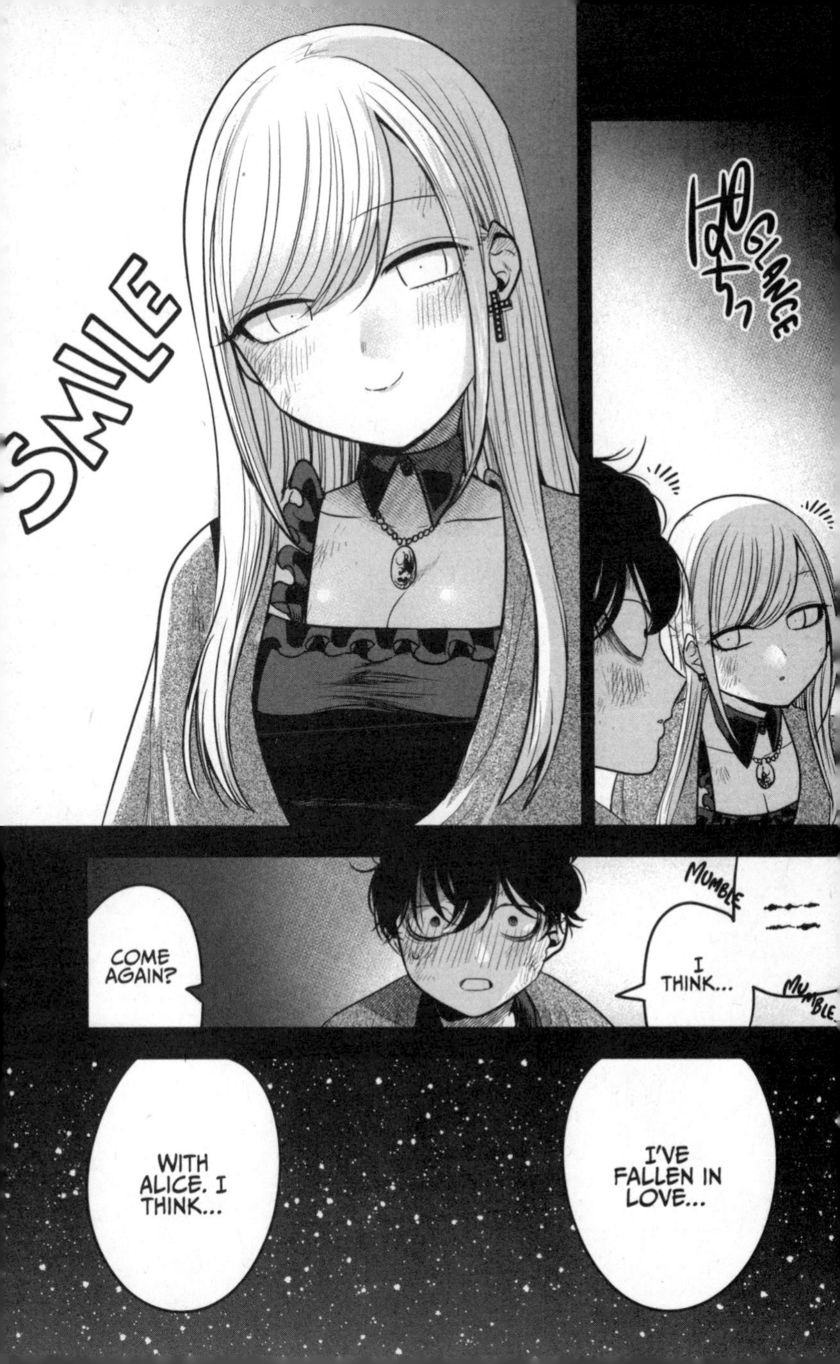
GLANCE
SMILE
MUMBLE
I THINK...
MUMBLE
COME AGAIN?
I'VE FALLEN IN LOVE...
WITH ALICE. I THINK...

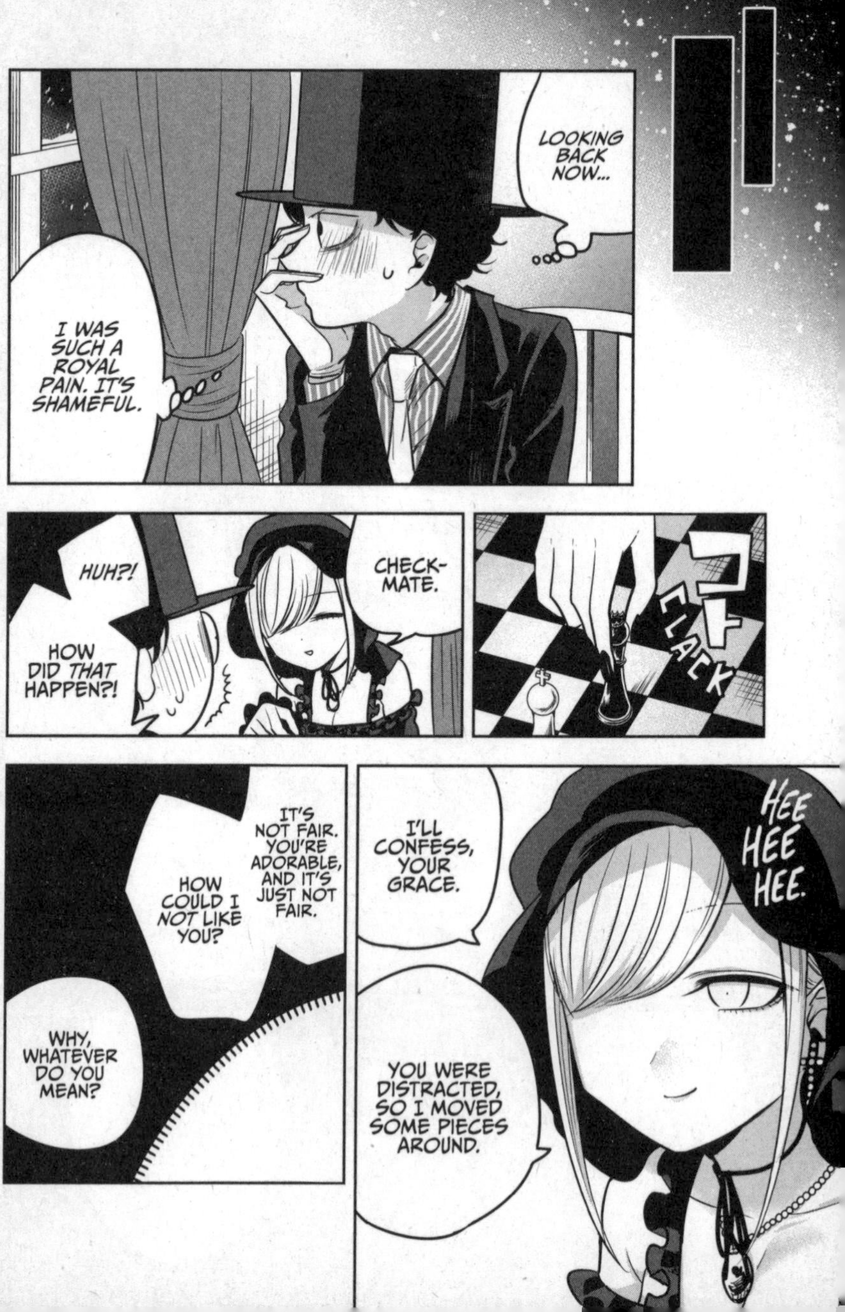

LOOKING BACK NOW...
I WAS SUCH A ROYAL PAIN. IT'S SHAMEFUL.
コト
CLACK
CHECK-MATE.
HUH?!
HOW DID *THAT* HAPPEN?!
HEE HEE HEE.
I'LL CONFESS, YOUR GRACE.
YOU WERE DISTRACTED, SO I MOVED SOME PIECES AROUND.
IT'S NOT FAIR. YOU'RE ADORABLE, AND IT'S JUST NOT FAIR.
HOW COULD I *NOT* LIKE YOU?
WHY, WHATEVER DO YOU MEAN?

THE DUKE OF DEATH AND HIS MAID

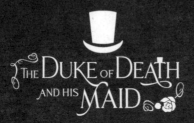

THE DUKE OF DEATH
AND HIS MAID

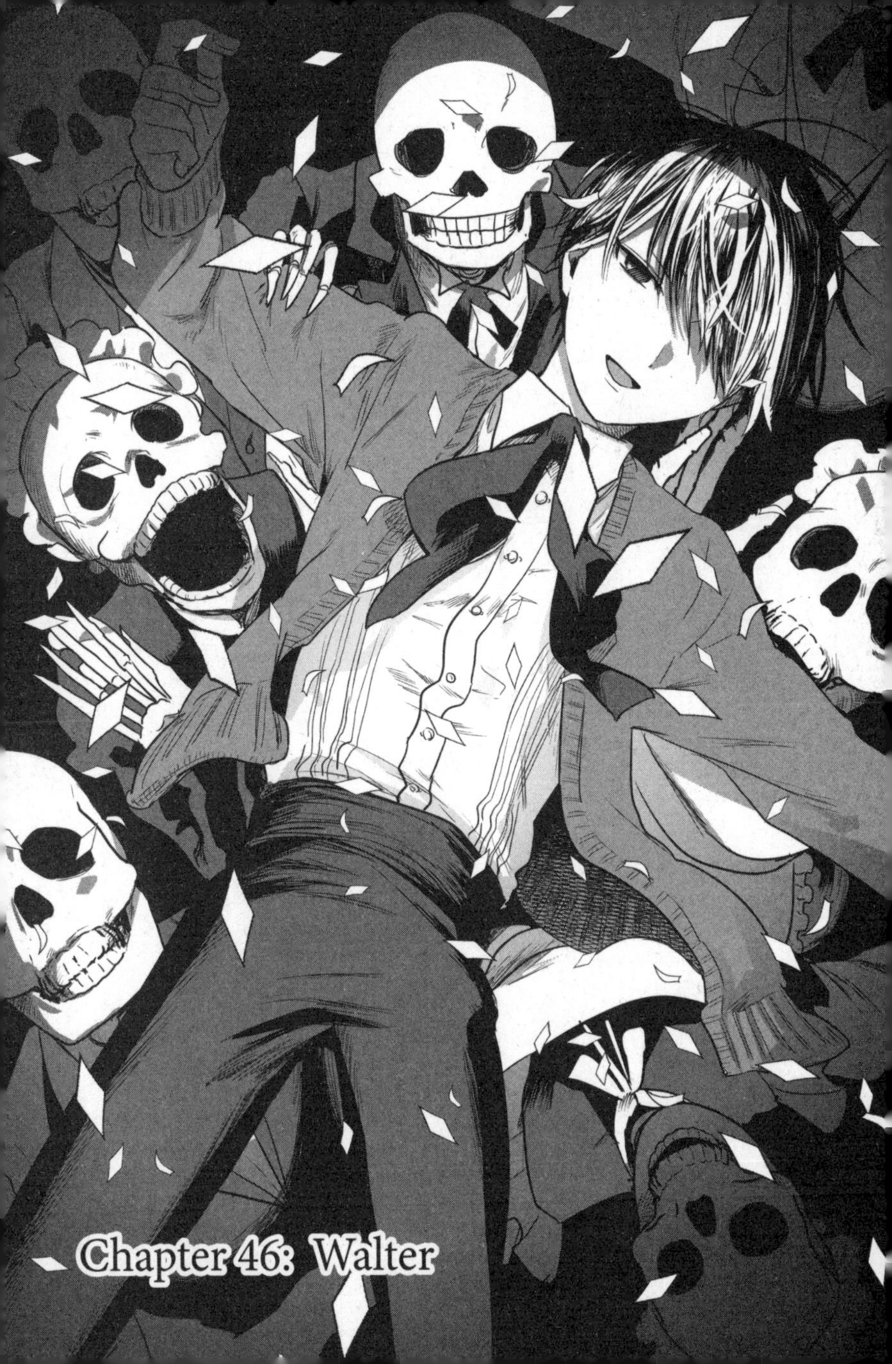
Chapter 46: Walter

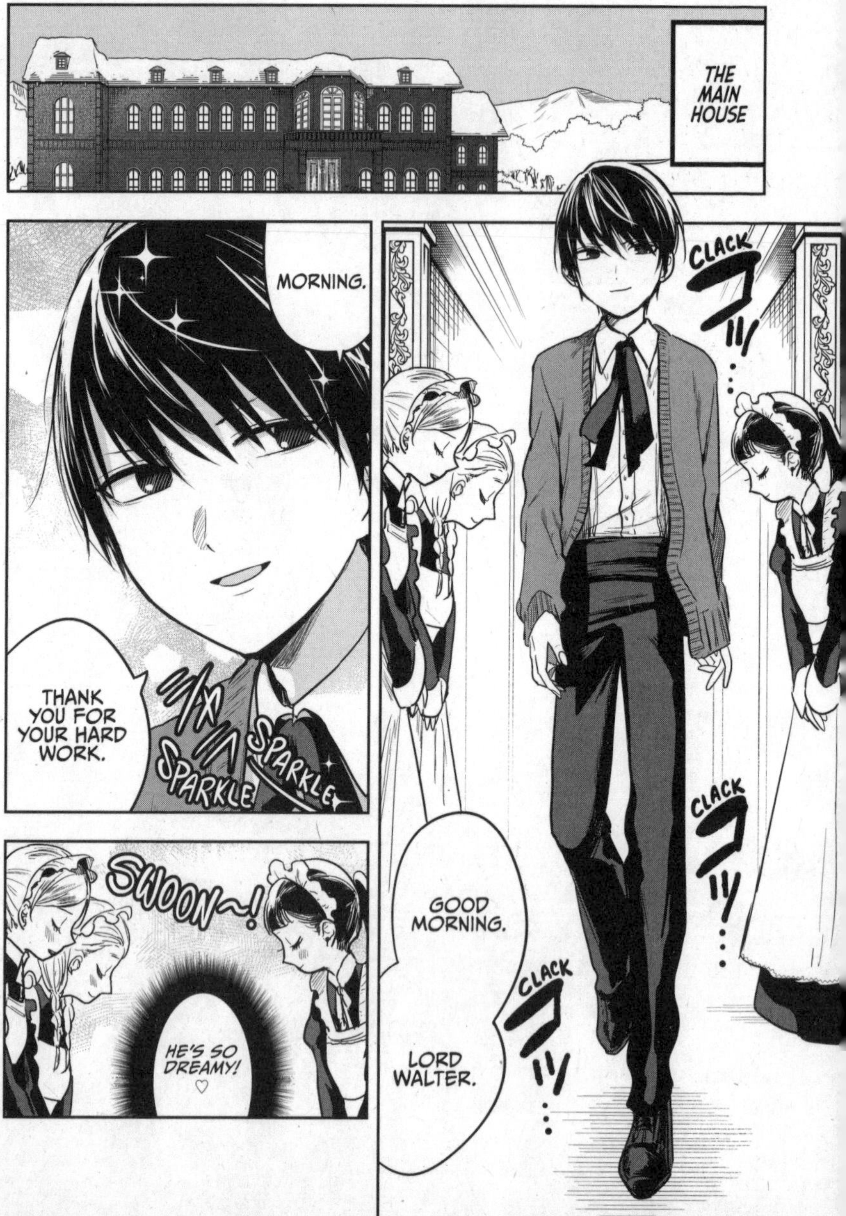
THE MAIN HOUSE
CLACK
CLACK
GOOD MORNING.
CLACK
LORD WALTER.
MORNING.
THANK YOU FOR YOUR HARD WORK.
SPARKLE
SPARKLE
SWOON~!
HE'S SO DREAMY! ♡

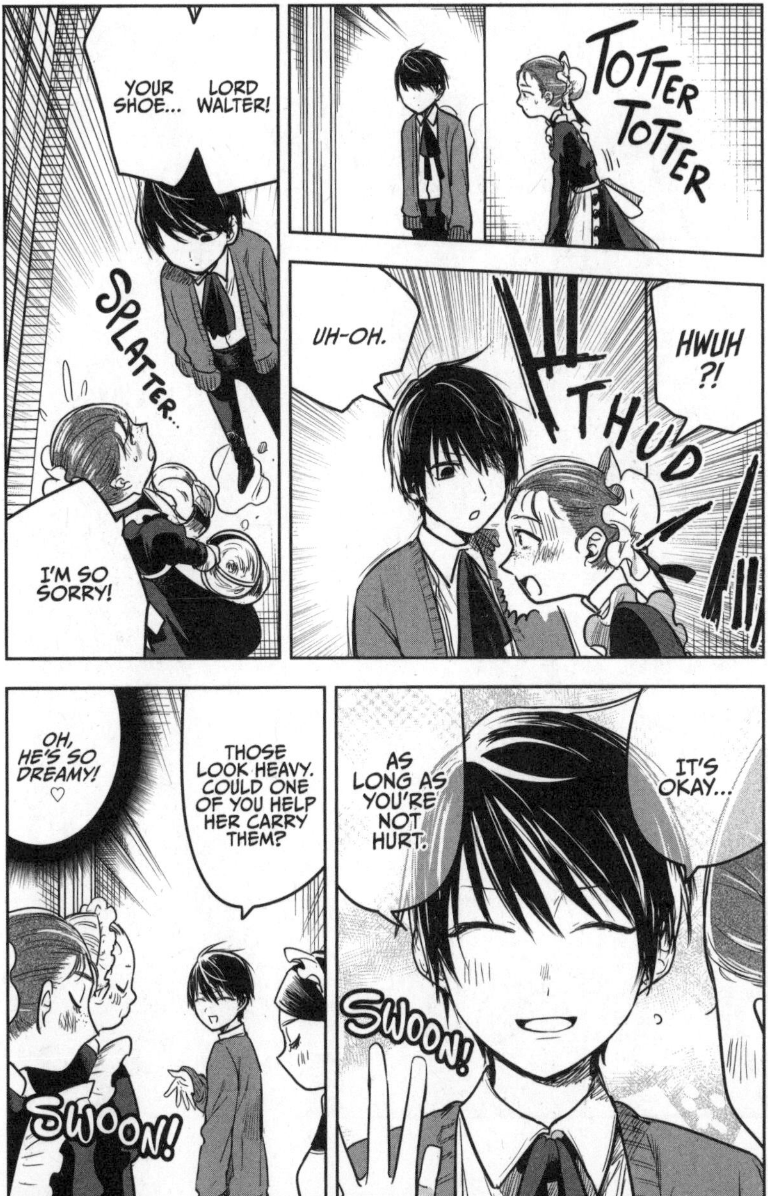
TOTTER TOTTER
LORD WALTER!
YOUR SHOE...
SPLATTER...
I'M SO SORRY!
HWUH ?!
THUD
UH-OH.
IT'S OKAY...
AS LONG AS YOU'RE NOT HURT.
SWOON!
THOSE LOOK HEAVY. COULD ONE OF YOU HELP HER CARRY THEM?
OH, HE'S SO DREAMY! ♡
SWOON!

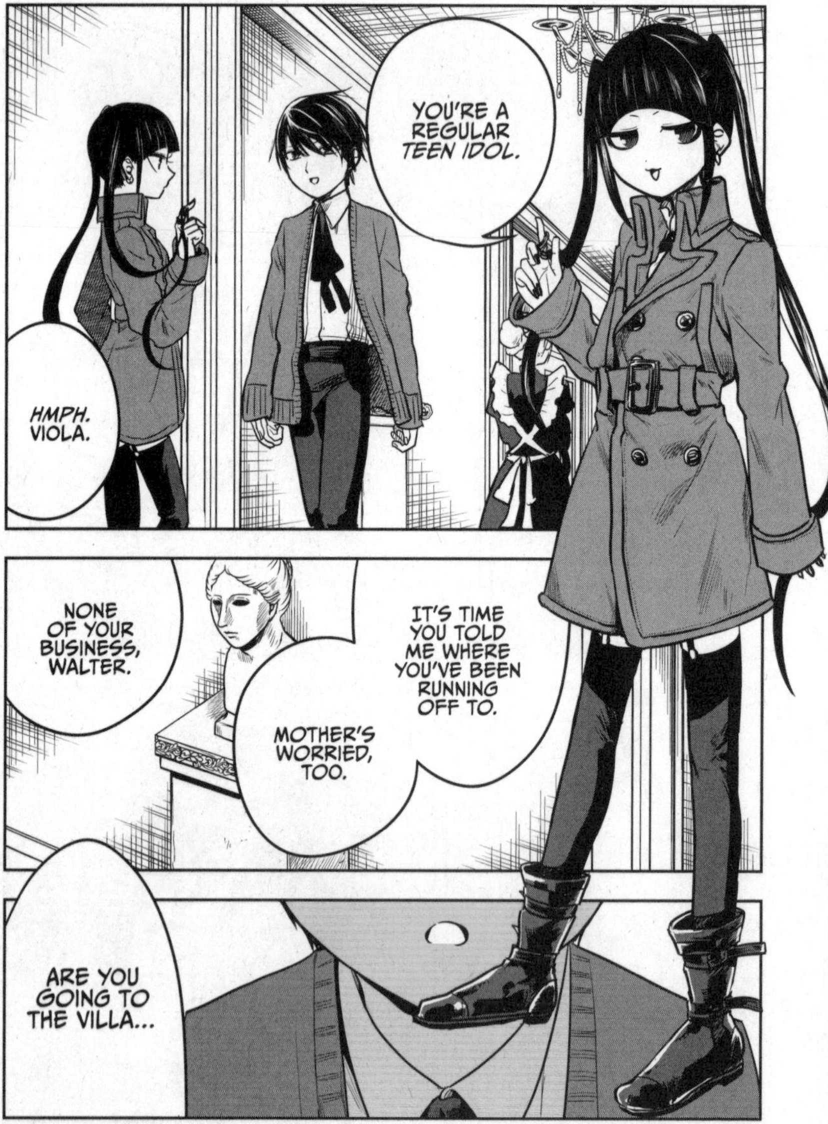
YOU'RE A REGULAR TEEN IDOL.
HMPH. VIOLA.
IT'S TIME YOU TOLD ME WHERE YOU'VE BEEN RUNNING OFF TO.
MOTHER'S WORRIED, TOO.
NONE OF YOUR BUSINESS, WALTER.
ARE YOU GOING TO THE VILLA...

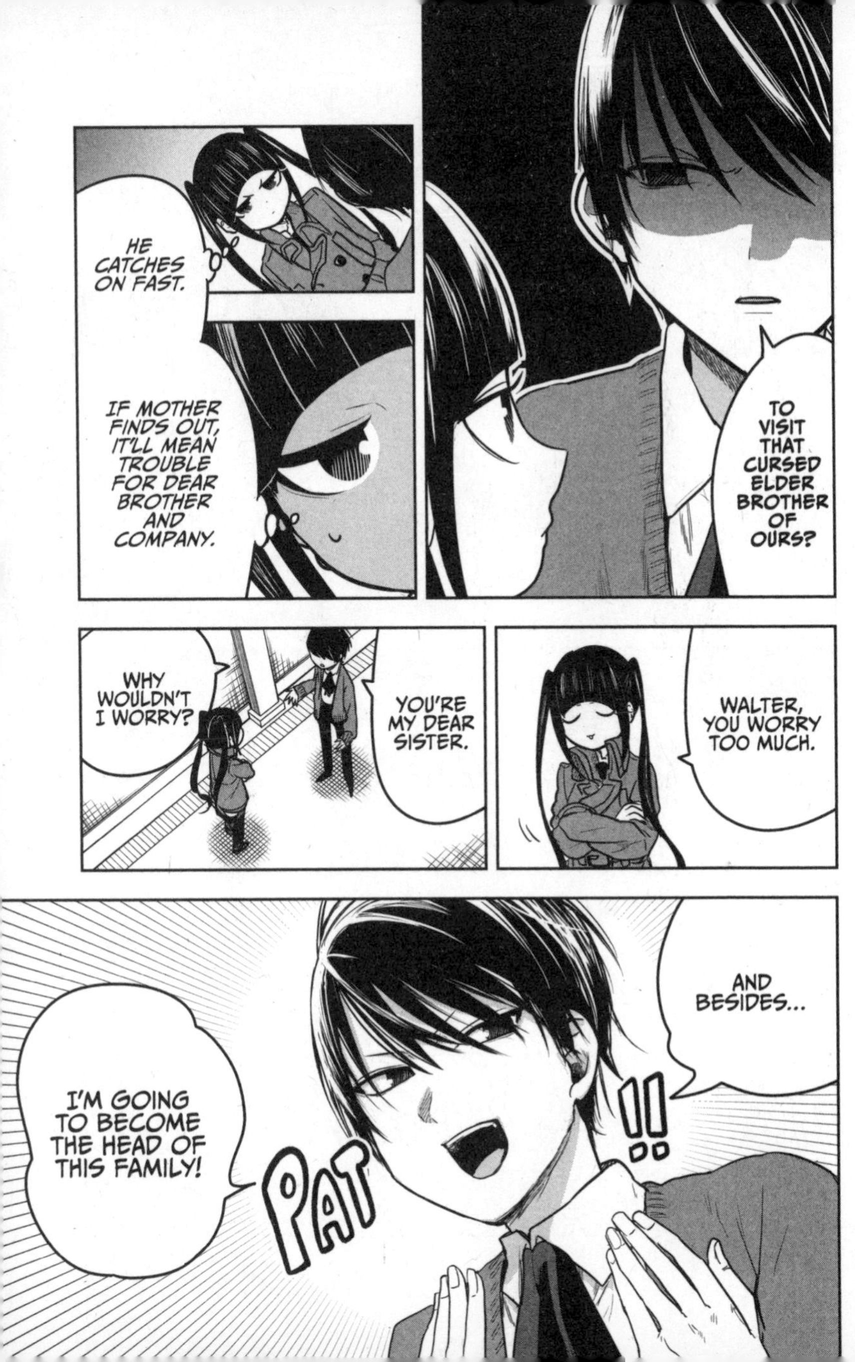
TO VISIT THAT CURSED ELDER BROTHER OF OURS?
HE CATCHES ON FAST.
IF MOTHER FINDS OUT, IT'LL MEAN TROUBLE FOR DEAR BROTHER AND COMPANY.
WALTER, YOU WORRY TOO MUCH.
WHY WOULDN'T I WORRY?
YOU'RE MY DEAR SISTER.
AND BESIDES...
!!
PAT
I'M GOING TO BECOME THE HEAD OF THIS FAMILY!

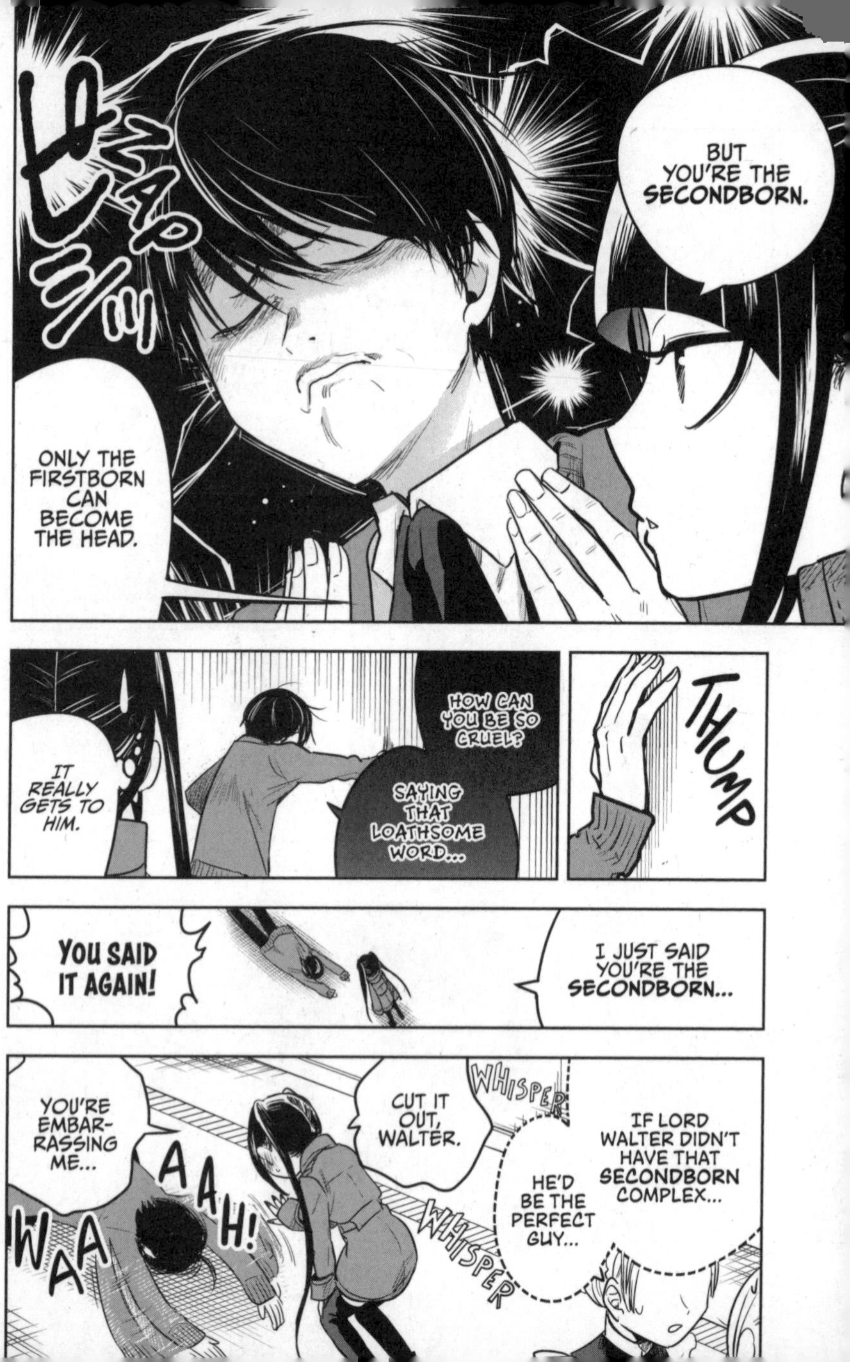

BUT YOU'RE THE SECONDBORN.
ZAP
ONLY THE FIRSTBORN CAN BECOME THE HEAD.
THUMP
HOW CAN YOU BE SO CRUEL?
SAYING THAT LOATHSOME WORD...
IT REALLY GETS TO HIM.
I JUST SAID YOU'RE THE SECONDBORN...
YOU SAID IT AGAIN!
WHISPER
IF LORD WALTER DIDN'T HAVE THAT SECONDBORN COMPLEX...
HE'D BE THE PERFECT GUY...
WHISPER
CUT IT OUT, WALTER.
YOU'RE EMBARRASSING ME...
WAAAAH!

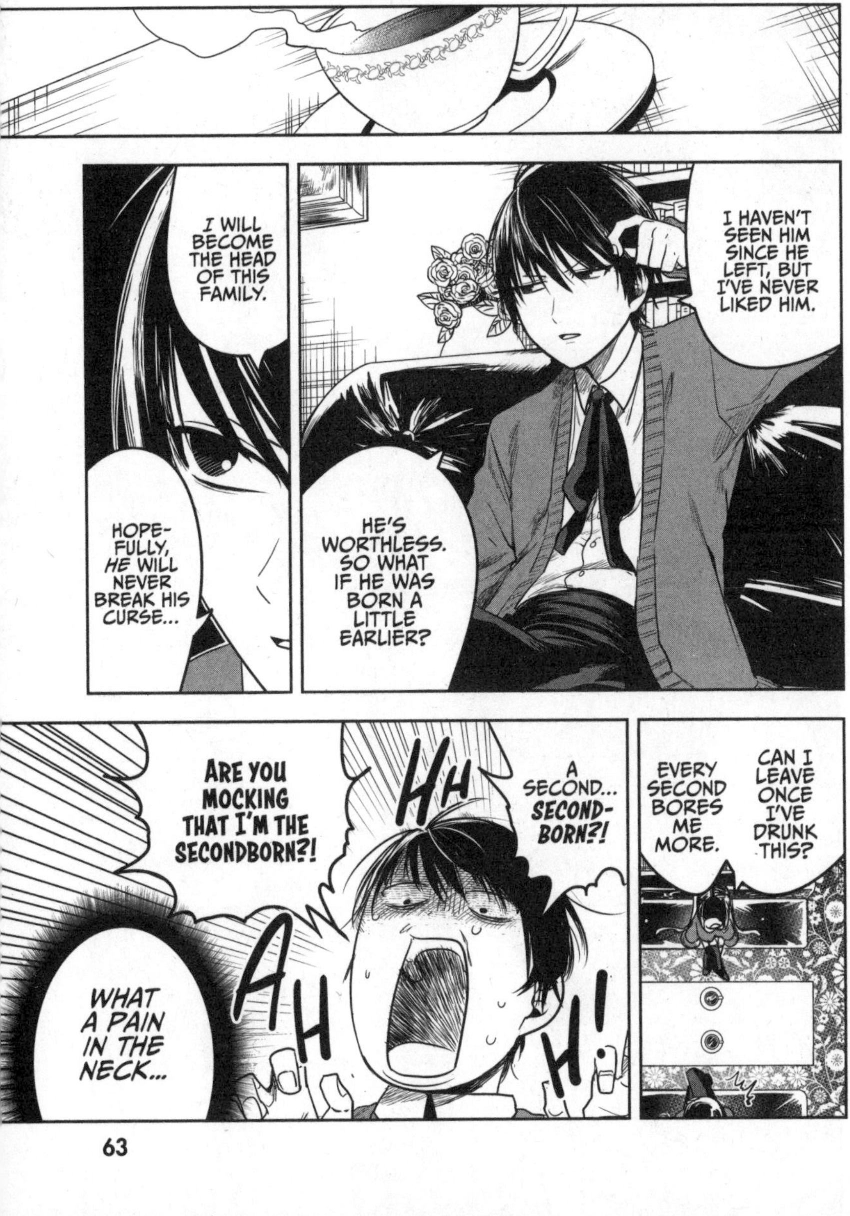
I HAVEN'T SEEN HIM SINCE HE LEFT, BUT I'VE NEVER LIKED HIM.
HE'S WORTHLESS. SO WHAT IF HE WAS BORN A LITTLE EARLIER?
I WILL BECOME THE HEAD OF THIS FAMILY.
HOPE-FULLY, *HE* WILL NEVER BREAK HIS CURSE...
CAN I LEAVE ONCE I'VE DRUNK THIS?
EVERY SECOND BORES ME MORE.
A SECOND... SECOND-BORN?!
HHAHHH!
ARE YOU MOCKING THAT I'M THE SECONDBORN?!
WHAT A PAIN IN THE NECK...

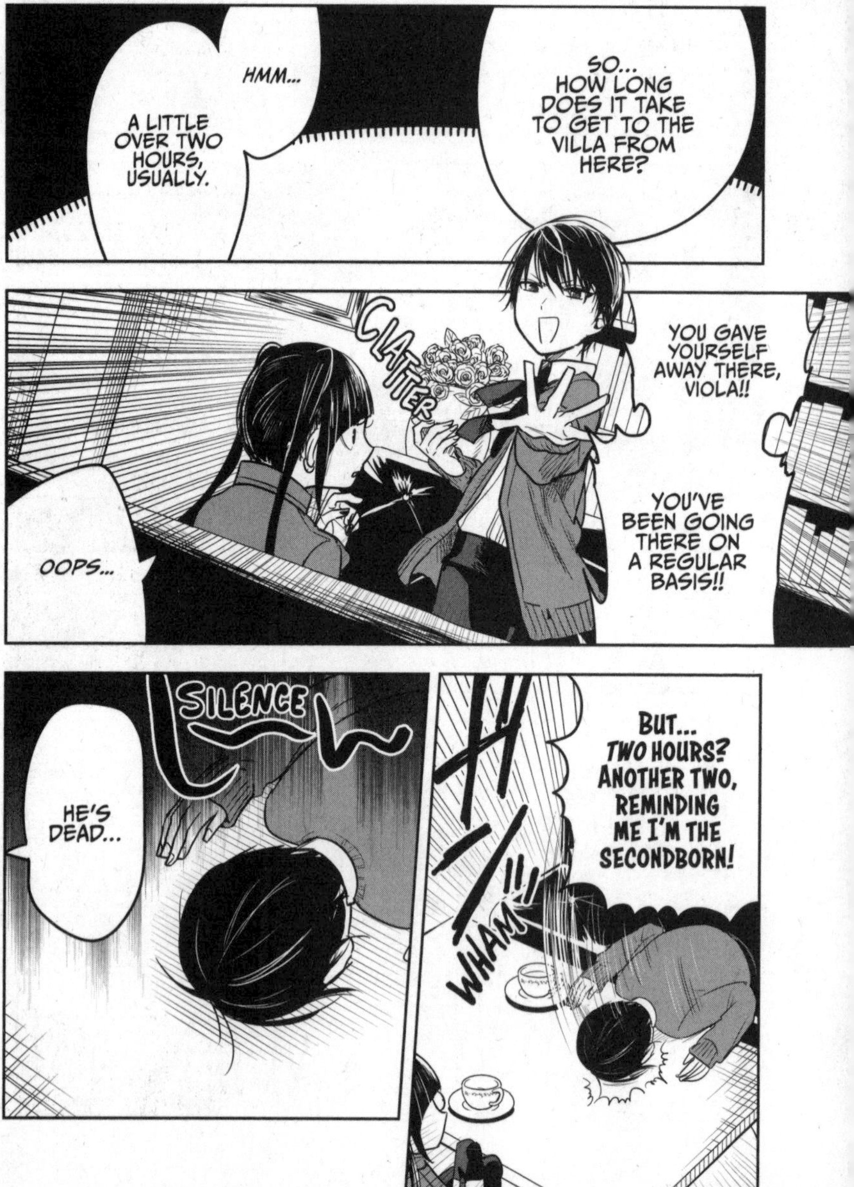
SO... HOW LONG DOES IT TAKE TO GET TO THE VILLA FROM HERE?
HMM...
A LITTLE OVER TWO HOURS, USUALLY.
YOU GAVE YOURSELF AWAY THERE, VIOLA!!
YOU'VE BEEN GOING THERE ON A REGULAR BASIS!!
CLATTER
OOPS...
BUT... TWO HOURS? ANOTHER TWO, REMINDING ME I'M THE SECONDBORN!
WHAM!!!
SILENCE
HE'S DEAD...

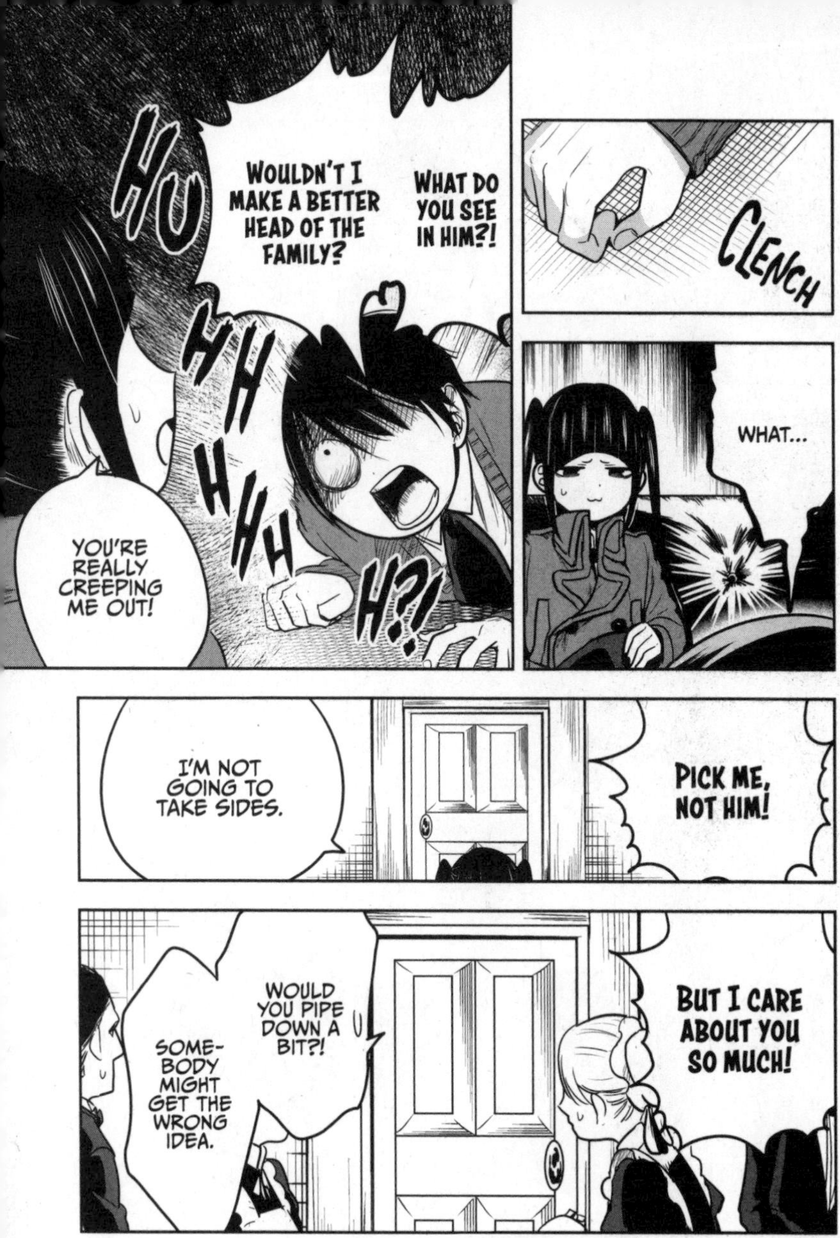
CLENCH
WHAT...
WHAT DO YOU SEE IN HIM?!
WOULDN'T I MAKE A BETTER HEAD OF THE FAMILY?
HUHHHHHHH?!
YOU'RE REALLY CREEPING ME OUT!
PICK ME, NOT HIM!
I'M NOT GOING TO TAKE SIDES.
BUT I CARE ABOUT YOU SO MUCH!
WOULD YOU PIPE DOWN A BIT?!
SOME-BODY MIGHT GET THE WRONG IDEA.

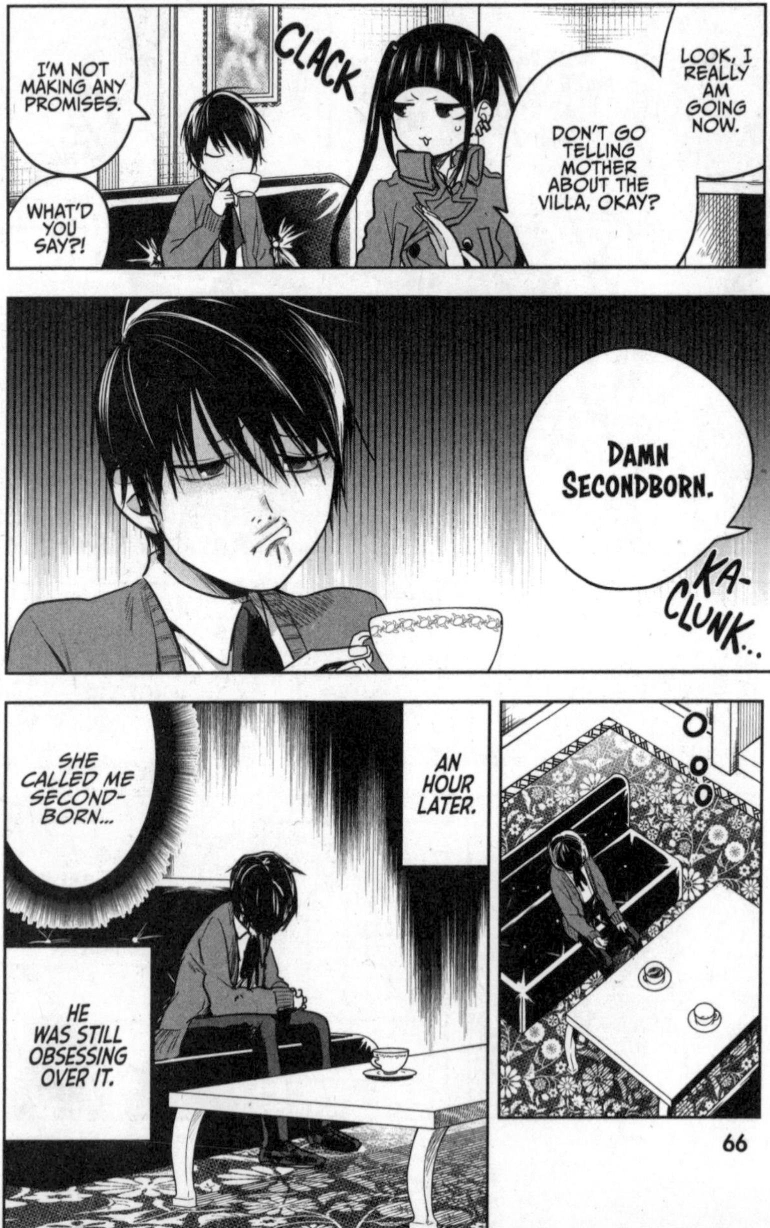
LOOK, I REALLY AM GOING NOW.
DON'T GO TELLING MOTHER ABOUT THE VILLA, OKAY?
CLACK
I'M NOT MAKING ANY PROMISES.
WHAT'D YOU SAY?!
DAMN SECONDBORN.
KA-CLUNK...
OOO
AN HOUR LATER.
SHE CALLED ME SECOND-BORN...
HE WAS STILL OBSESSING OVER IT.

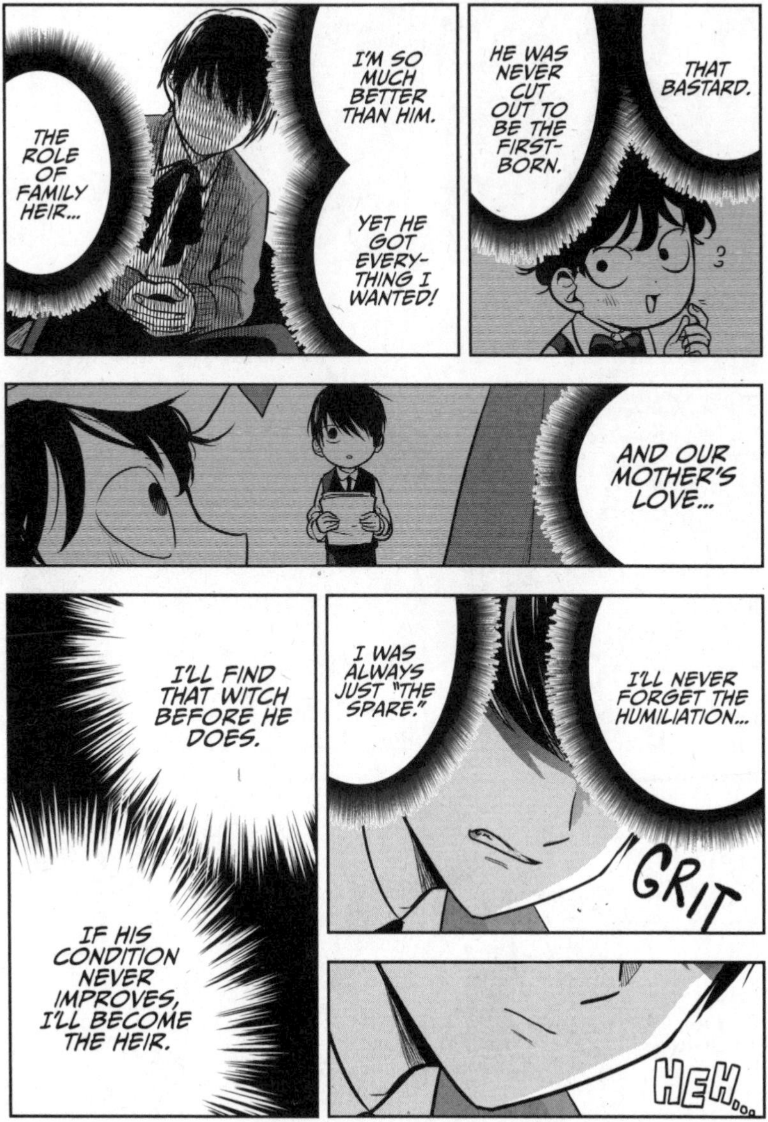
THAT BASTARD.
HE WAS NEVER CUT OUT TO BE THE FIRST-BORN.
I'M SO MUCH BETTER THAN HIM.
YET HE GOT EVERYTHING I WANTED!
THE ROLE OF FAMILY HEIR...
AND OUR MOTHER'S LOVE...
I'LL NEVER FORGET THE HUMILIATION...
I WAS ALWAYS JUST "THE SPARE."
GRIT
HEH...
I'LL FIND THAT WITCH BEFORE HE DOES.
IF HIS CONDITION NEVER IMPROVES, I'LL BECOME THE HEIR.

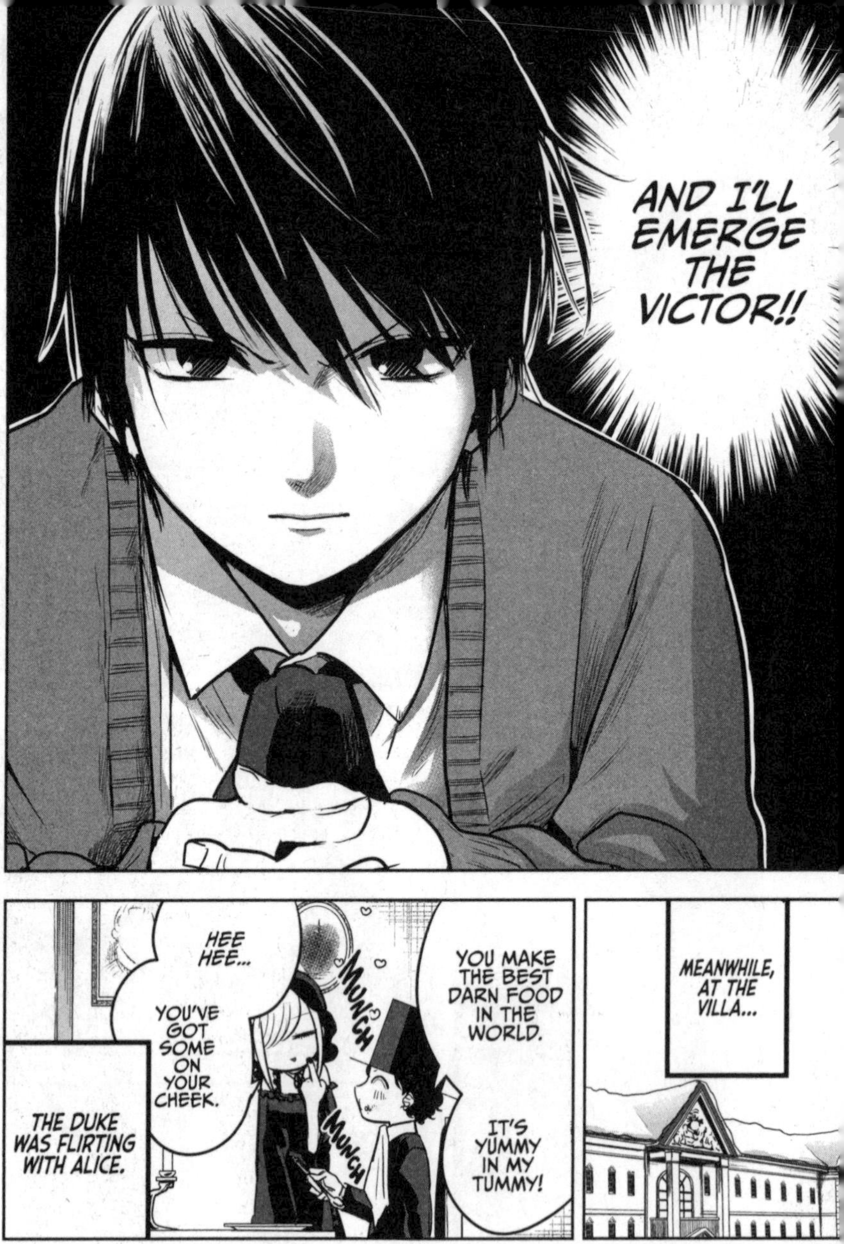
AND I'LL EMERGE THE VICTOR!!
MEANWHILE, AT THE VILLA...
YOU MAKE THE BEST DARN FOOD IN THE WORLD.
IT'S YUMMY IN MY TUMMY!
MUNCH
MUNCH
HEE HEE...
YOU'VE GOT SOME ON YOUR CHEEK.
THE DUKE WAS FLIRTING WITH ALICE.

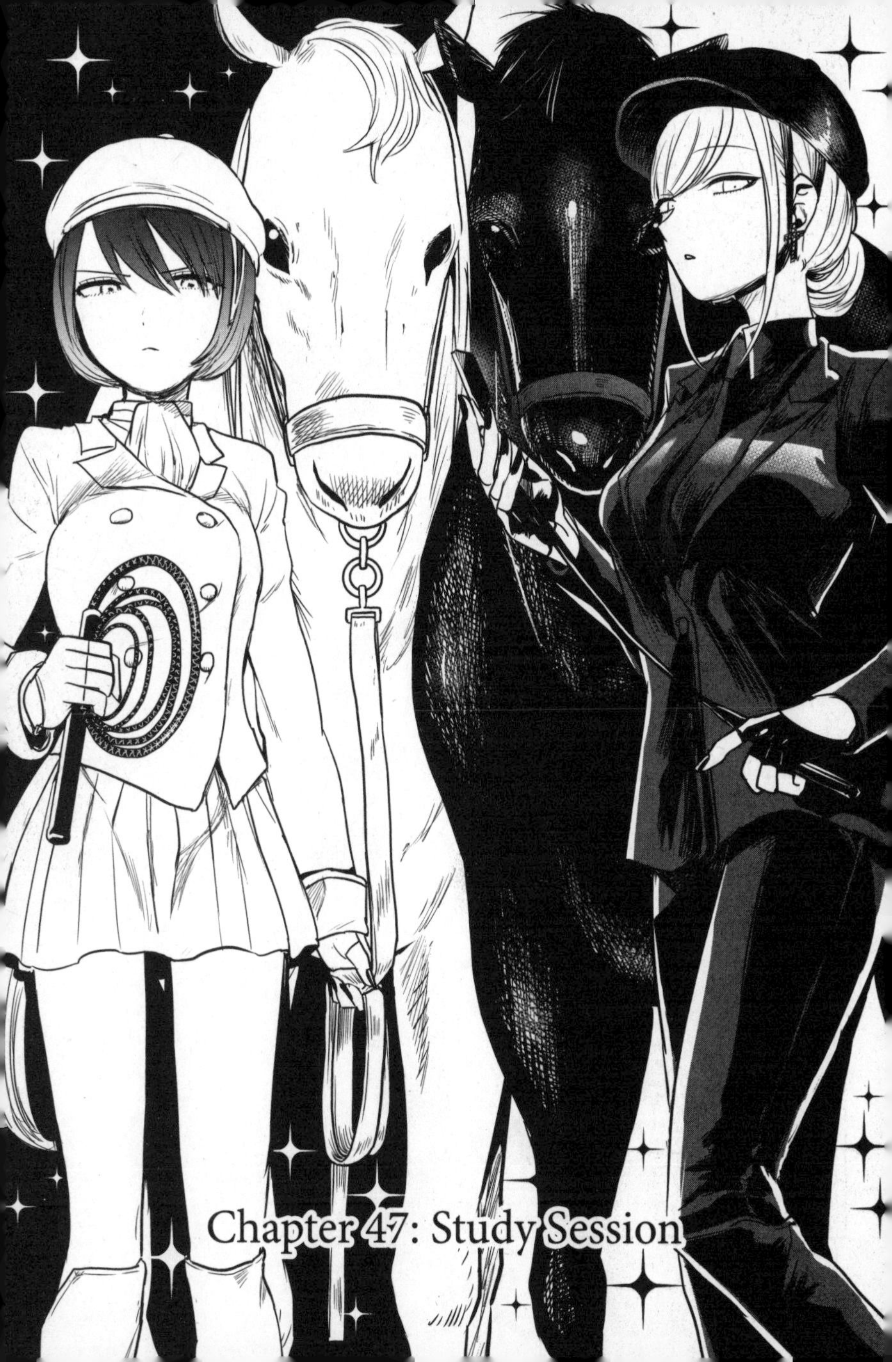
Chapter 47: Study Session

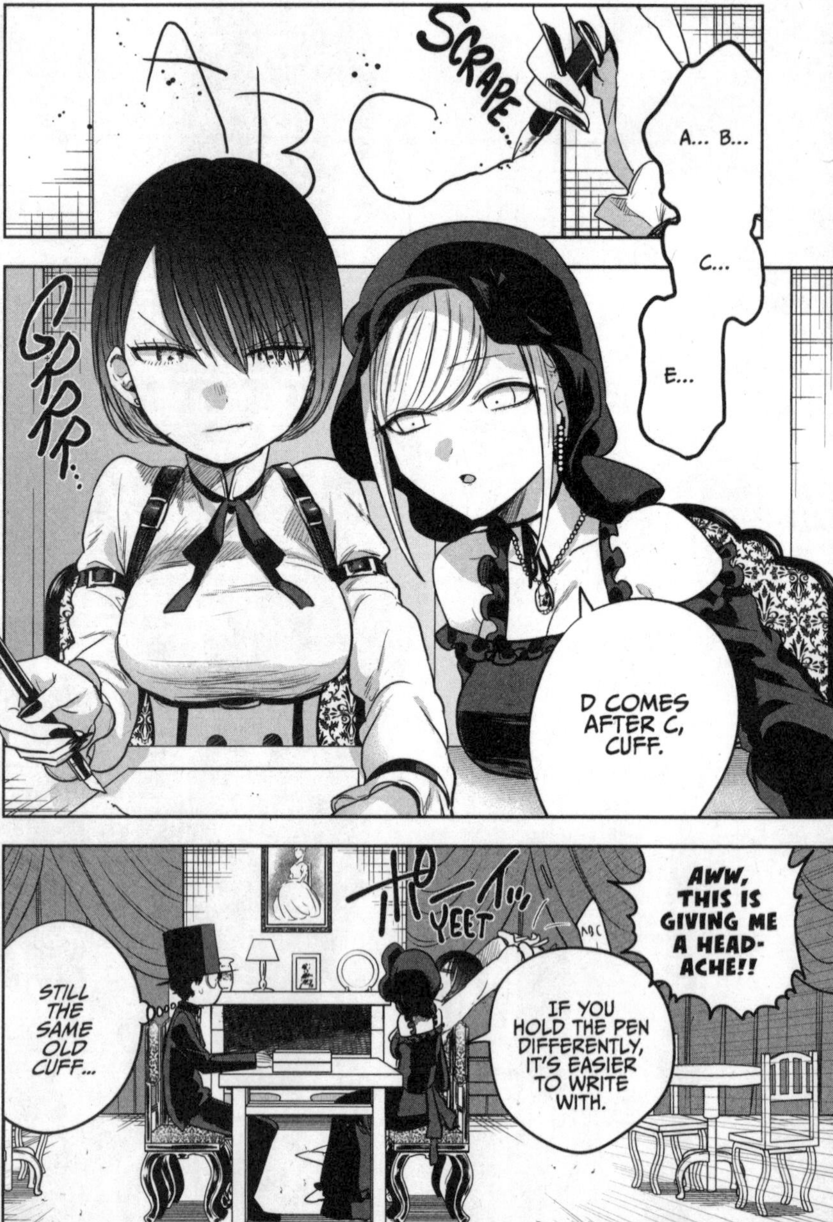
SCRAPE...
A... B...
C...
E...
ABC
GRRRR...
D COMES AFTER C, CUFF.
AWW, THIS IS GIVING ME A HEAD-ACHE!!
YEET
ABC
IF YOU HOLD THE PEN DIFFERENTLY, IT'S EASIER TO WRITE WITH.
STILL THE SAME OLD CUFF...

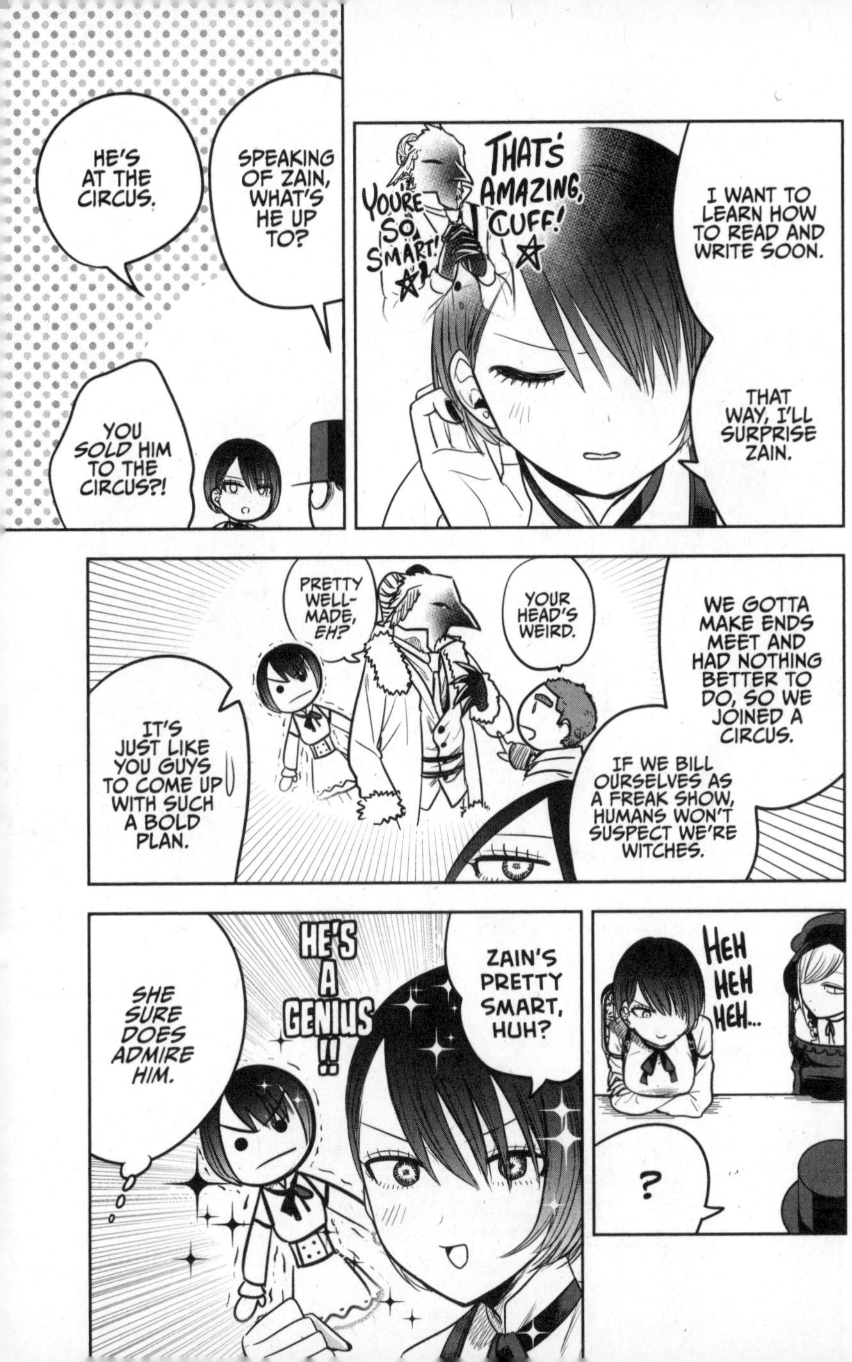
I WANT TO LEARN HOW TO READ AND WRITE SOON.
THAT WAY, I'LL SURPRISE ZAIN.
THAT'S AMAZING, CUFF!
YOU'RE SO SMART!
SPEAKING OF ZAIN, WHAT'S HE UP TO?
HE'S AT THE CIRCUS.
YOU SOLD HIM TO THE CIRCUS?!
WE GOTTA MAKE ENDS MEET AND HAD NOTHING BETTER TO DO, SO WE JOINED A CIRCUS.
IF WE BILL OURSELVES AS A FREAK SHOW, HUMANS WON'T SUSPECT WE'RE WITCHES.
YOUR HEAD'S WEIRD.
PRETTY WELL-MADE, EH?
IT'S JUST LIKE YOU GUYS TO COME UP WITH SUCH A BOLD PLAN.
HEH HEH HEH...
?
ZAIN'S PRETTY SMART, HUH?
HE'S A GENIUS!!
SHE SURE DOES ADMIRE HIM.

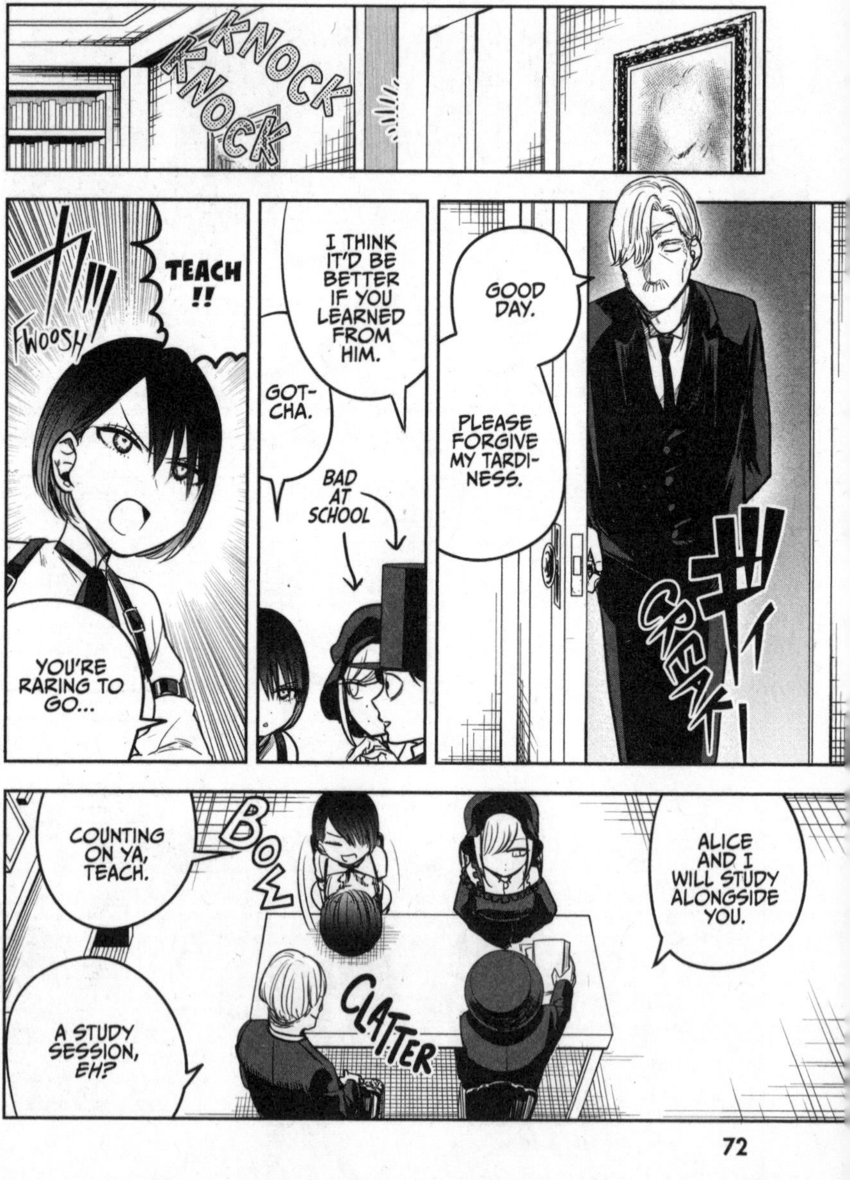
KNOCK KNOCK
GOOD DAY.
PLEASE FORGIVE MY TARDINESS.
CREAK
I THINK IT'D BE BETTER IF YOU LEARNED FROM HIM.
GOT-CHA.
BAD AT SCHOOL
TEACH!!
FWOOSH
YOU'RE RARING TO GO...
ALICE AND I WILL STUDY ALONGSIDE YOU.
CLATTER
BOW
COUNTING ON YA, TEACH.
A STUDY SESSION, EH?

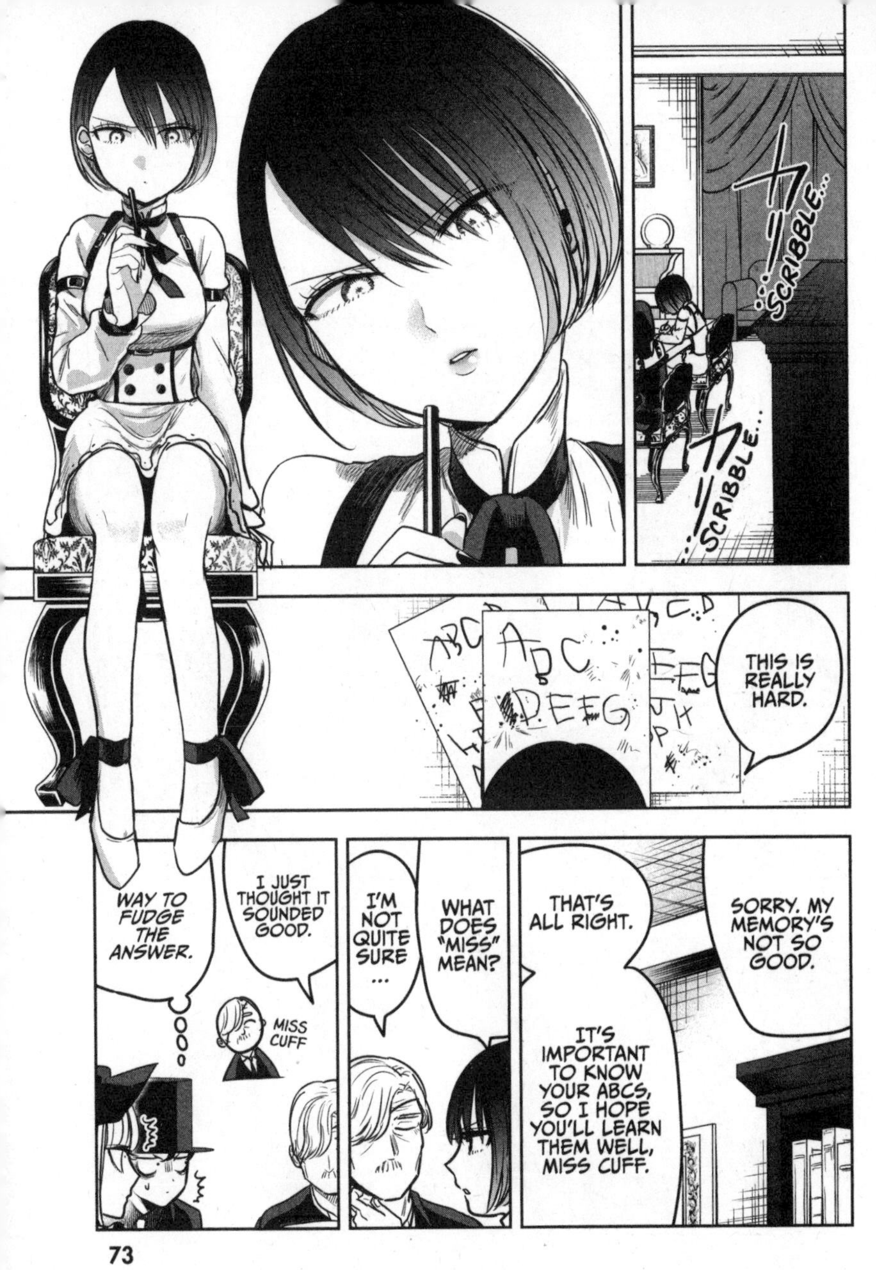
SCRIBBLE...
SCRIBBLE...
THIS IS REALLY HARD.
SORRY. MY MEMORY'S NOT SO GOOD.
THAT'S ALL RIGHT.
IT'S IMPORTANT TO KNOW YOUR ABCS, SO I HOPE YOU'LL LEARN THEM WELL, MISS CUFF.
WHAT DOES "MISS" MEAN?
I'M NOT QUITE SURE ...
I JUST THOUGHT IT SOUNDED GOOD.
WAY TO FUDGE THE ANSWER.
MISS CUFF

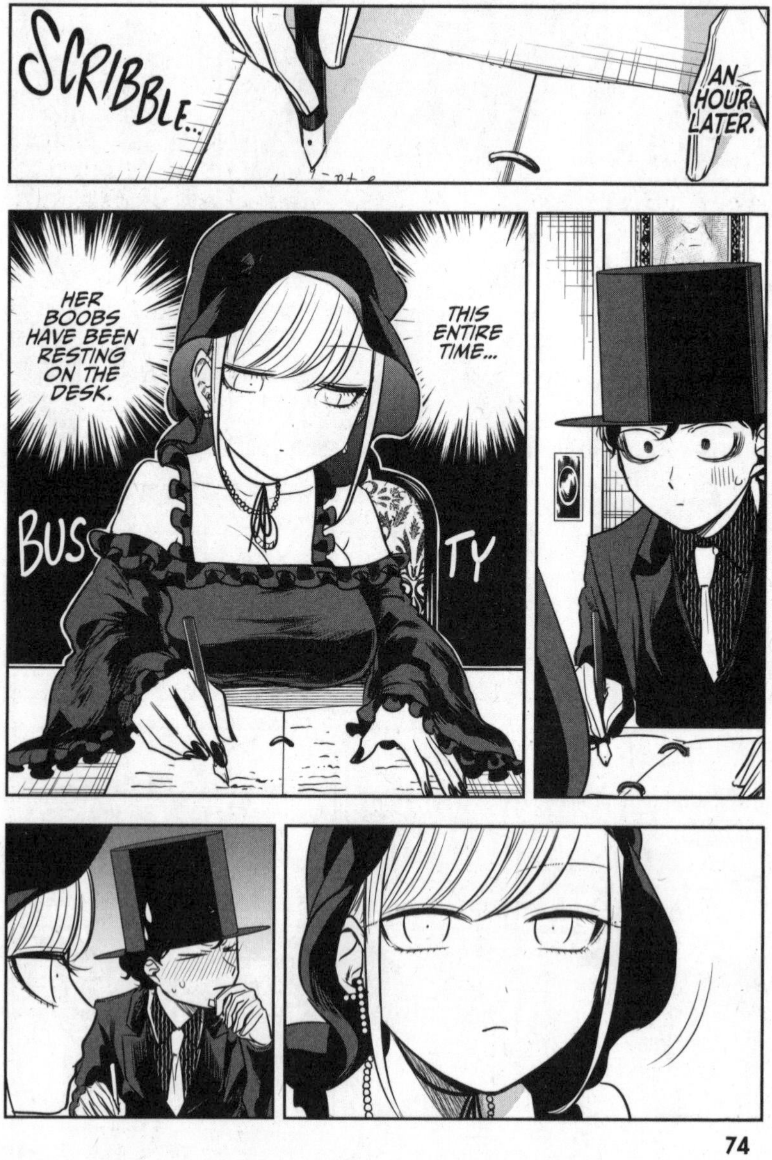
AN HOUR LATER.
SCRIBBLE...
THIS ENTIRE TIME...
HER BOOBS HAVE BEEN RESTING ON THE DESK.
BUSTY

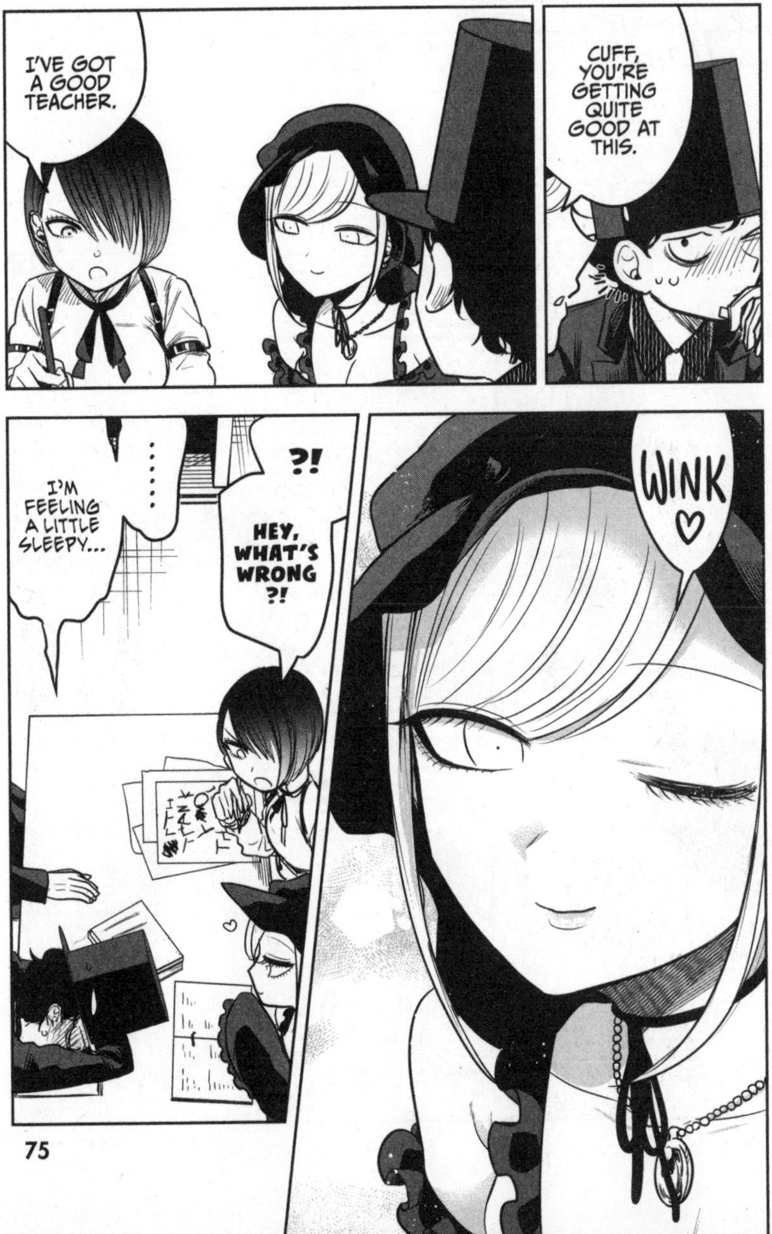
CUFF, YOU'RE GETTING QUITE GOOD AT THIS.
I'VE GOT A GOOD TEACHER.
WINK ♡
?!
HEY, WHAT'S WRONG?!
......
I'M FEELING A LITTLE SLEEPY...

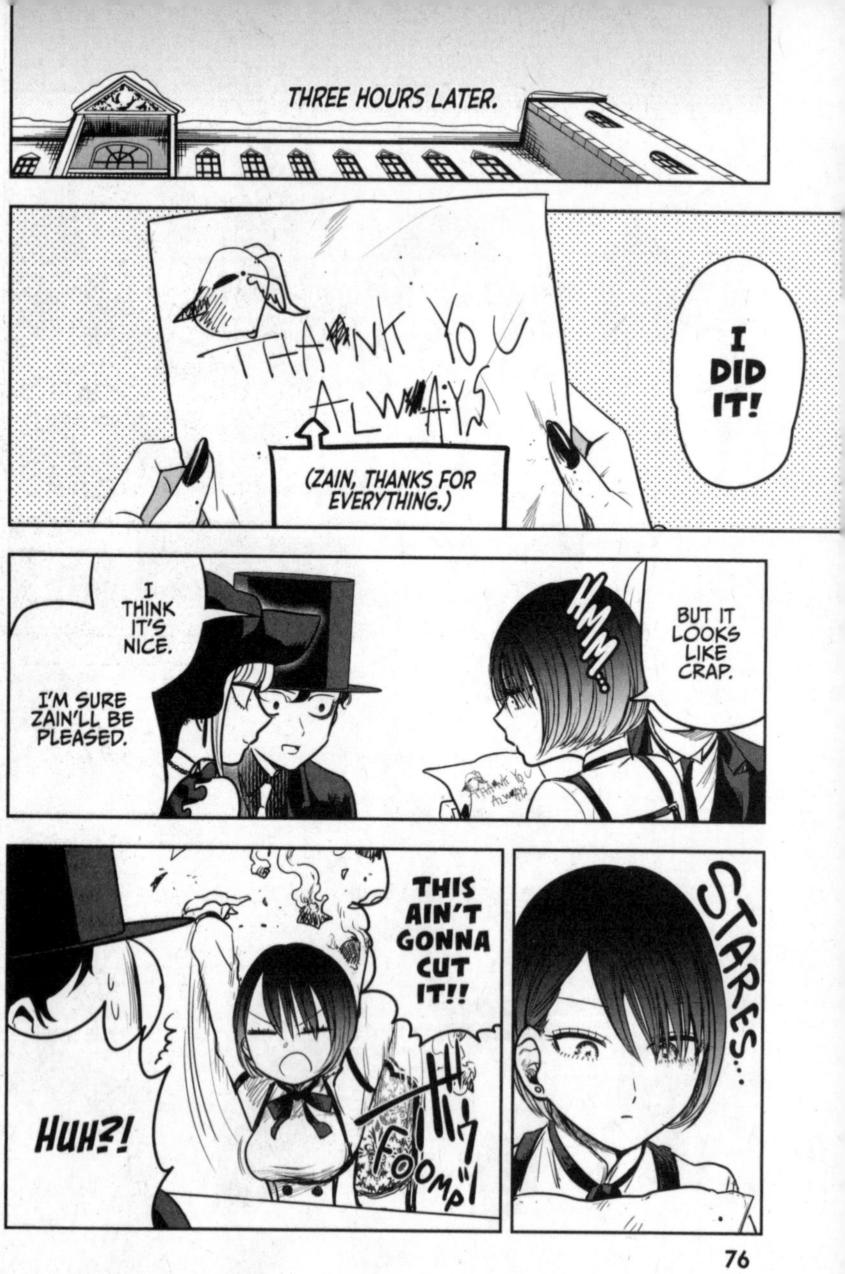
THREE HOURS LATER.
I DID IT!
THANK YOU ALWAYS
(ZAIN, THANKS FOR EVERYTHING.)
HMM...
BUT IT LOOKS LIKE CRAP.
I THINK IT'S NICE.
I'M SURE ZAIN'LL BE PLEASED.
STARES...
THIS AIN'T GONNA CUT IT!!
FOOMP
HUH?!

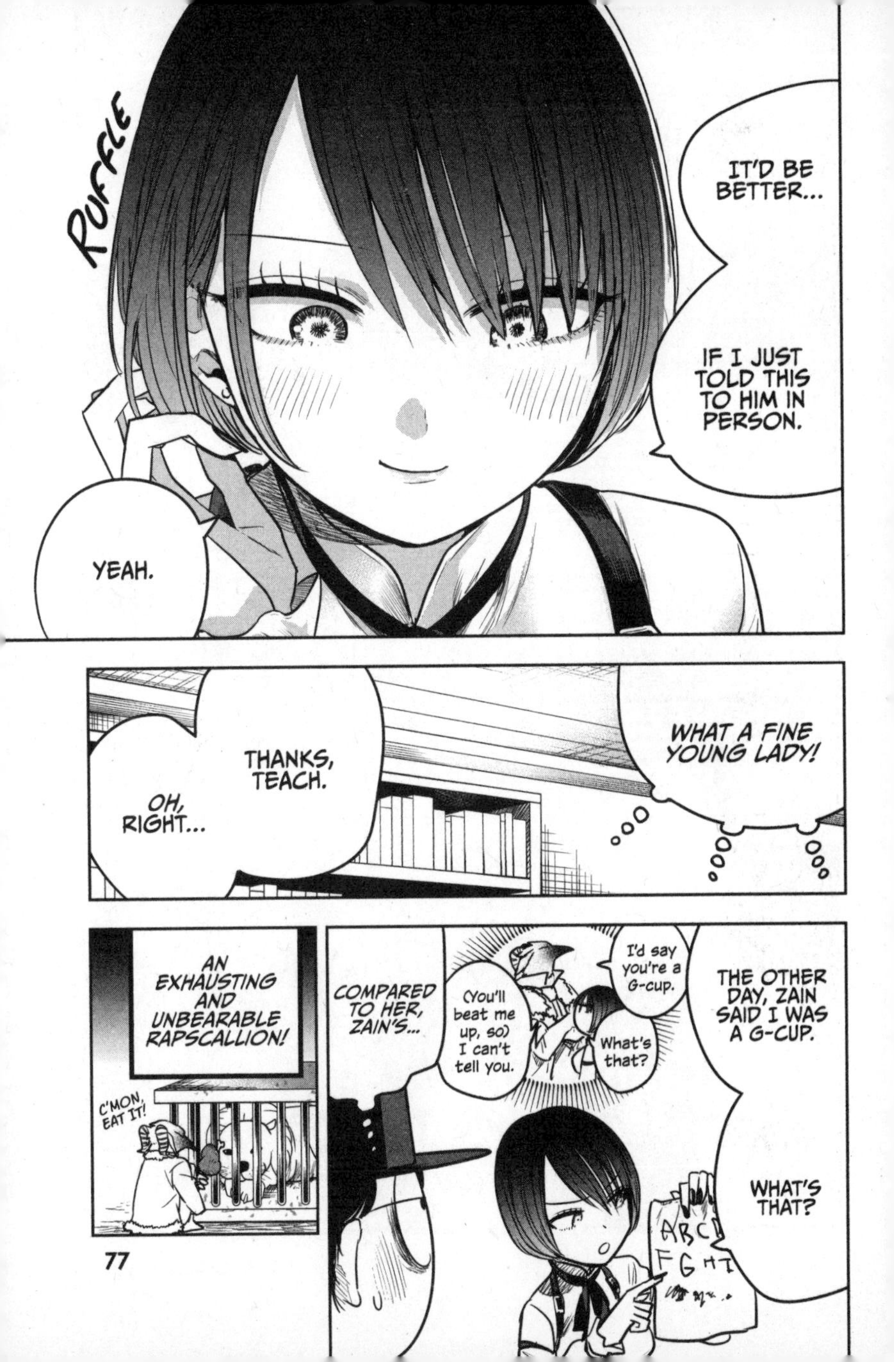
IT'D BE BETTER...
IF I JUST TOLD THIS TO HIM IN PERSON.
RUFFLE
YEAH.
WHAT A FINE YOUNG LADY!
OH, RIGHT... THANKS, TEACH.
THE OTHER DAY, ZAIN SAID I WAS A G-CUP.
WHAT'S THAT?
I'd say you're a G-cup.
What's that?
(You'll beat me up, so) I can't tell you.
COMPARED TO HER, ZAIN'S...
AN EXHAUSTING AND UNBEARABLE RAPSCALLION!
C'MON, EAT IT!

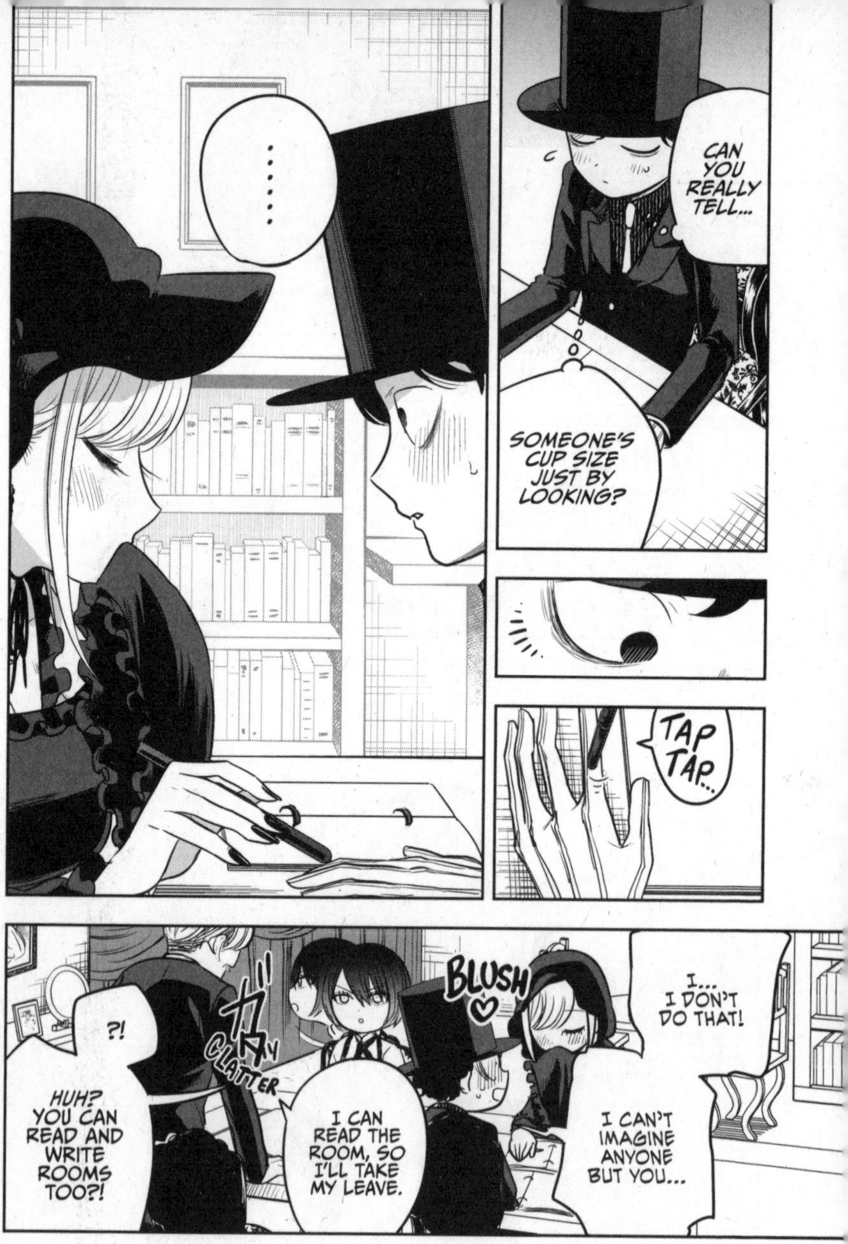
CAN YOU REALLY TELL...
SOMEONE'S CUP SIZE JUST BY LOOKING?
TAP TAP...
......
I... I DON'T DO THAT!
I CAN'T IMAGINE ANYONE BUT YOU...
BLUSH
I CAN READ THE ROOM, SO I'LL TAKE MY LEAVE.
CLATTER
?!
HUH? YOU CAN READ AND WRITE ROOMS TOO?!

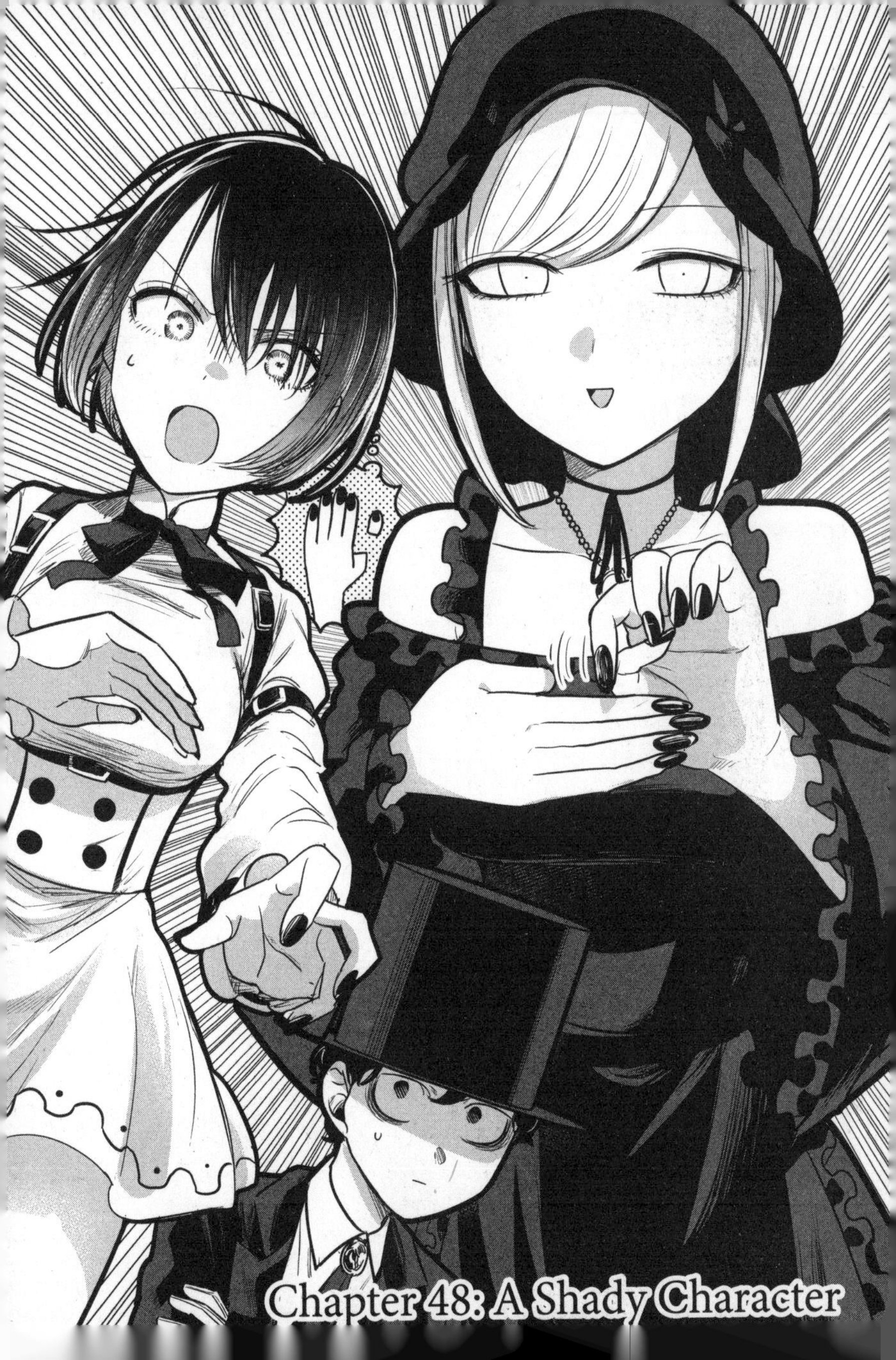
Chapter 48: A Shady Character

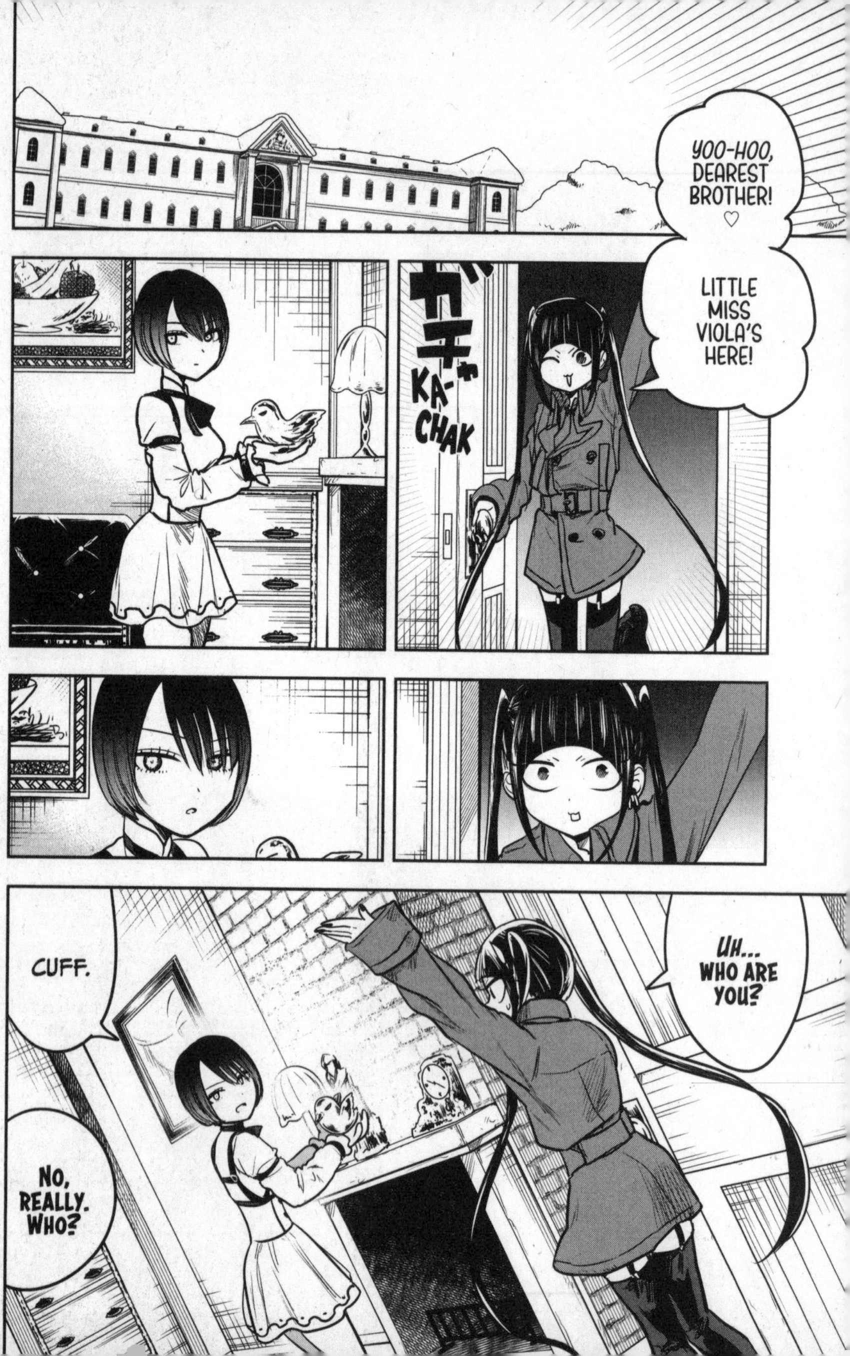
YOO-HOO, DEAREST BROTHER! ♡
LITTLE MISS VIOLA'S HERE!
カチャ
KA-CHAK
UH... WHO ARE YOU?
CUFF.
NO, REALLY. WHO?

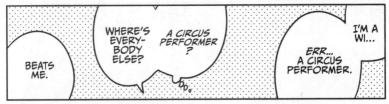

I'M A WI...
ERR... A CIRCUS PERFORMER.
A CIRCUS PERFORMER?
WHERE'S EVERY-BODY ELSE?
BEATS ME.
WHY DON'T YOU MAKE YOURSELF AT HOME?
THERE'S SOMETHING SHADY ABOUT HER...
WHO IS THIS GIRL?
DID SHE COME IN UNAN-NOUNCED?
※SO DID VIOLA.
COULD SHE BE...
A BURG-LAR?
THIS LOOKS LIKE ZAIN.
A SHINY, GOLD ZAIN.
GRIN
SHE IS!

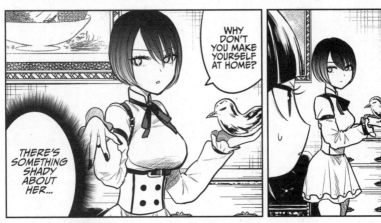

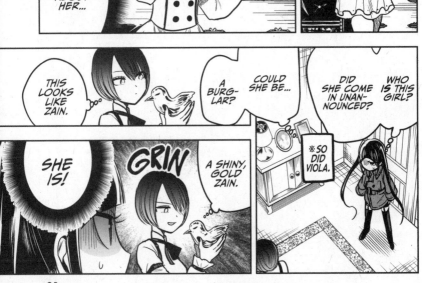

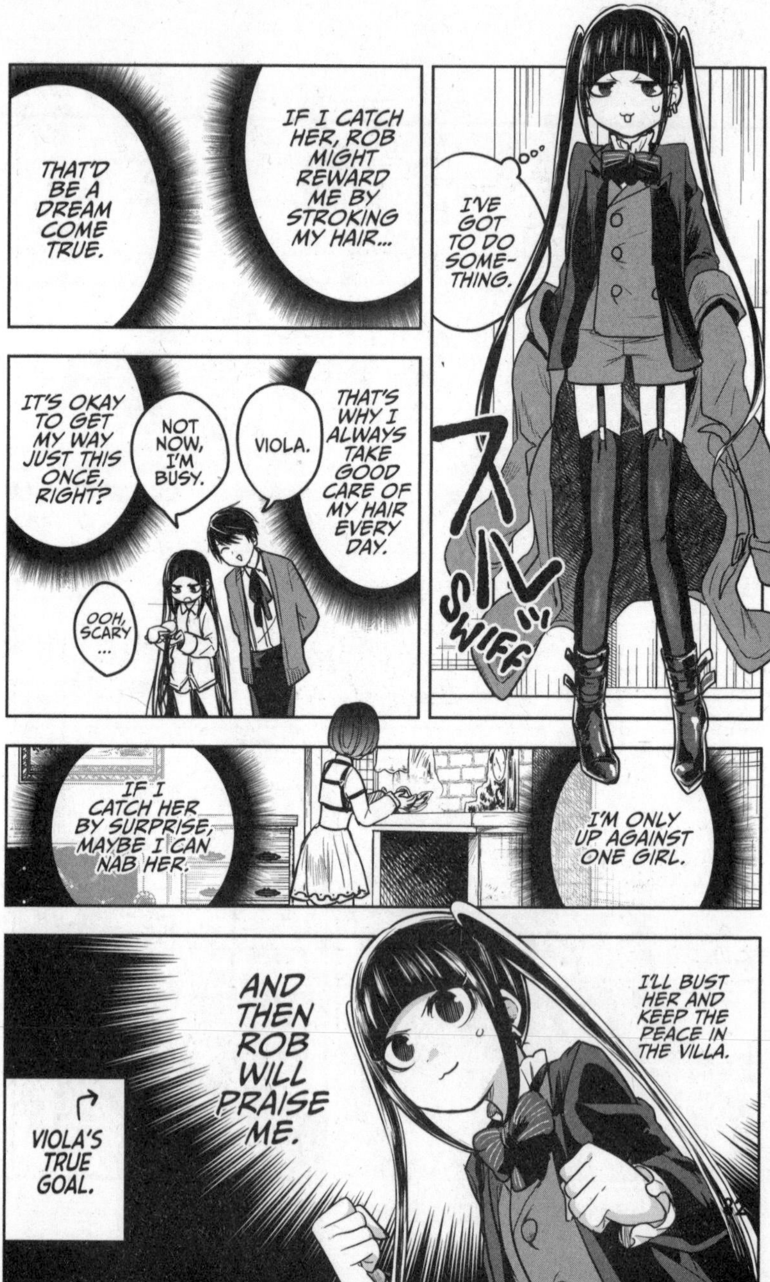
I'VE GOT TO DO SOME-THING.
スル
SWIFF
IF I CATCH HER, ROB MIGHT REWARD ME BY STROKING MY HAIR...
THAT'D BE A DREAM COME TRUE.
THAT'S WHY I ALWAYS TAKE GOOD CARE OF MY HAIR EVERY DAY.
VIOLA.
NOT NOW, I'M BUSY.
IT'S OKAY TO GET MY WAY JUST THIS ONCE, RIGHT?
OOH, SCARY...
I'M ONLY UP AGAINST ONE GIRL.
IF I CATCH HER BY SURPRISE, MAYBE I CAN NAB HER.
I'LL BUST HER AND KEEP THE PEACE IN THE VILLA.
AND THEN ROB WILL PRAISE ME.
VIOLA'S TRUE GOAL.

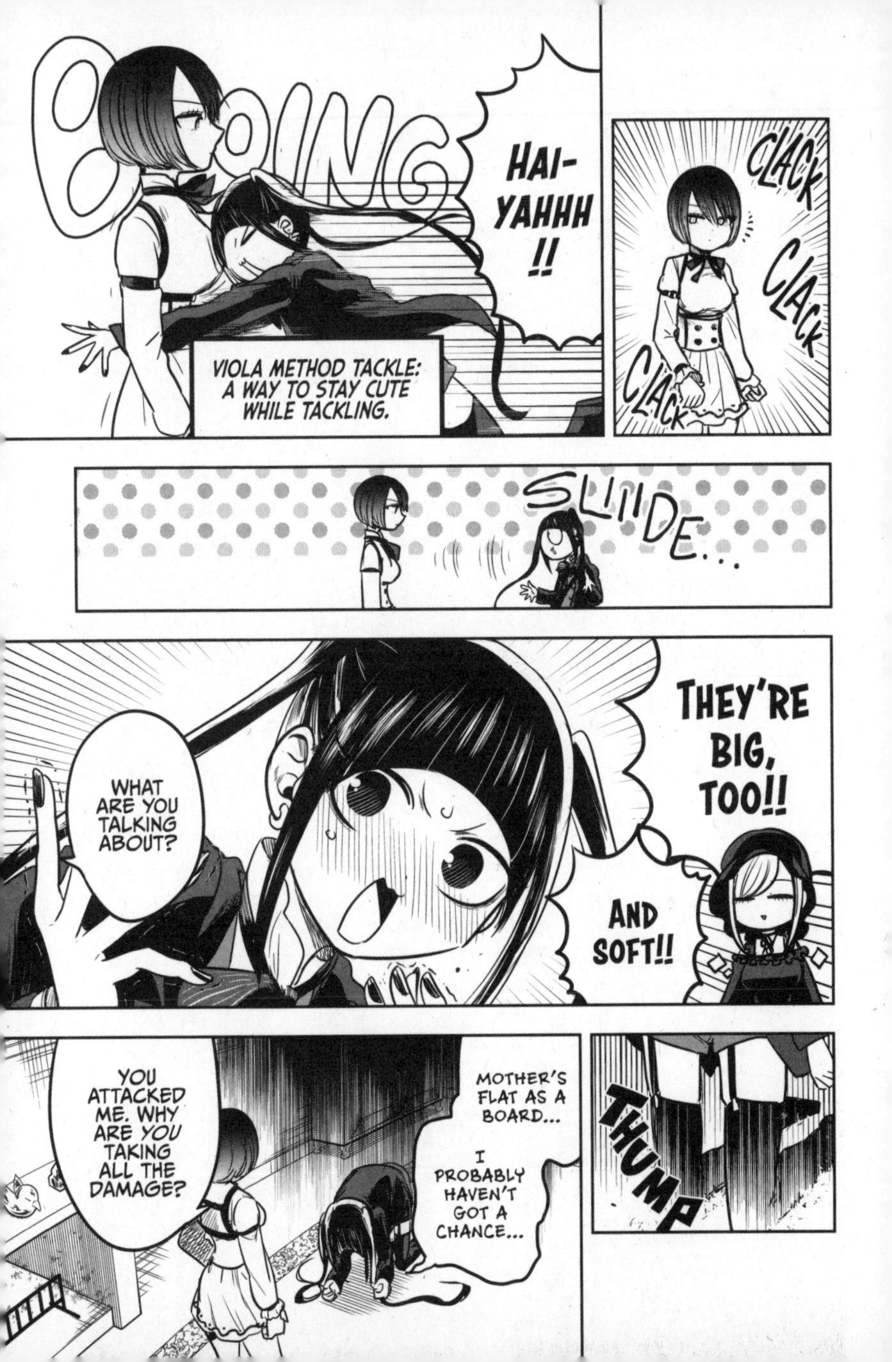
CLACK
CLACK
CLACK
HAI-YAHHH!!
BOING
VIOLA METHOD TACKLE: A WAY TO STAY CUTE WHILE TACKLING.
SLIIDE...
THEY'RE BIG, TOO!!
AND SOFT!!
WHAT ARE YOU TALKING ABOUT?
THUMP
MOTHER'S FLAT AS A BOARD...
I PROBABLY HAVEN'T GOT A CHANCE...
YOU ATTACKED ME. WHY ARE *YOU* TAKING ALL THE DAMAGE?

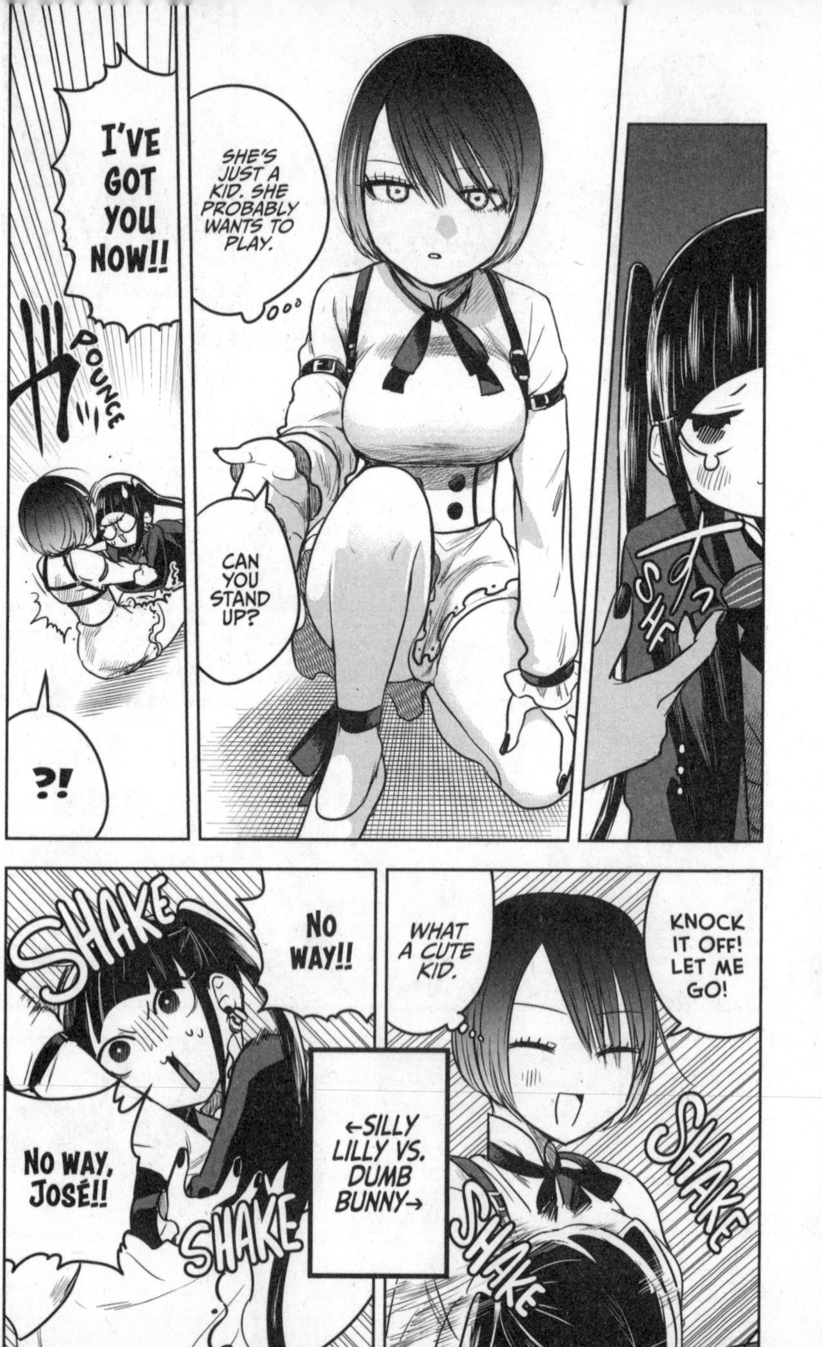
SHF
SHF
SHE'S JUST A KID. SHE PROBABLY WANTS TO PLAY.
CAN YOU STAND UP?
I'VE GOT YOU NOW!!
POUNCE
?!
KNOCK IT OFF! LET ME GO!
WHAT A CUTE KID.
SHAKE
SHAKE
←SILLY LILLY VS. DUMB BUNNY→
NO WAY!!
SHAKE
NO WAY, JOSÉ!!
SHAKE

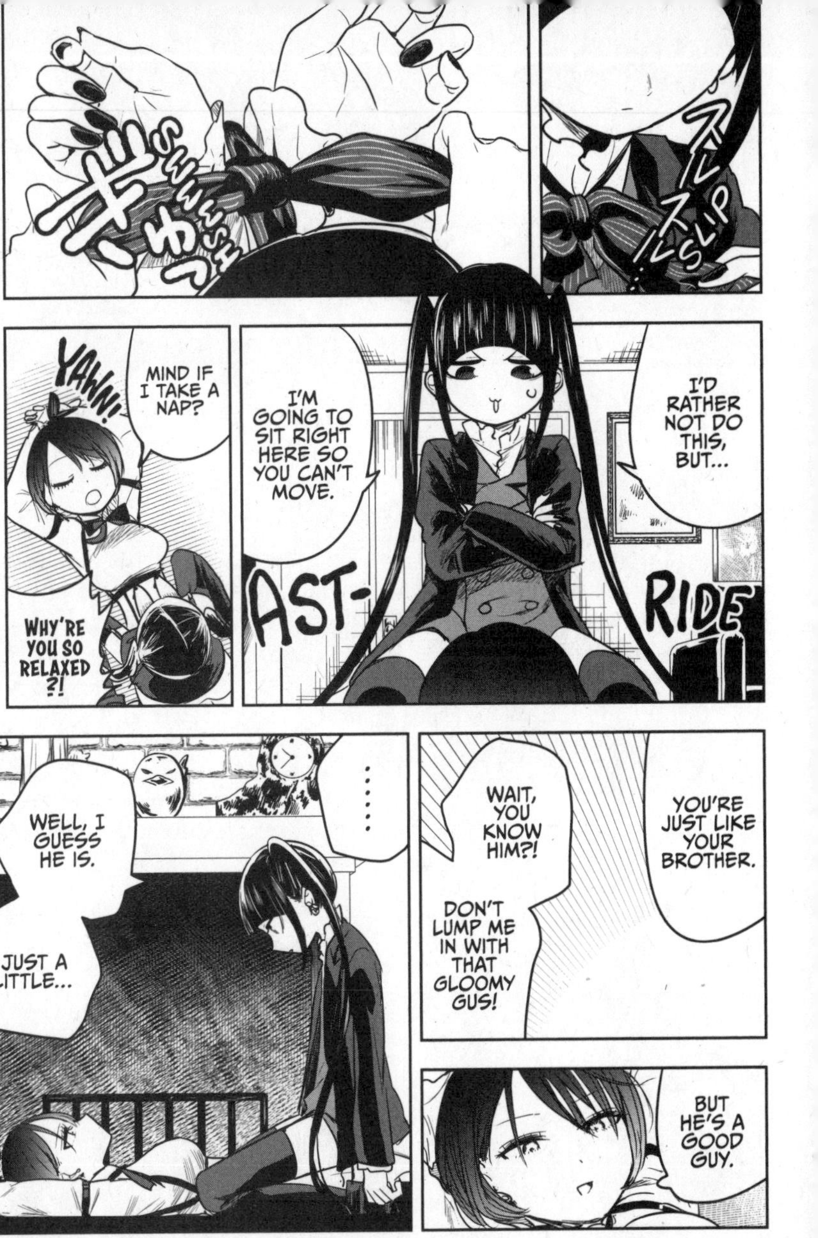
スルッ
SLIP
ギュッ
SWWESH
I'D RATHER NOT DO THIS, BUT...
I'M GOING TO SIT RIGHT HERE SO YOU CAN'T MOVE.
AST-
RIDE
YAWN!
MIND IF I TAKE A NAP?
WHY'RE YOU SO RELAXED?!
YOU'RE JUST LIKE YOUR BROTHER.
WAIT, YOU KNOW HIM?!
DON'T LUMP ME IN WITH THAT GLOOMY GUS!
BUT HE'S A GOOD GUY.
......
WELL, I GUESS HE IS.
JUST A LITTLE...

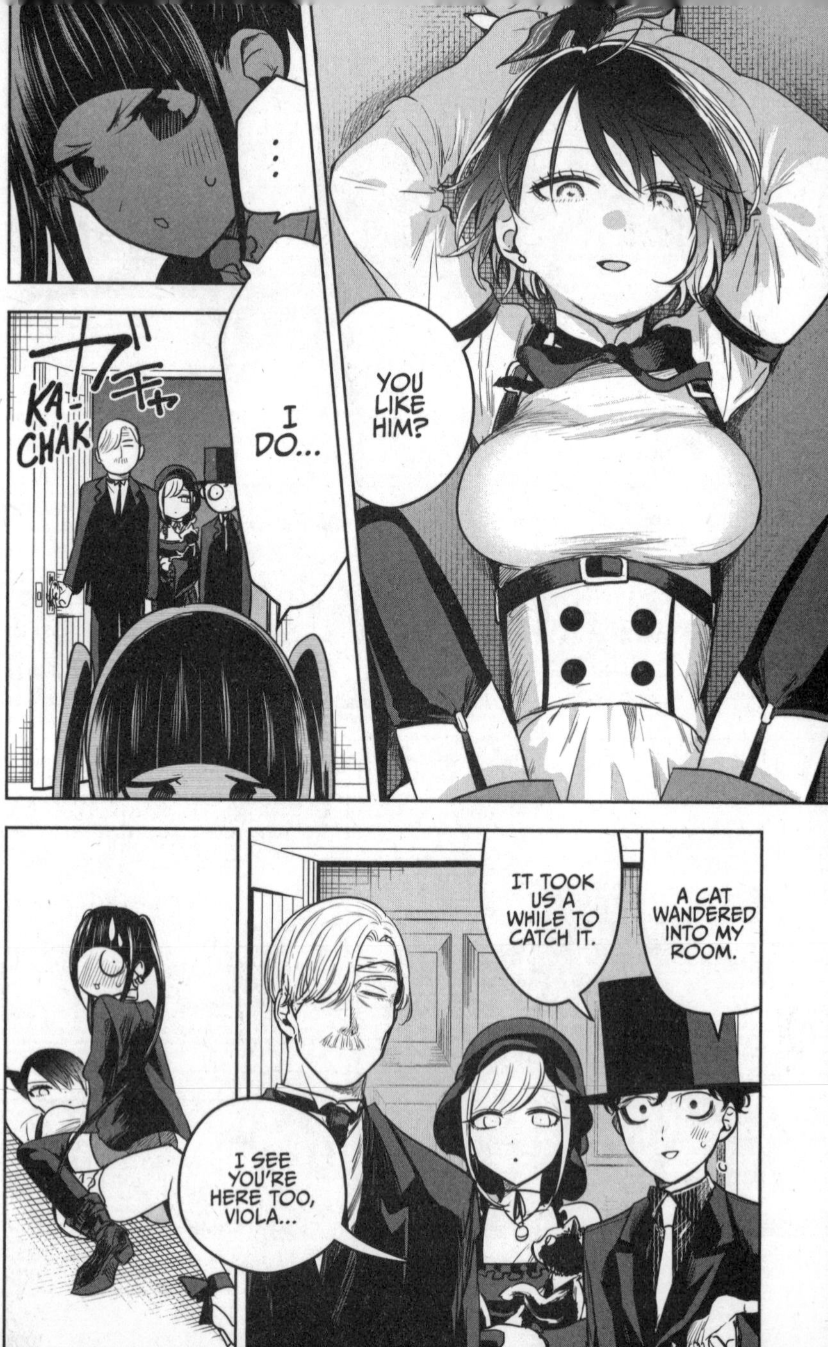
YOU LIKE HIM?
...
I DO...
KA-CHAK
ガチャ
A CAT WANDERED INTO MY ROOM.
IT TOOK US A WHILE TO CATCH IT.
I SEE YOU'RE HERE TOO, VIOLA...

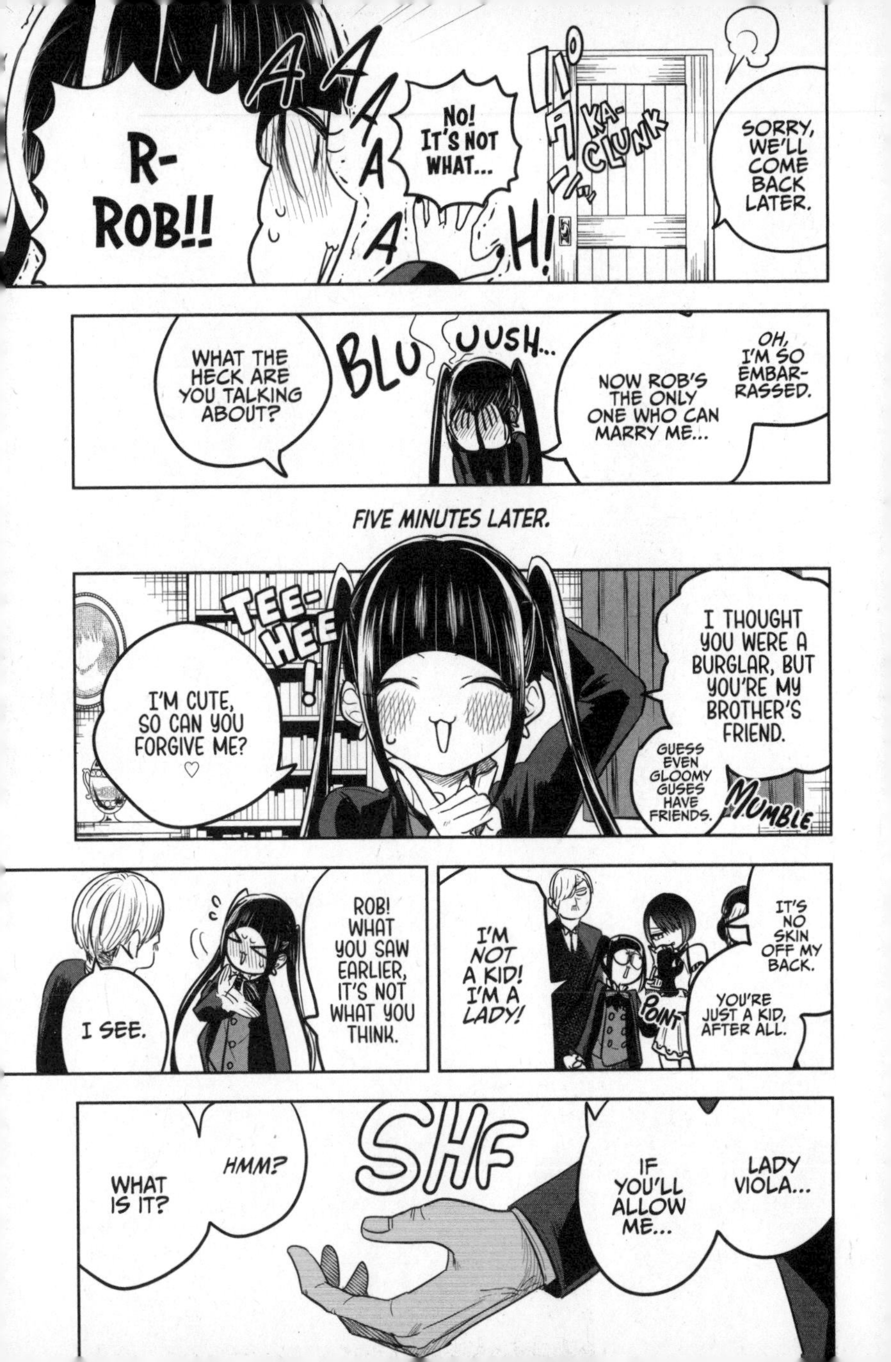
SORRY, WE'LL COME BACK LATER.
KA-CLUNK
No! IT'S NOT WHAT...
AAAAAAH!
R-ROB!!
OH, I'M SO EMBARRASSED.
NOW ROB'S THE ONLY ONE WHO CAN MARRY ME...
BLUUSH...
WHAT THE HECK ARE YOU TALKING ABOUT?
FIVE MINUTES LATER.
I THOUGHT YOU WERE A BURGLAR, BUT YOU'RE MY BROTHER'S FRIEND.
GUESS EVEN GLOOMY GUSES HAVE FRIENDS.
MUMBLE
TEE-HEE!
I'M CUTE, SO CAN YOU FORGIVE ME? ♡
IT'S NO SKIN OFF MY BACK.
YOU'RE JUST A KID, AFTER ALL.
POINT
I'M NOT A KID! I'M A LADY!
ROB! WHAT YOU SAW EARLIER, IT'S NOT WHAT YOU THINK.
I SEE.
LADY VIOLA...
IF YOU'LL ALLOW ME...
SHF
HMM?
WHAT IS IT?

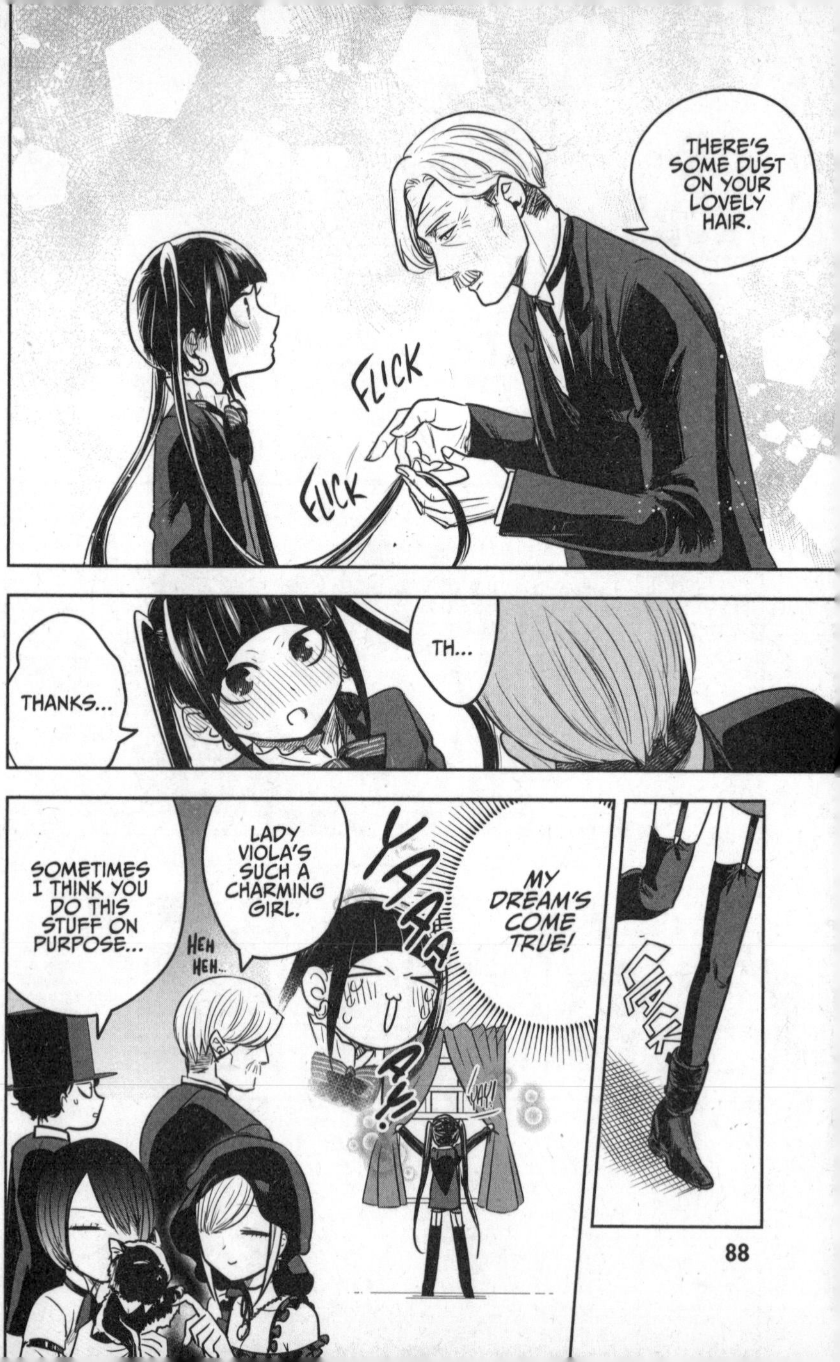
THERE'S SOME DUST ON YOUR LOVELY HAIR.
FLICK
FLICK
TH...
THANKS...
CLACK
MY DREAM'S COME TRUE!
YAAAAAY!
YAY!
LADY VIOLA'S SUCH A CHARMING GIRL.
HEH HEH...
SOMETIMES I THINK YOU DO THIS STUFF ON PURPOSE...

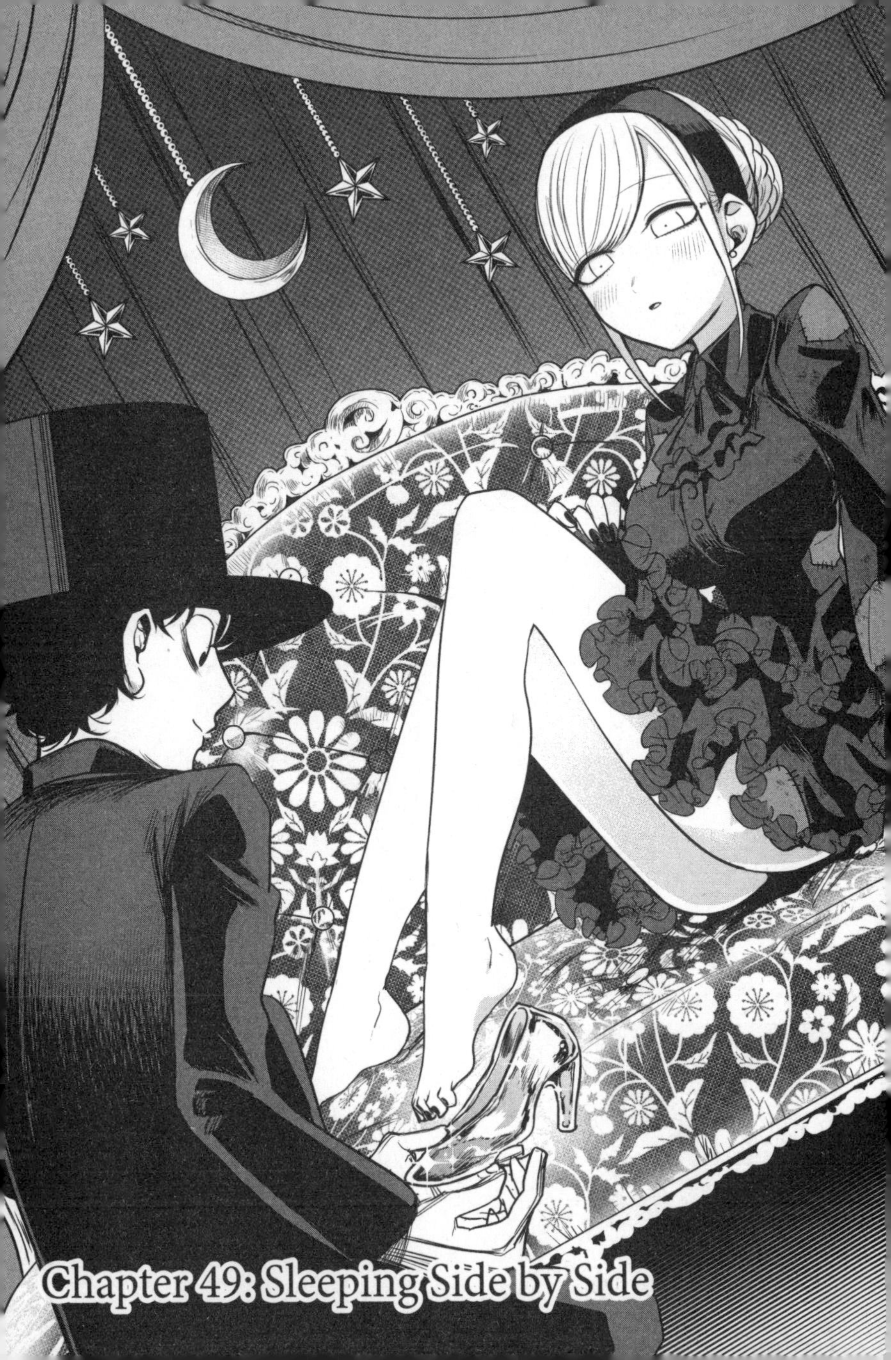

Chapter 49: Sleeping Side by Side

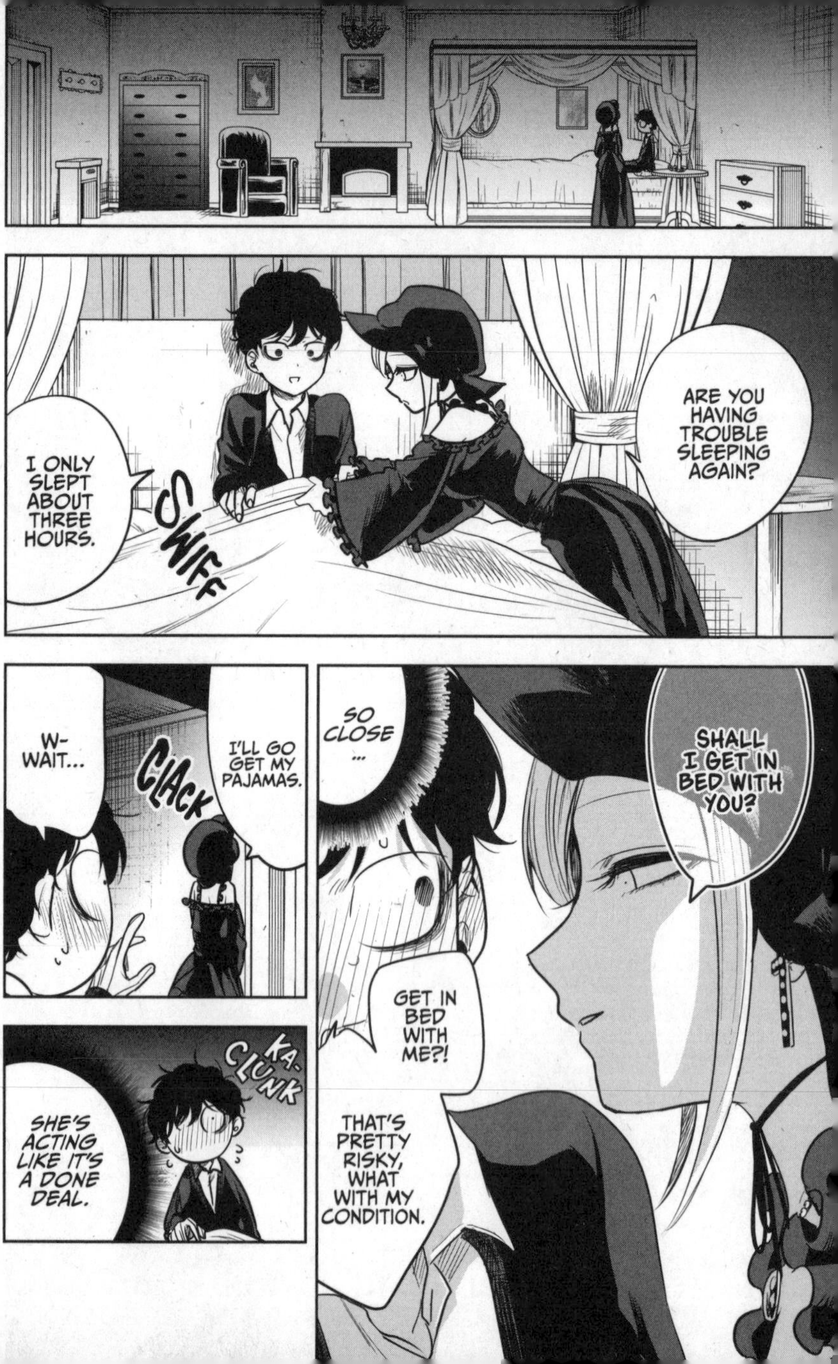
ARE YOU HAVING TROUBLE SLEEPING AGAIN?
SWIFF
I ONLY SLEPT ABOUT THREE HOURS.
SHALL I GET IN BED WITH YOU?
SO CLOSE ...
GET IN BED WITH ME?!
THAT'S PRETTY RISKY, WHAT WITH MY CONDITION.
I'LL GO GET MY PAJAMAS.
CLACK
W-WAIT...
KA-CLUNK
SHE'S ACTING LIKE IT'S A DONE DEAL.

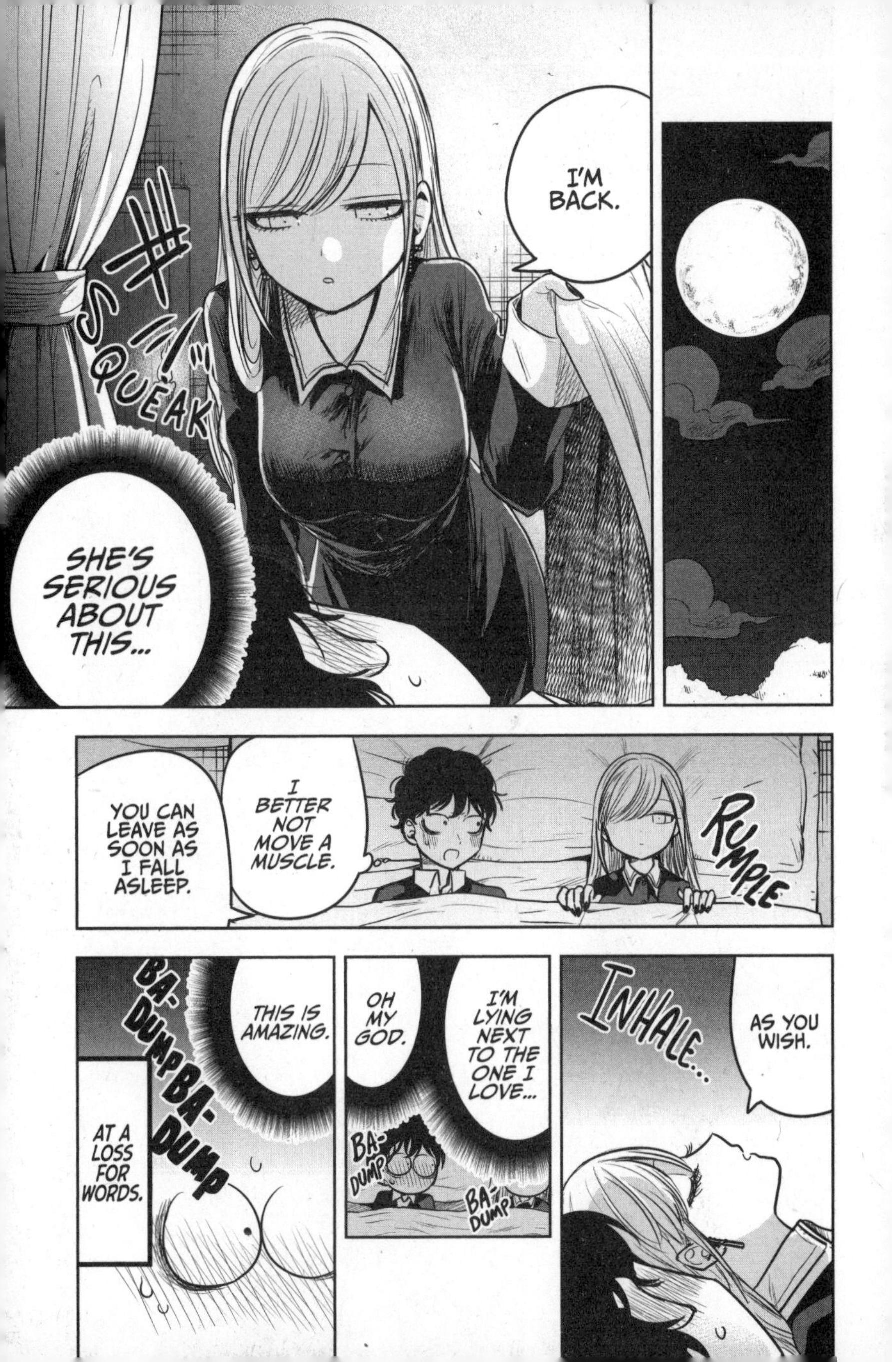
I'M BACK.
SQUEAK
SHE'S SERIOUS ABOUT THIS...
RUMPLE
I BETTER NOT MOVE A MUSCLE.
YOU CAN LEAVE AS SOON AS I FALL ASLEEP.
AS YOU WISH.
INHALE...
I'M LYING NEXT TO THE ONE I LOVE...
OH MY GOD.
BA-DUMP
BA-DUMP
THIS IS AMAZING.
BA-DUMP BA-DUMP
AT A LOSS FOR WORDS.

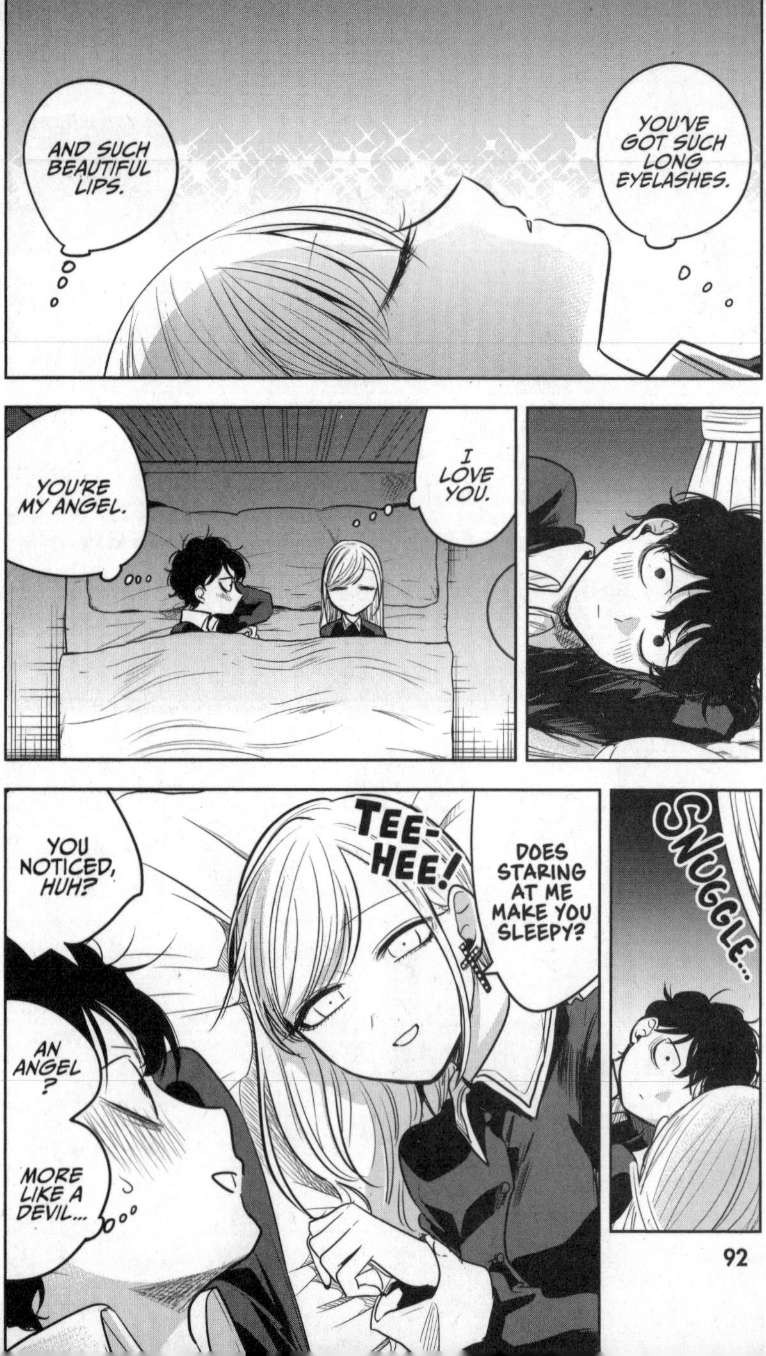
YOU'VE GOT SUCH LONG EYELASHES.
AND SUCH BEAUTIFUL LIPS.
I LOVE YOU.
YOU'RE MY ANGEL.
SNUGGLE...
DOES STARING AT ME MAKE YOU SLEEPY?
TEE-HEE!
YOU NOTICED, HUH?
AN ANGEL?
MORE LIKE A DEVIL...

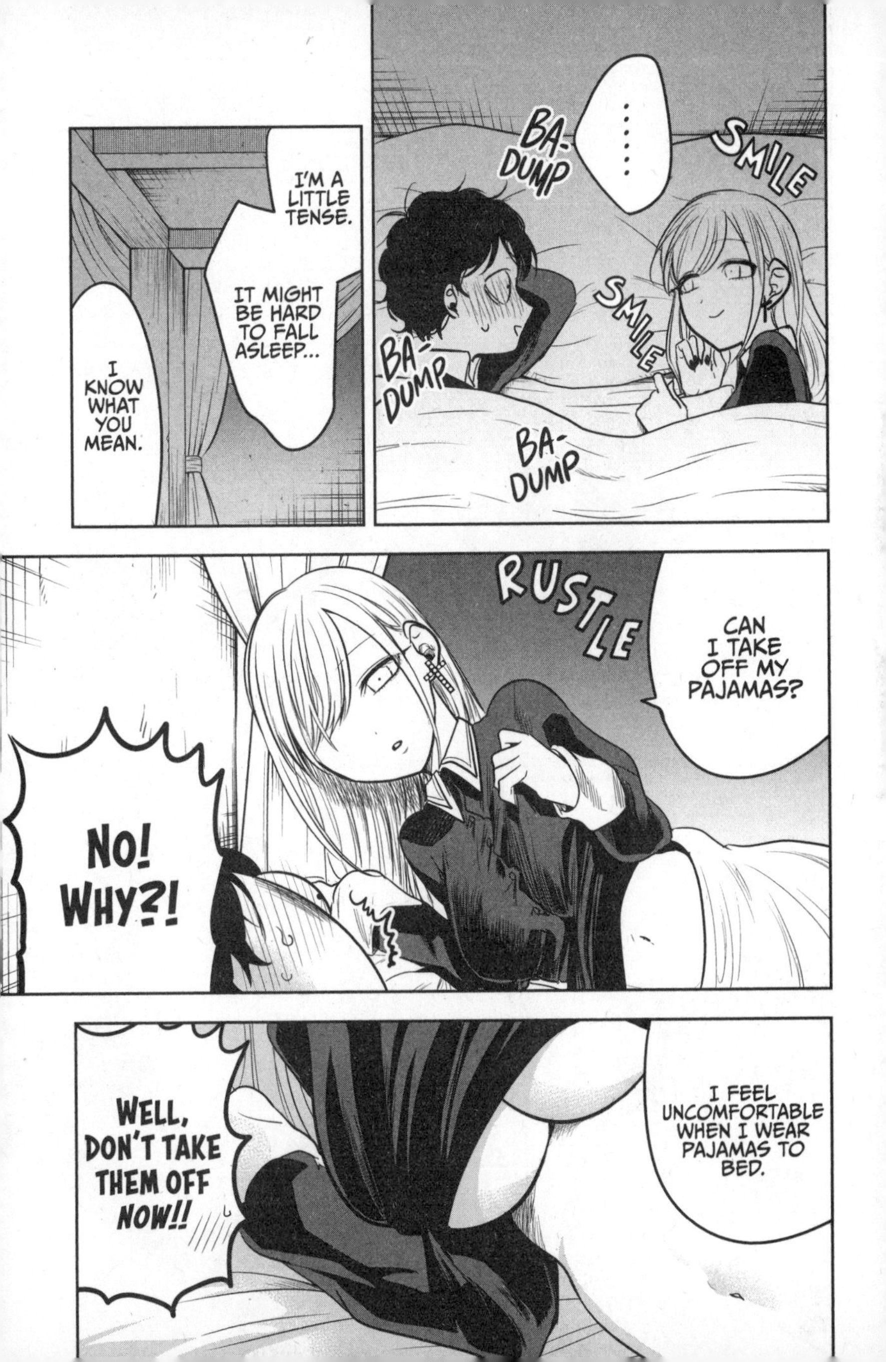
......
BA-DUMP
SMILE
SMILE
BA-DUMP
BA-DUMP
I'M A LITTLE TENSE.
IT MIGHT BE HARD TO FALL ASLEEP...
I KNOW WHAT YOU MEAN.
RUSTLE
CAN I TAKE OFF MY PAJAMAS?
NO! WHY?!
I FEEL UNCOMFORTABLE WHEN I WEAR PAJAMAS TO BED.
WELL, DON'T TAKE THEM OFF NOW!!

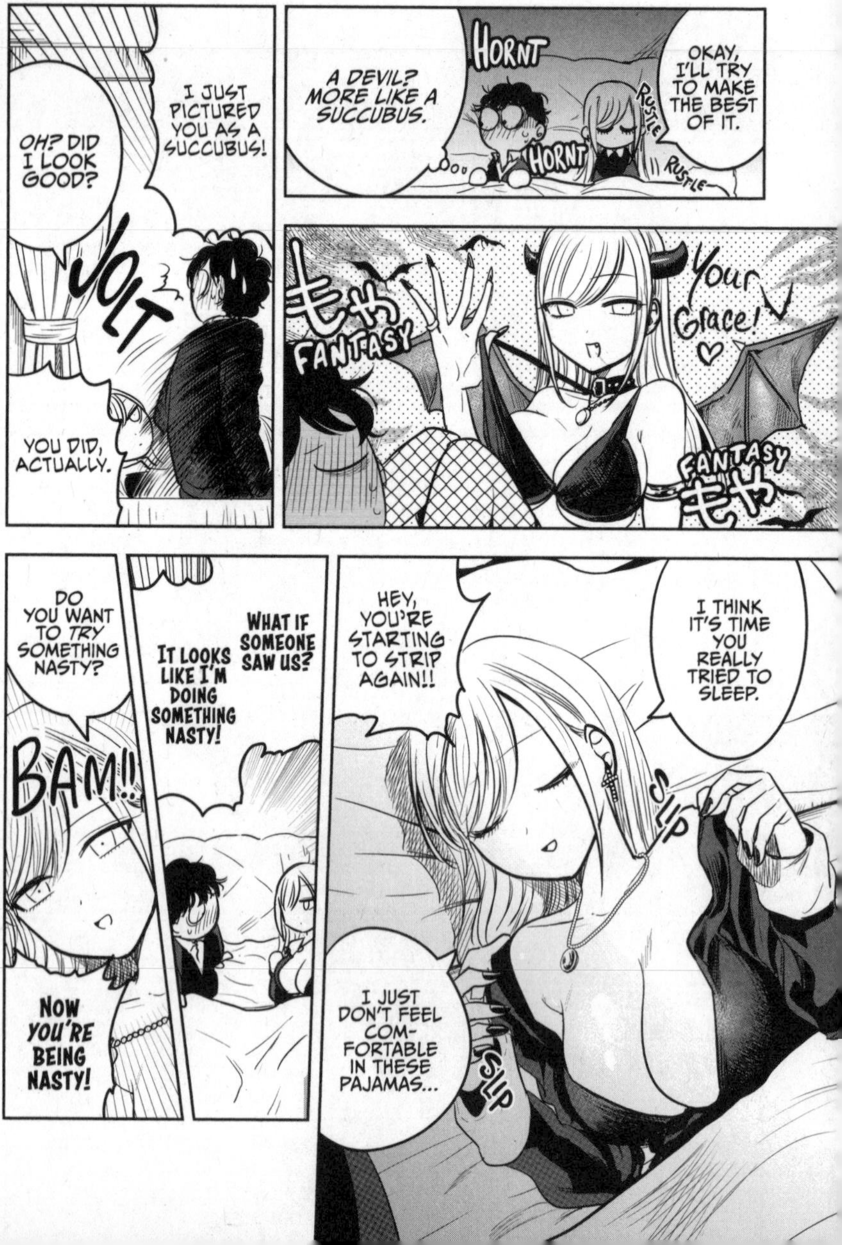
OKAY, I'LL TRY TO MAKE THE BEST OF IT.
RUSTLE
RUSTLE
HORNT
HORNT
A DEVIL? MORE LIKE A SUCCUBUS.
Your Grace! ♥
FANTASY もや
もや FANTASY
I JUST PICTURED YOU AS A SUCCUBUS!
OH? DID I LOOK GOOD?
JOLT
YOU DID, ACTUALLY.
I THINK IT'S TIME YOU REALLY TRIED TO SLEEP.
HEY, YOU'RE STARTING TO STRIP AGAIN!!
SLIP
I JUST DON'T FEEL COM-FORTABLE IN THESE PAJAMAS...
SLIP
WHAT IF SOMEONE SAW US?
IT LOOKS LIKE I'M DOING SOMETHING NASTY!
DO YOU WANT TO *TRY* SOMETHING NASTY?
BAM!!
NOW *YOU'RE* BEING NASTY!

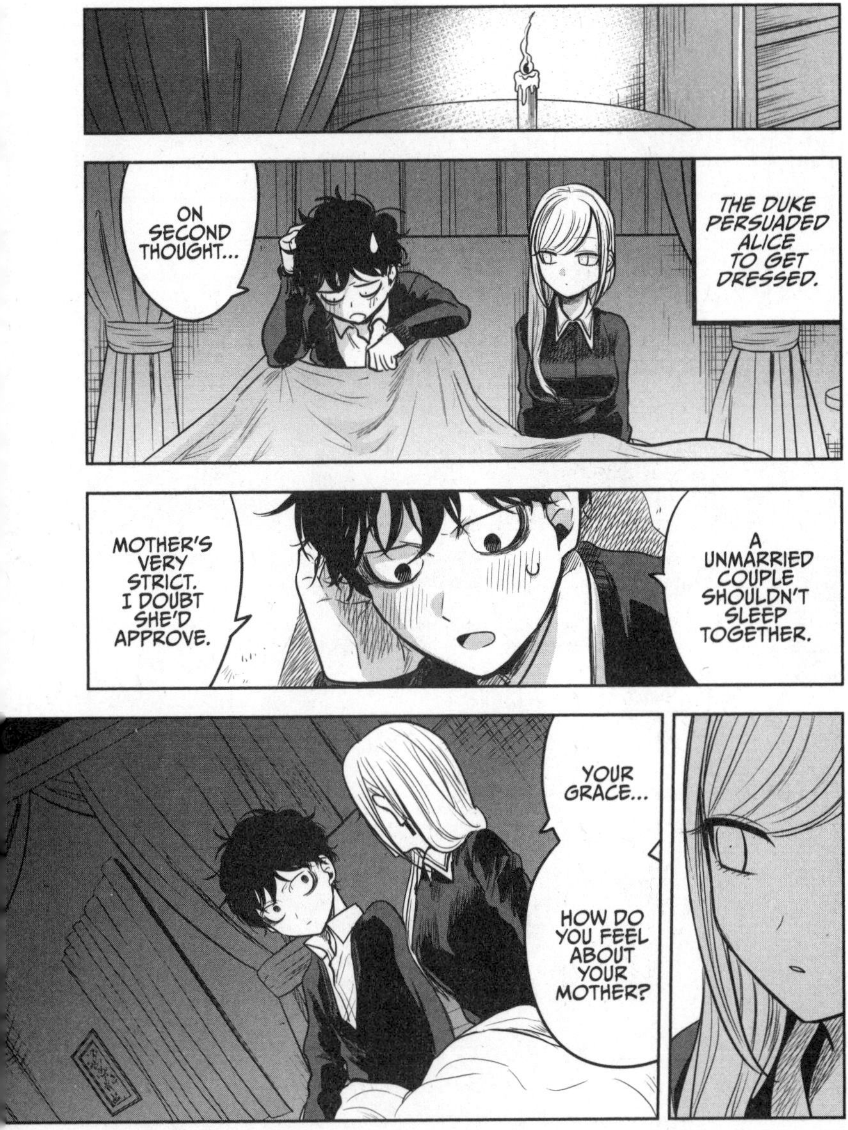
THE DUKE PERSUADED ALICE TO GET DRESSED.
ON SECOND THOUGHT...
A UNMARRIED COUPLE SHOULDN'T SLEEP TOGETHER.
MOTHER'S VERY STRICT. I DOUBT SHE'D APPROVE.
YOUR GRACE...
HOW DO YOU FEEL ABOUT YOUR MOTHER?

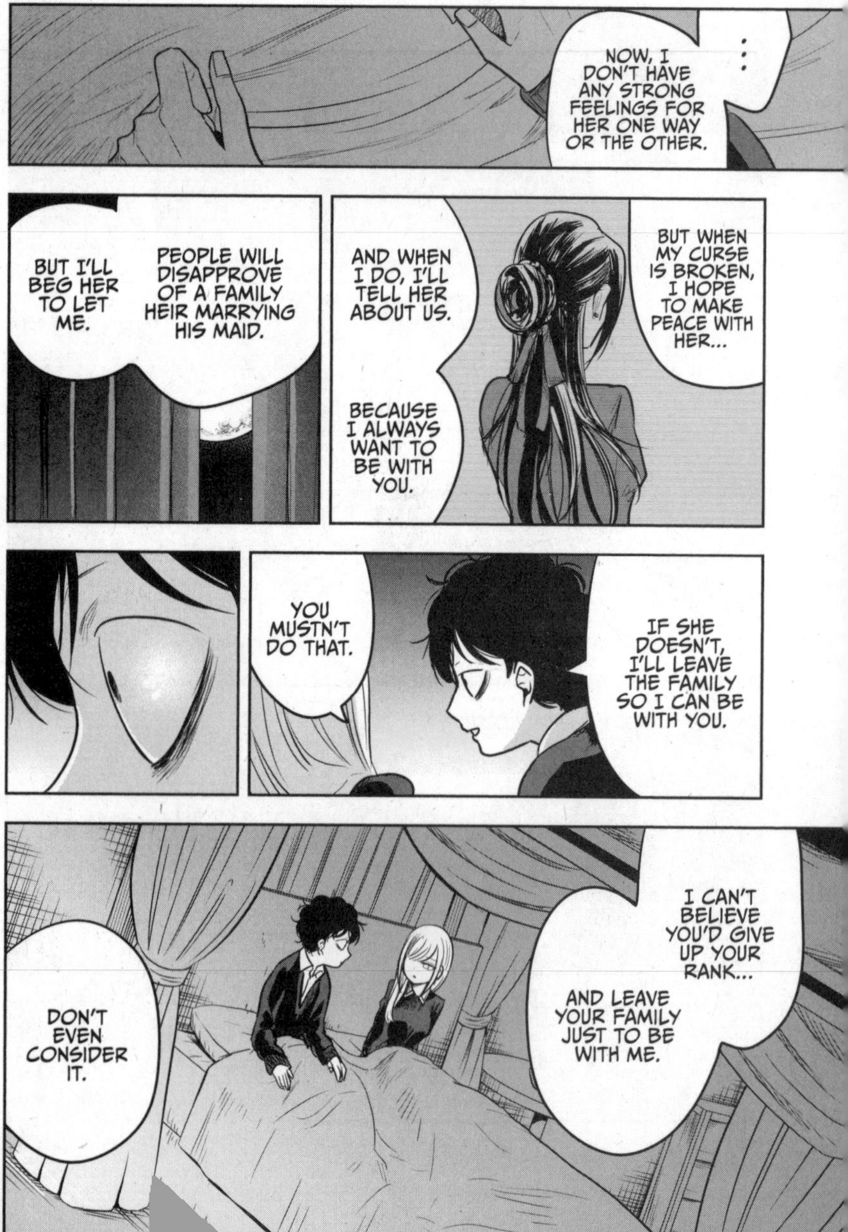
...
NOW, I DON'T HAVE ANY STRONG FEELINGS FOR HER ONE WAY OR THE OTHER.
BUT WHEN MY CURSE IS BROKEN, I HOPE TO MAKE PEACE WITH HER...
AND WHEN I DO, I'LL TELL HER ABOUT US.
BECAUSE I ALWAYS WANT TO BE WITH YOU.
PEOPLE WILL DISAPPROVE OF A FAMILY HEIR MARRYING HIS MAID.
BUT I'LL BEG HER TO LET ME.
IF SHE DOESN'T, I'LL LEAVE THE FAMILY SO I CAN BE WITH YOU.
YOU MUSTN'T DO THAT.
I CAN'T BELIEVE YOU'D GIVE UP YOUR RANK...
AND LEAVE YOUR FAMILY JUST TO BE WITH ME.
DON'T EVEN CONSIDER IT.

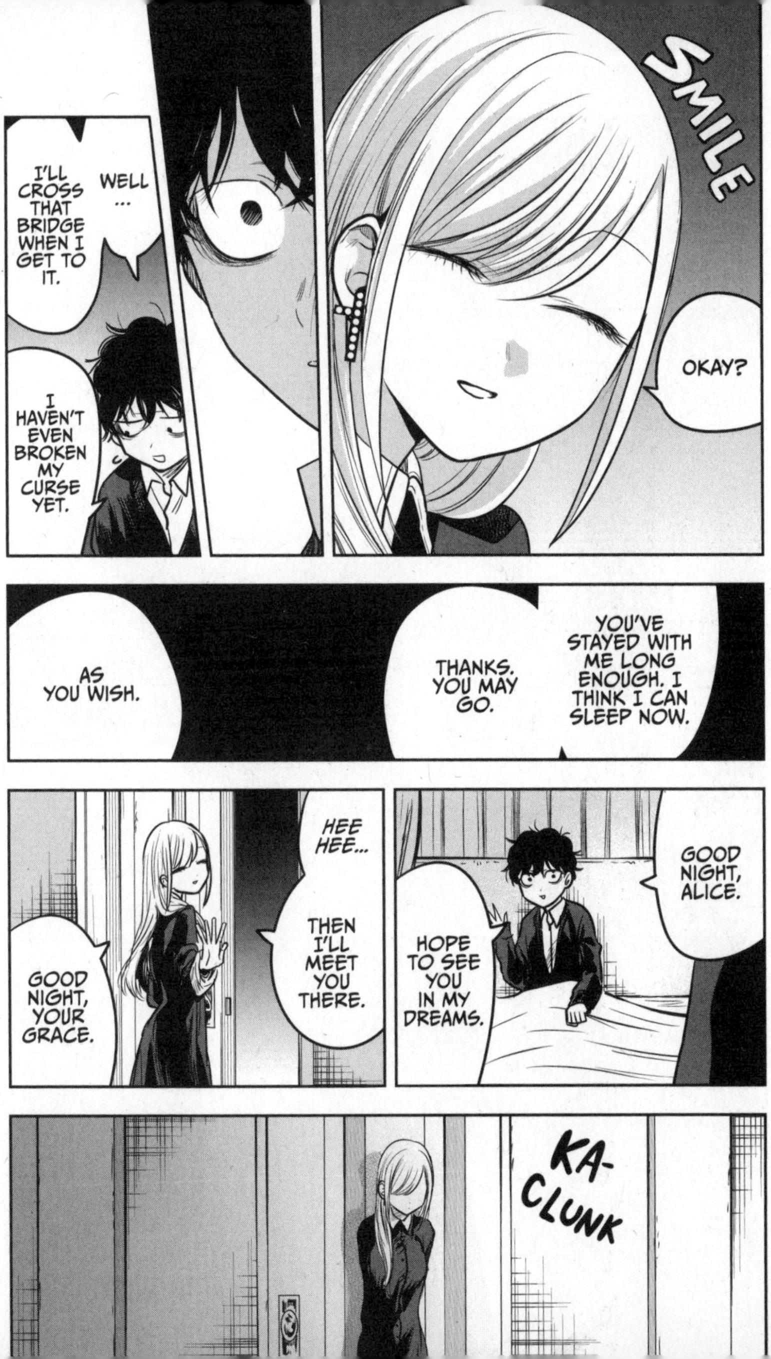
SMILE
OKAY?
WELL ...
I'LL CROSS THAT BRIDGE WHEN I GET TO IT.
I HAVEN'T EVEN BROKEN MY CURSE YET.
YOU'VE STAYED WITH ME LONG ENOUGH. I THINK I CAN SLEEP NOW.
THANKS. YOU MAY GO.
AS YOU WISH.
GOOD NIGHT, ALICE.
HOPE TO SEE YOU IN MY DREAMS.
HEE HEE...
THEN I'LL MEET YOU THERE.
GOOD NIGHT, YOUR GRACE.
KA-CLUNK

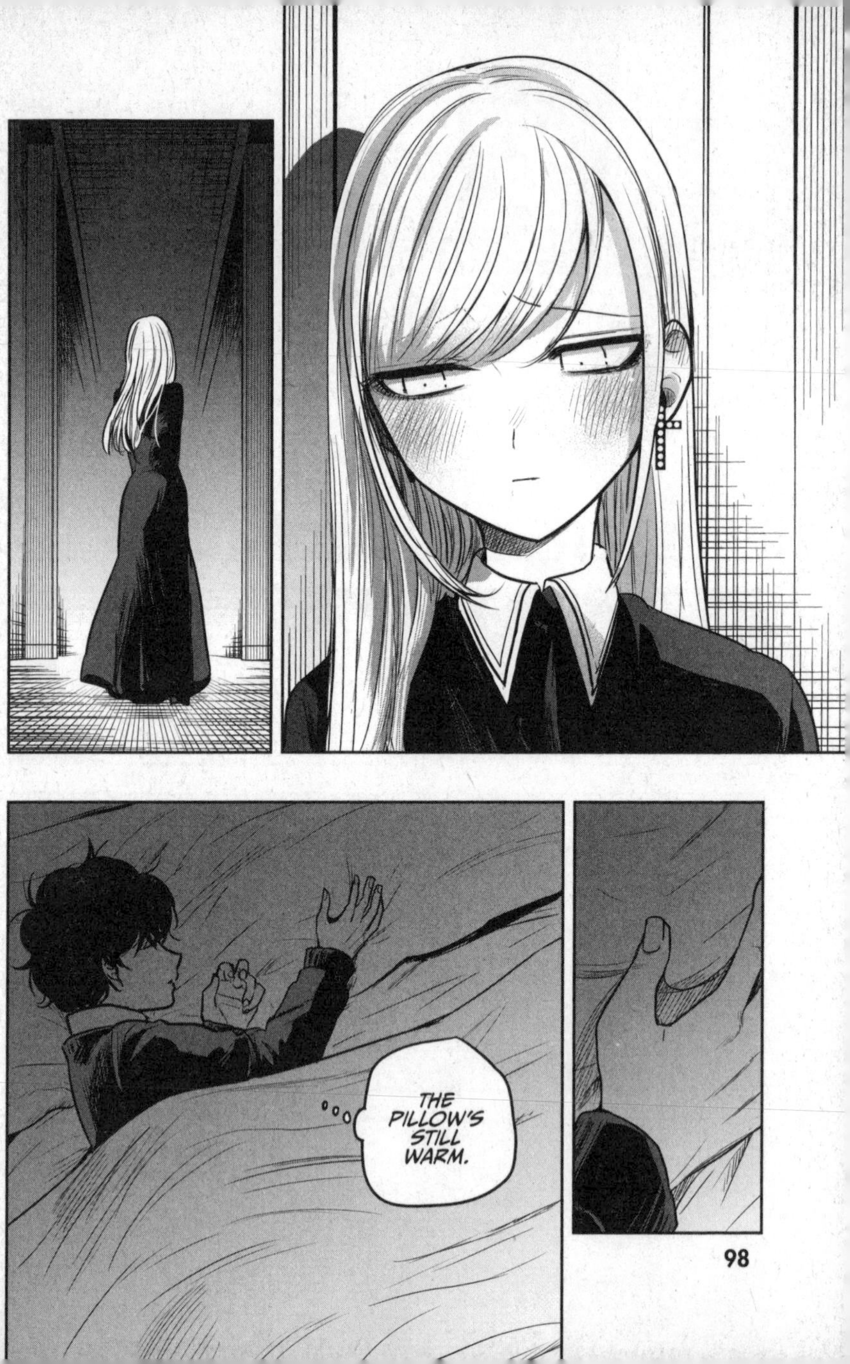
THE PILLOW'S STILL WARM.

THE DUKE OF DEATH AND HIS MAID

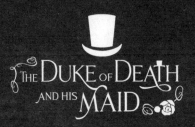

THE DUKE OF DEATH AND HIS MAID

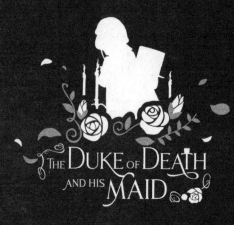

Chapter 50: Christmas Pt. 1

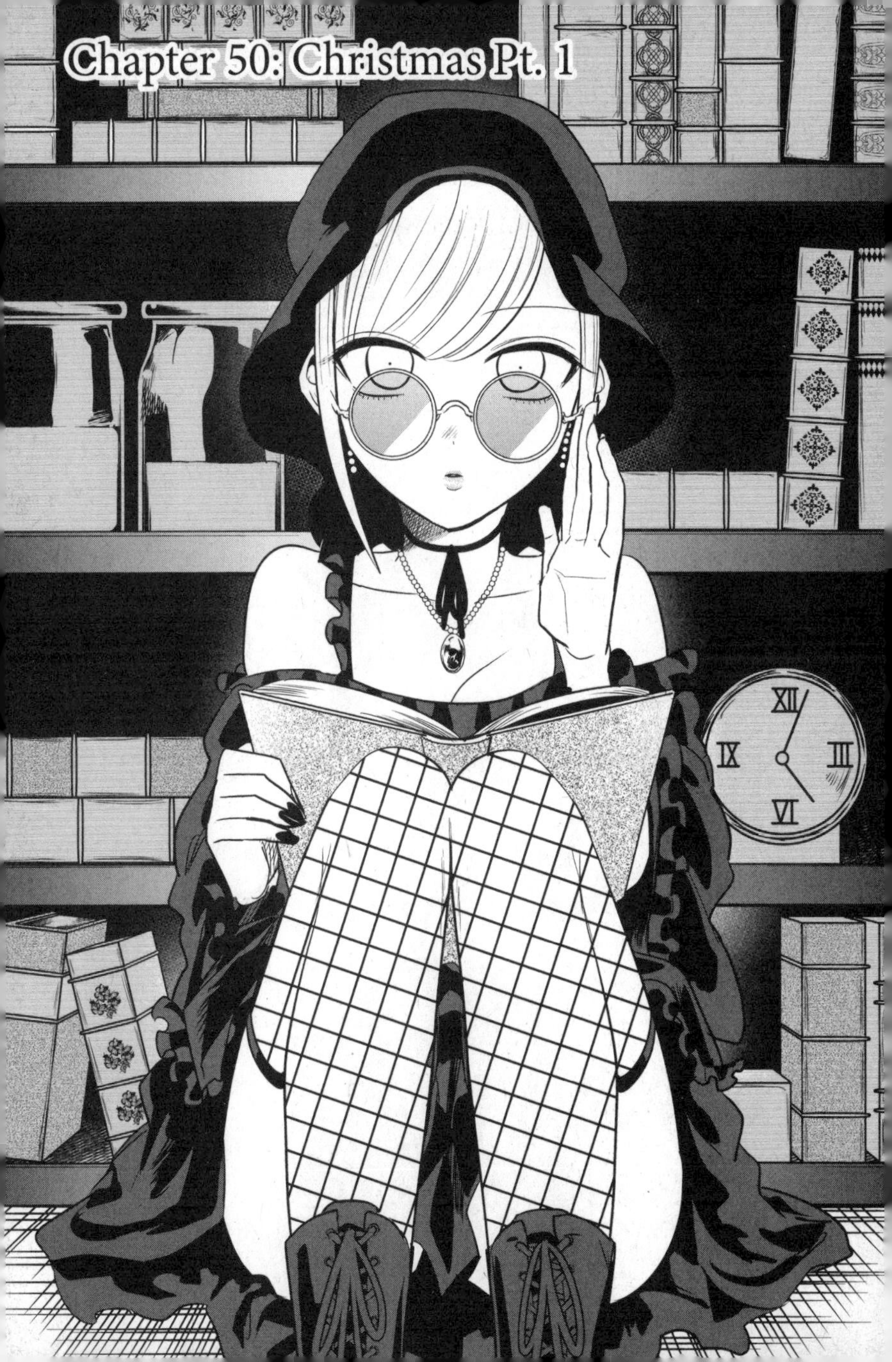

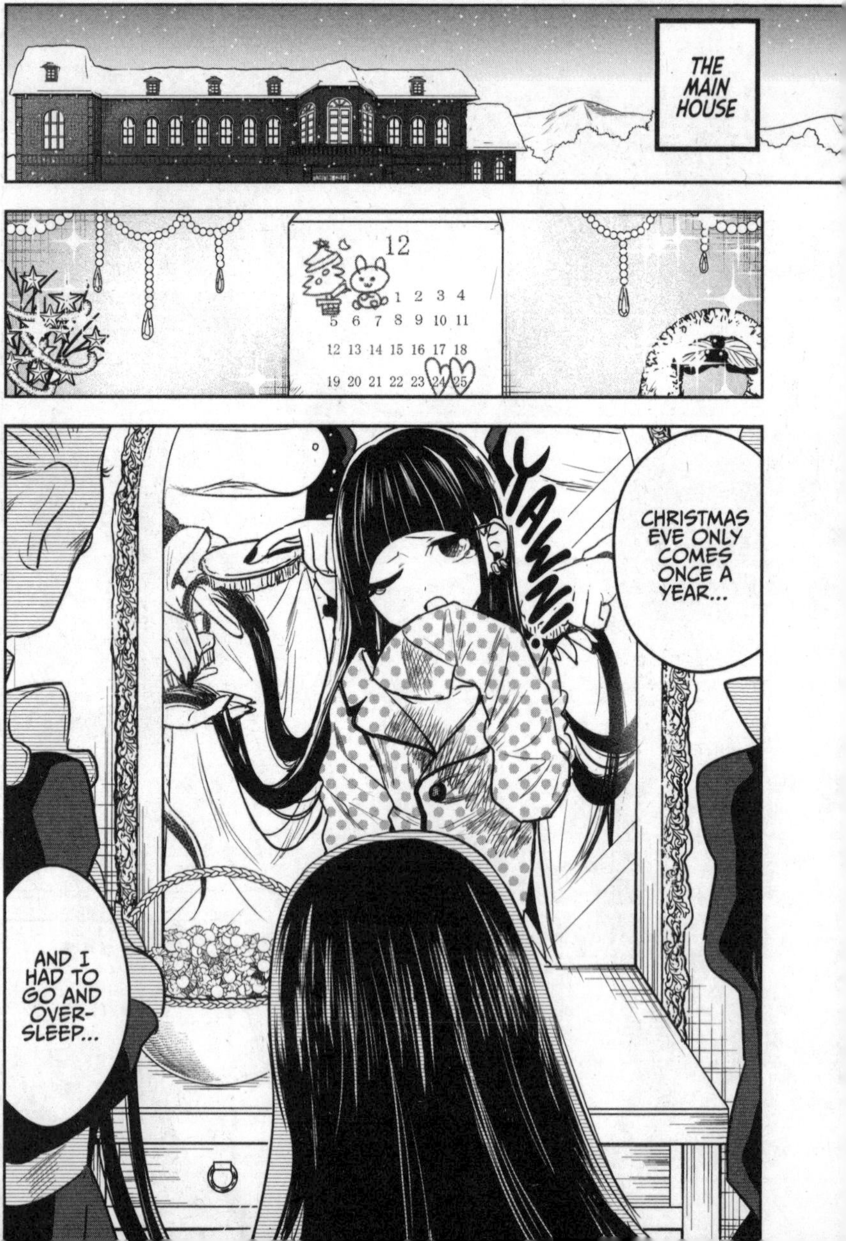
THE MAIN HOUSE
12
1 2 3 4
5 6 7 8 9 10 11
12 13 14 15 16 17 18
19 20 21 22 23 24 25
CHRISTMAS EVE ONLY COMES ONCE A YEAR...
YAWN!
AND I HAD TO GO AND OVER-SLEEP...

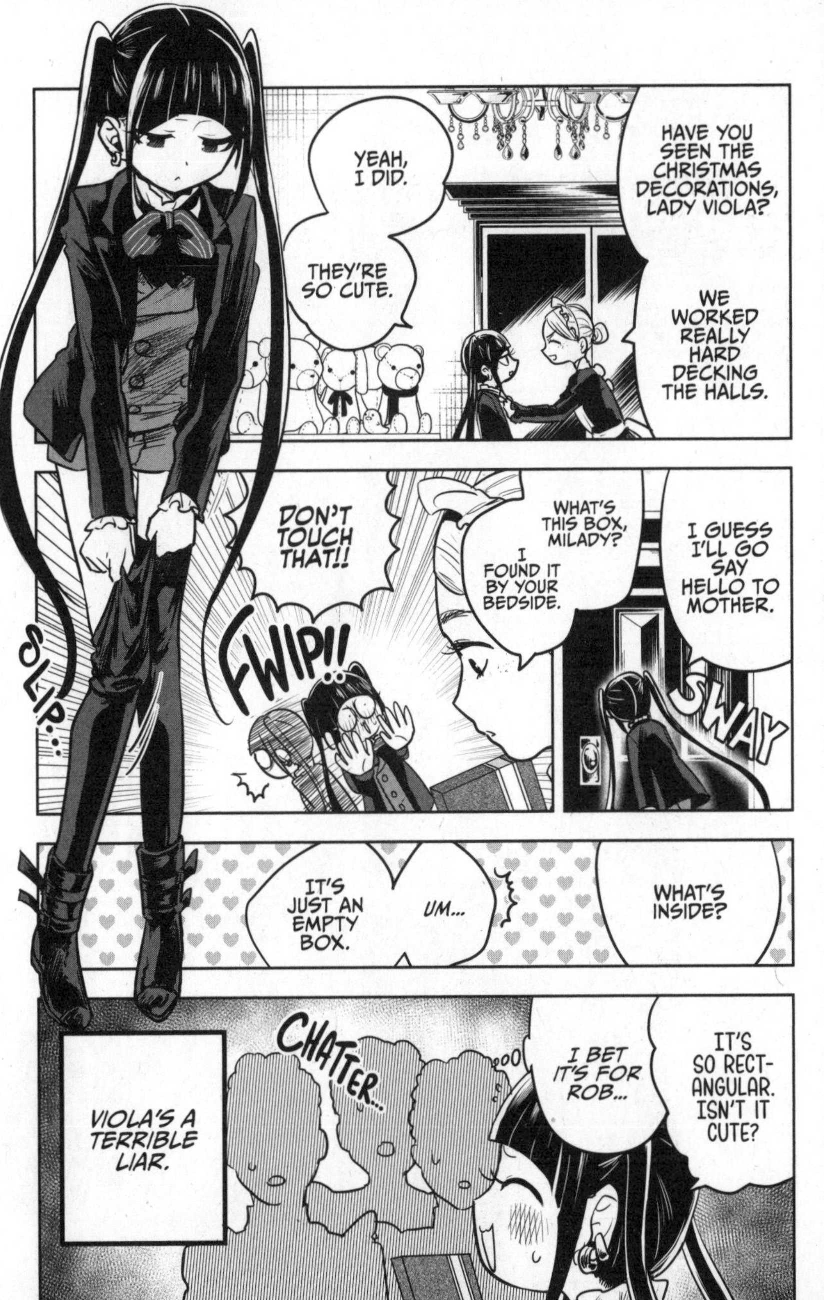
HAVE YOU SEEN THE CHRISTMAS DECORATIONS, LADY VIOLA?
WE WORKED REALLY HARD DECKING THE HALLS.
YEAH, I DID.
THEY'RE SO CUTE.
I GUESS I'LL GO SAY HELLO TO MOTHER.
SWAY
WHAT'S THIS BOX, MILADY?
I FOUND IT BY YOUR BEDSIDE.
DON'T TOUCH THAT!!
FWIP!!
SLIP...
WHAT'S INSIDE?
UM...
IT'S JUST AN EMPTY BOX.
IT'S SO RECT-ANGULAR. ISN'T IT CUTE?
I BET IT'S FOR ROB...
CHATTER...
VIOLA'S A TERRIBLE LIAR.

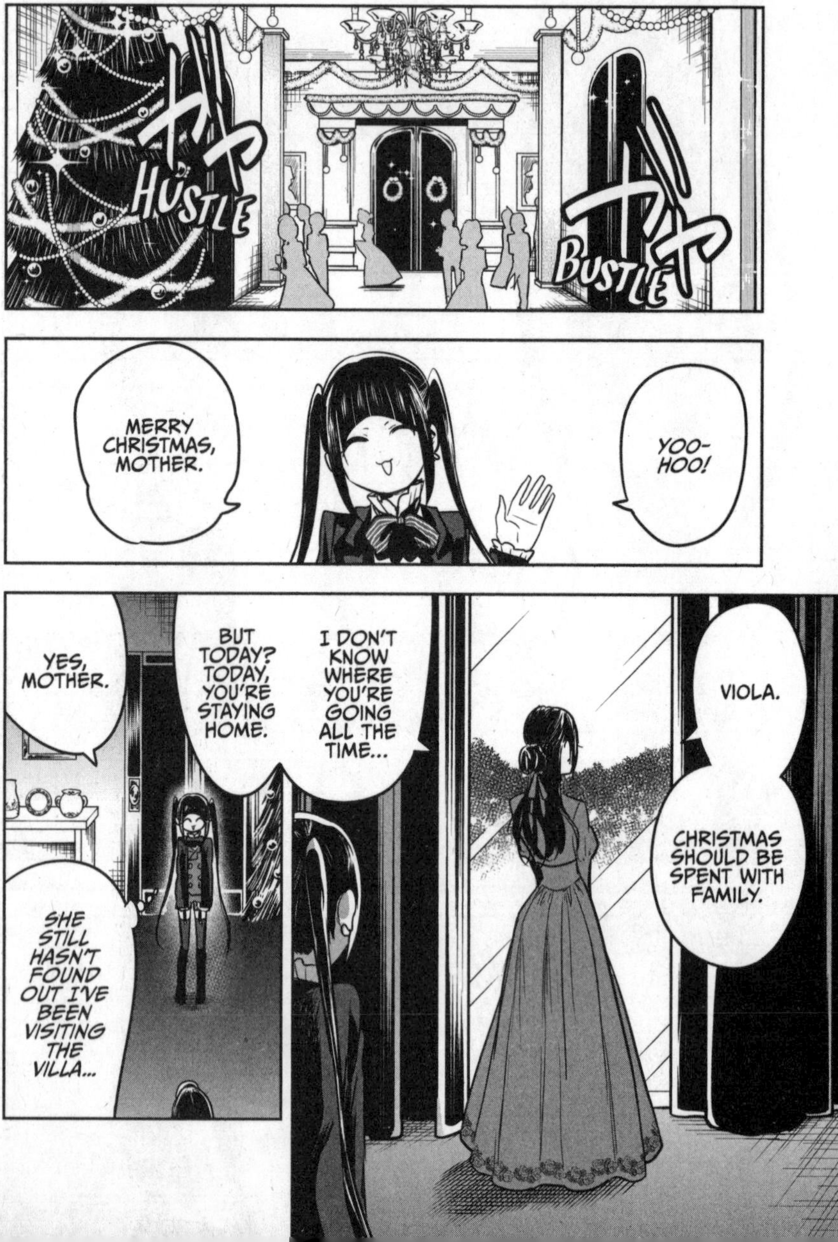
BUSTLE
HUSTLE
YOO-HOO!
MERRY CHRISTMAS, MOTHER.
VIOLA.
CHRISTMAS SHOULD BE SPENT WITH FAMILY.
I DON'T KNOW WHERE YOU'RE GOING ALL THE TIME...
BUT TODAY? TODAY, YOU'RE STAYING HOME.
YES, MOTHER.
SHE STILL HASN'T FOUND OUT I'VE BEEN VISITING THE VILLA...

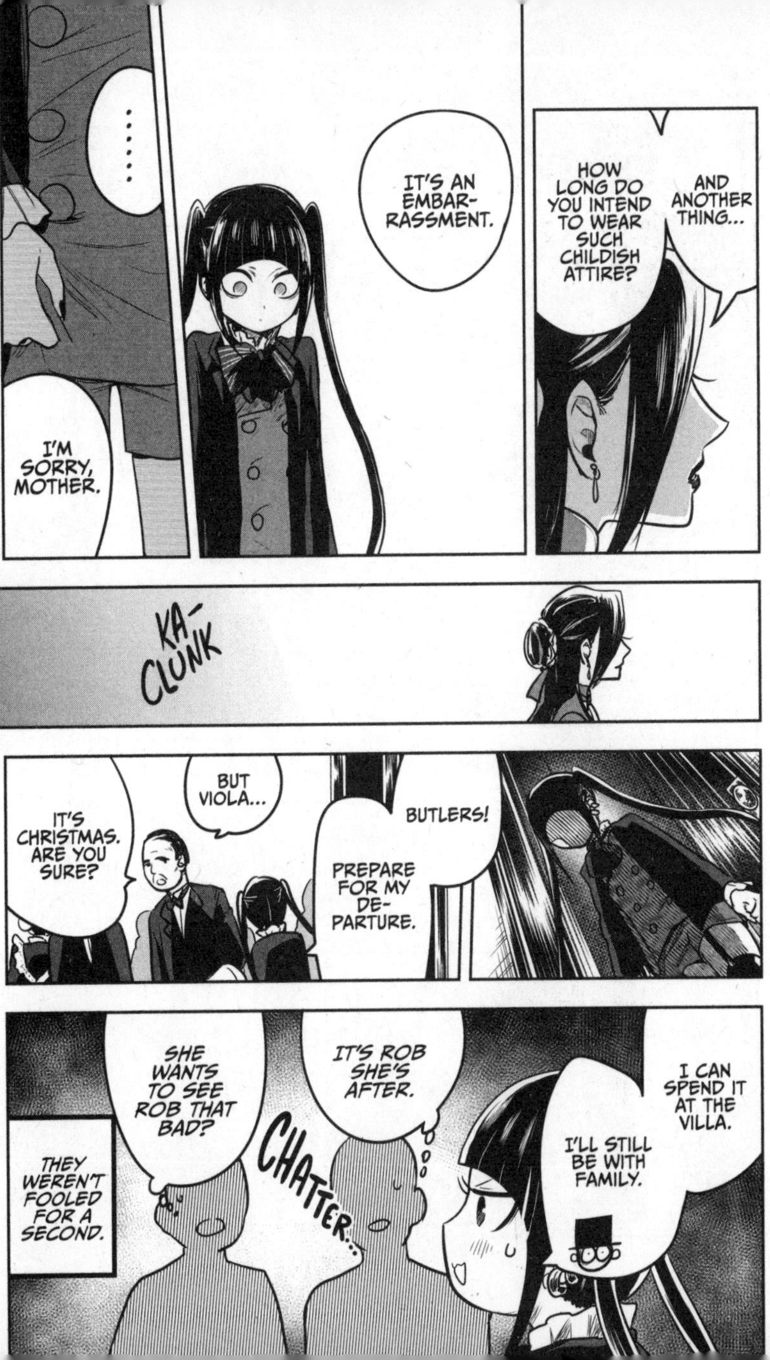
AND ANOTHER THING...
HOW LONG DO YOU INTEND TO WEAR SUCH CHILDISH ATTIRE?
IT'S AN EMBARRASSMENT.
......
I'M SORRY, MOTHER.
KA-CLUNK
BUTLERS!
PREPARE FOR MY DEPARTURE.
BUT VIOLA...
IT'S CHRISTMAS. ARE YOU SURE?
I CAN SPEND IT AT THE VILLA.
I'LL STILL BE WITH FAMILY.
IT'S ROB SHE'S AFTER.
SHE WANTS TO SEE ROB THAT BAD?
CHATTER...
THEY WEREN'T FOOLED FOR A SECOND.

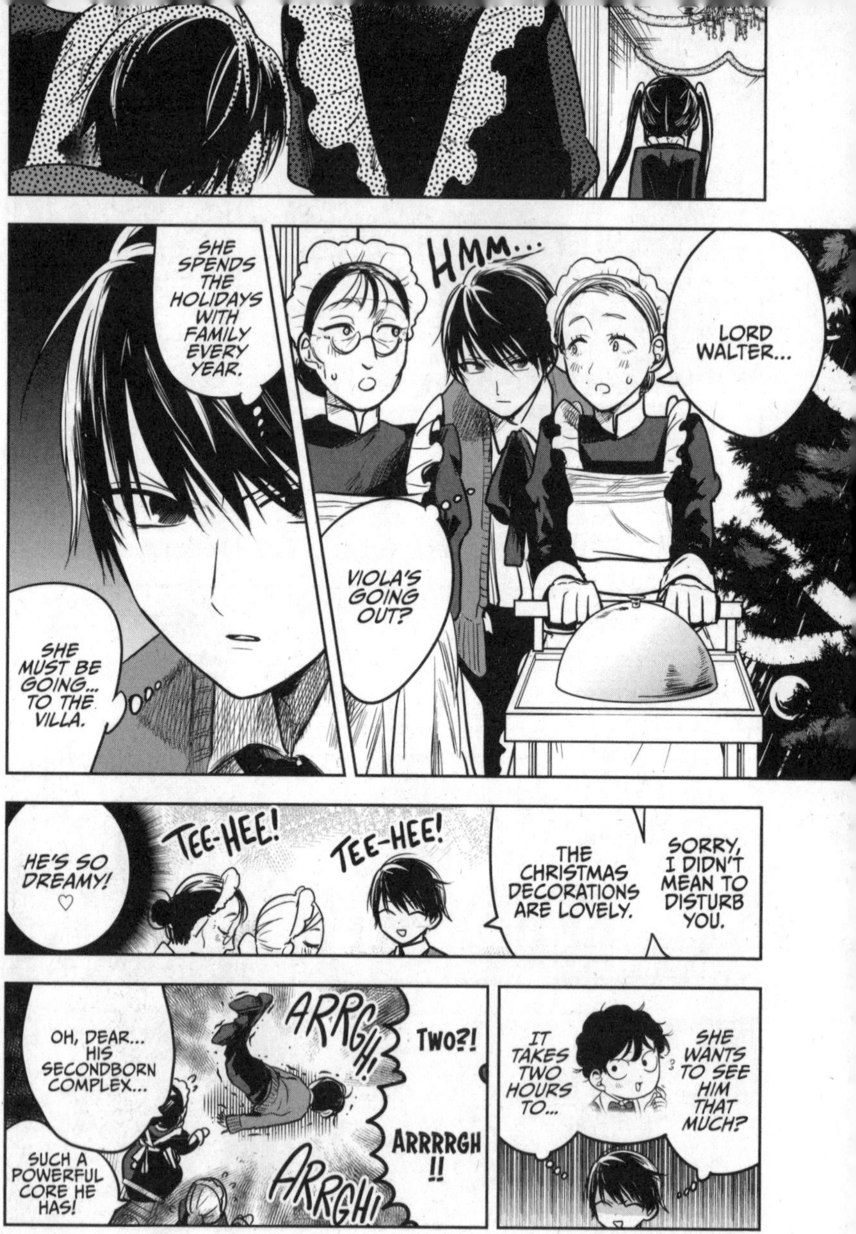
LORD WALTER...
HMM...
VIOLA'S GOING OUT?
SHE SPENDS THE HOLIDAYS WITH FAMILY EVERY YEAR.
SHE MUST BE GOING... TO THE VILLA.
SORRY, I DIDN'T MEAN TO DISTURB YOU.
THE CHRISTMAS DECORATIONS ARE LOVELY.
TEE-HEE!
TEE-HEE!
HE'S SO DREAMY! ♡
SHE WANTS TO SEE HIM THAT MUCH?
IT TAKES TWO HOURS TO...
TWO?!
ARRGH!
ARRRRGH!!
ARRGH!
OH, DEAR... HIS SECONDBORN COMPLEX...
SUCH A POWERFUL CORE HE HAS!

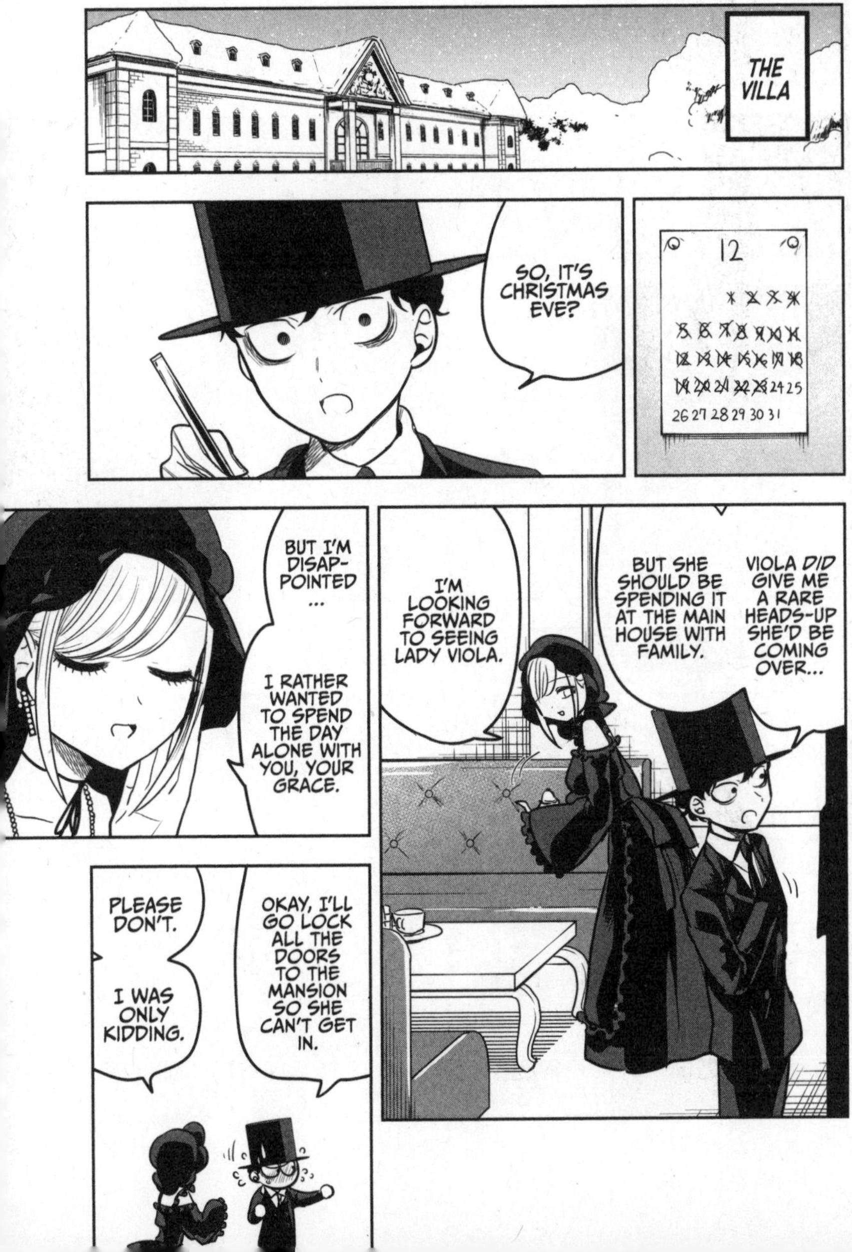
THE VILLA
12
SO, IT'S CHRISTMAS EVE?
VIOLA *DID* GIVE ME A RARE HEADS-UP SHE'D BE COMING OVER...
BUT SHE SHOULD BE SPENDING IT AT THE MAIN HOUSE WITH FAMILY.
I'M LOOKING FORWARD TO SEEING LADY VIOLA.
BUT I'M DISAP-POINTED ...
I RATHER WANTED TO SPEND THE DAY ALONE WITH YOU, YOUR GRACE.
OKAY, I'LL GO LOCK ALL THE DOORS TO THE MANSION SO SHE CAN'T GET IN.
PLEASE DON'T.
I WAS ONLY KIDDING.

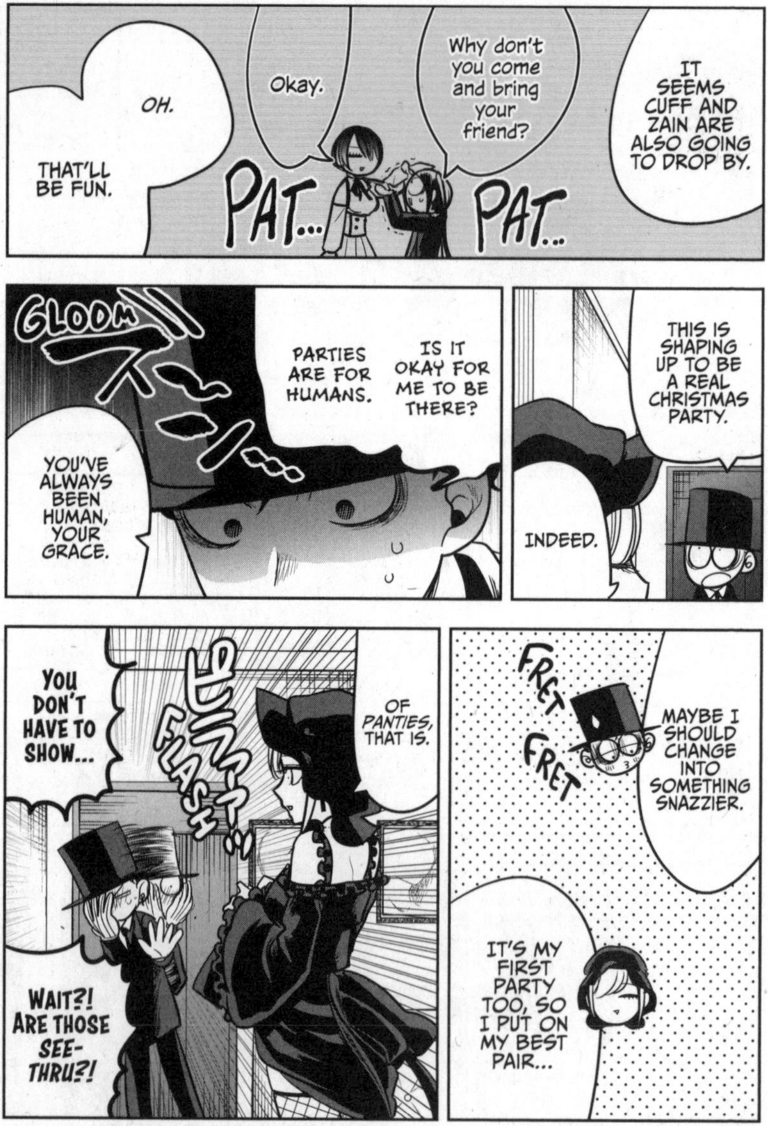
IT SEEMS CUFF AND ZAIN ARE ALSO GOING TO DROP BY.
Why don't you come and bring your friend?
PAT... PAT...
Okay.
OH.
THAT'LL BE FUN.
THIS IS SHAPING UP TO BE A REAL CHRISTMAS PARTY.
INDEED.
IS IT OKAY FOR ME TO BE THERE?
PARTIES ARE FOR HUMANS.
GLOOM
YOU'VE ALWAYS BEEN HUMAN, YOUR GRACE.
MAYBE I SHOULD CHANGE INTO SOMETHING SNAZZIER.
FRET FRET
IT'S MY FIRST PARTY TOO, SO I PUT ON MY BEST PAIR...
OF PANTIES, THAT IS.
FLASH
YOU DON'T HAVE TO SHOW...
WAIT?! ARE THOSE SEE-THRU?!

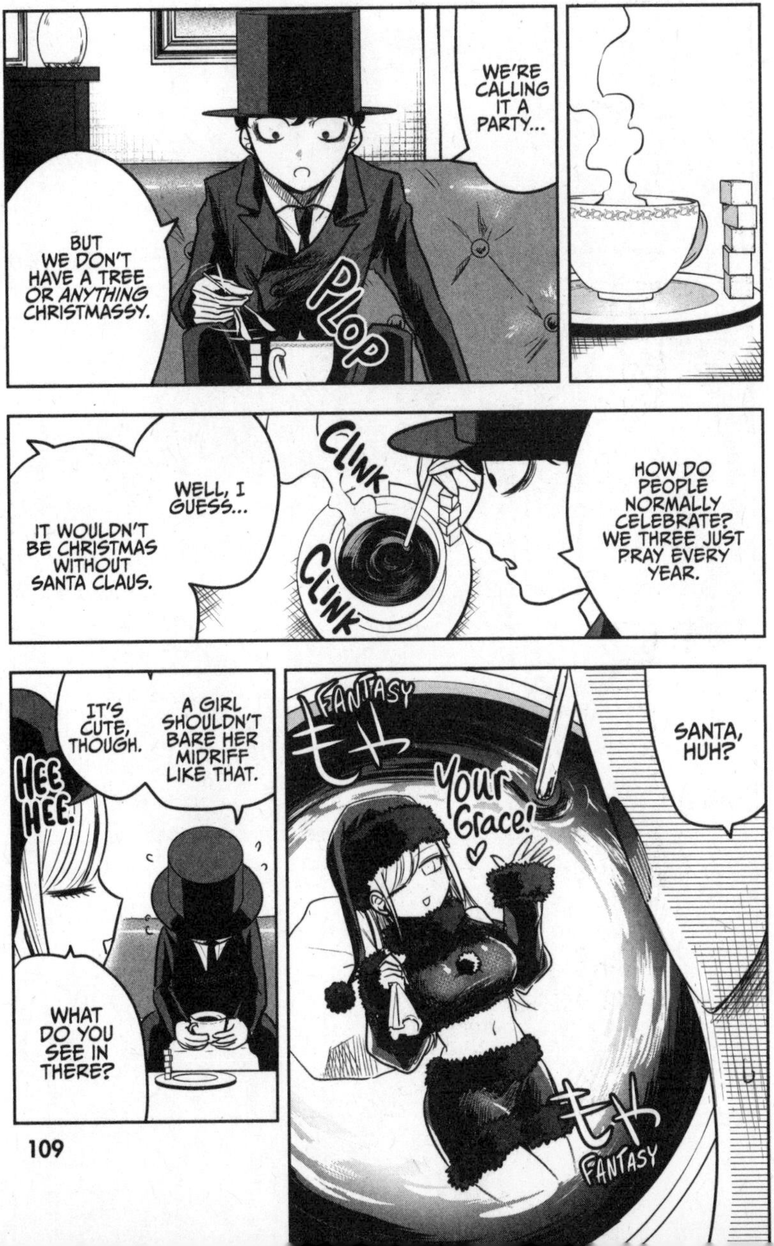
WE'RE CALLING IT A PARTY...
BUT WE DON'T HAVE A TREE OR *ANYTHING* CHRISTMASSY.
PLOP
HOW DO PEOPLE NORMALLY CELEBRATE? WE THREE JUST PRAY EVERY YEAR.
CLINK
CLINK
WELL, I GUESS...
IT WOULDN'T BE CHRISTMAS WITHOUT SANTA CLAUS.
SANTA, HUH?
FANTASY
Your Grace!
FANTASY
A GIRL SHOULDN'T BARE HER MIDRIFF LIKE THAT.
IT'S CUTE, THOUGH.
HEE HEE.
WHAT DO YOU SEE IN THERE?

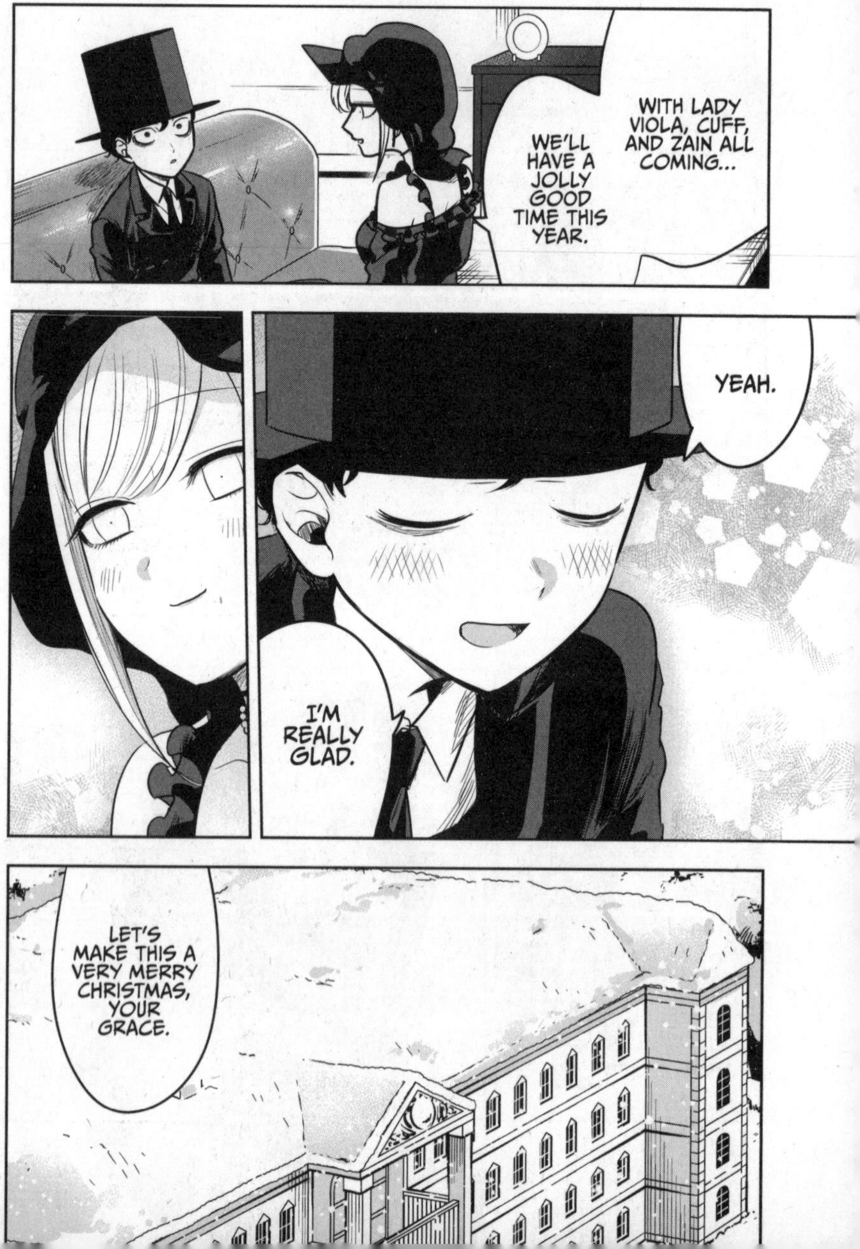
WITH LADY VIOLA, CUFF, AND ZAIN ALL COMING...
WE'LL HAVE A JOLLY GOOD TIME THIS YEAR.
YEAH.
I'M REALLY GLAD.
LET'S MAKE THIS A VERY MERRY CHRISTMAS, YOUR GRACE.

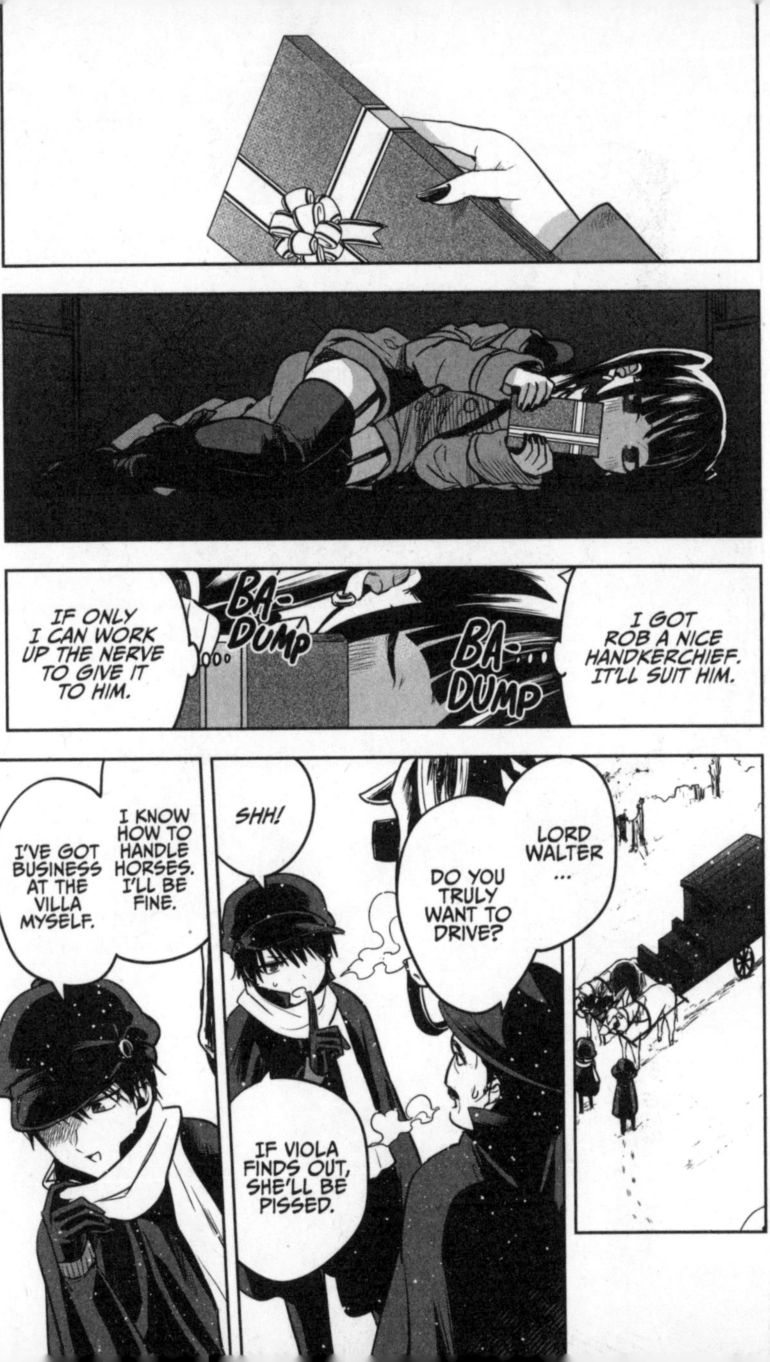
I GOT ROB A NICE HANDKERCHIEF. IT'LL SUIT HIM.
BA-DUMP
BA-DUMP
IF ONLY I CAN WORK UP THE NERVE TO GIVE IT TO HIM.
LORD WALTER ...
DO YOU TRULY WANT TO DRIVE?
SHH!
IF VIOLA FINDS OUT, SHE'LL BE PISSED.
I KNOW HOW TO HANDLE HORSES. I'LL BE FINE.
I'VE GOT BUSINESS AT THE VILLA MYSELF.

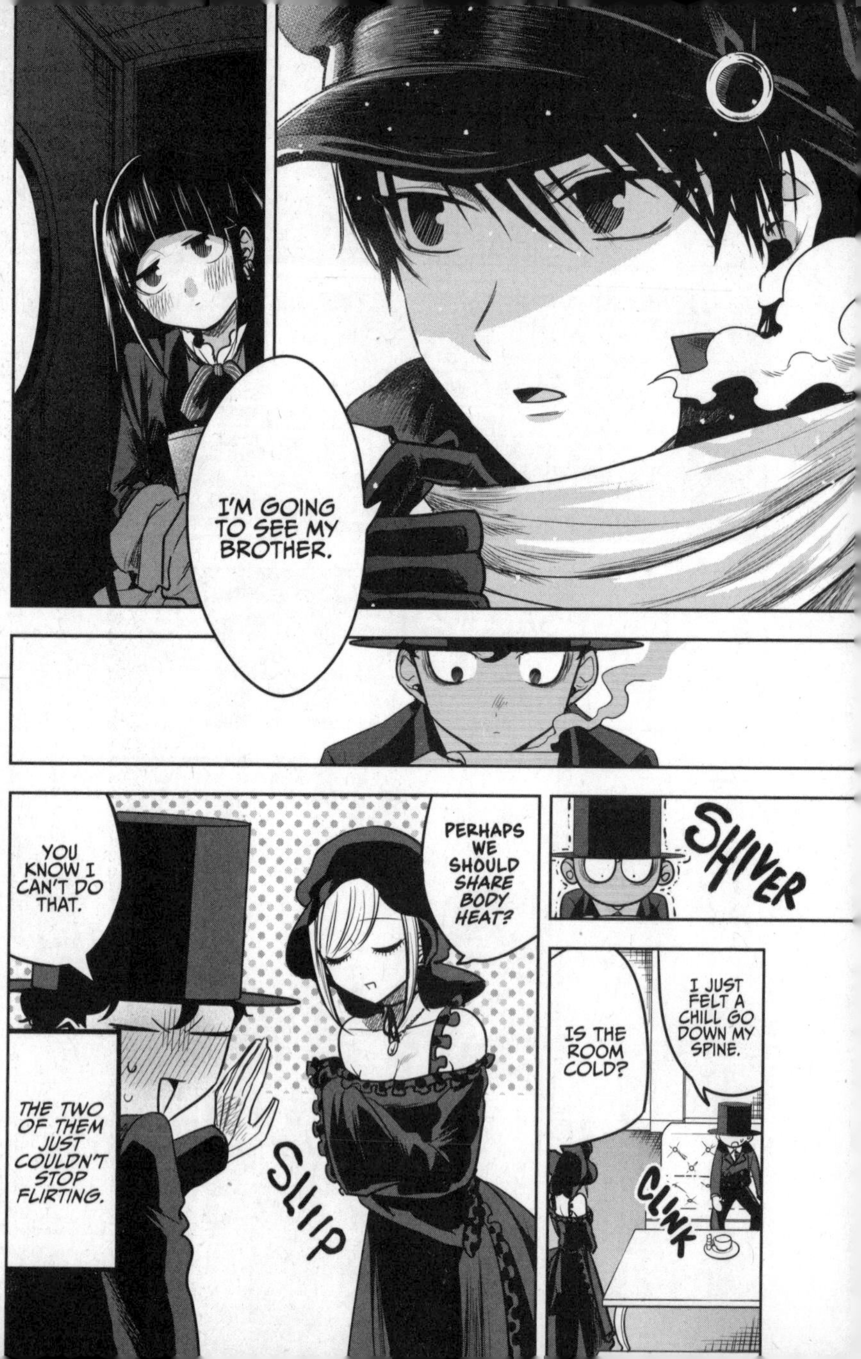
I'M GOING TO SEE MY BROTHER.
SHIVER
I JUST FELT A CHILL GO DOWN MY SPINE.
IS THE ROOM COLD?
CLINK
PERHAPS WE SHOULD SHARE BODY HEAT?
YOU KNOW I CAN'T DO THAT.
SLIIP
THE TWO OF THEM JUST COULDN'T STOP FLIRTING.

Chapter 51: Christmas Pt. 2

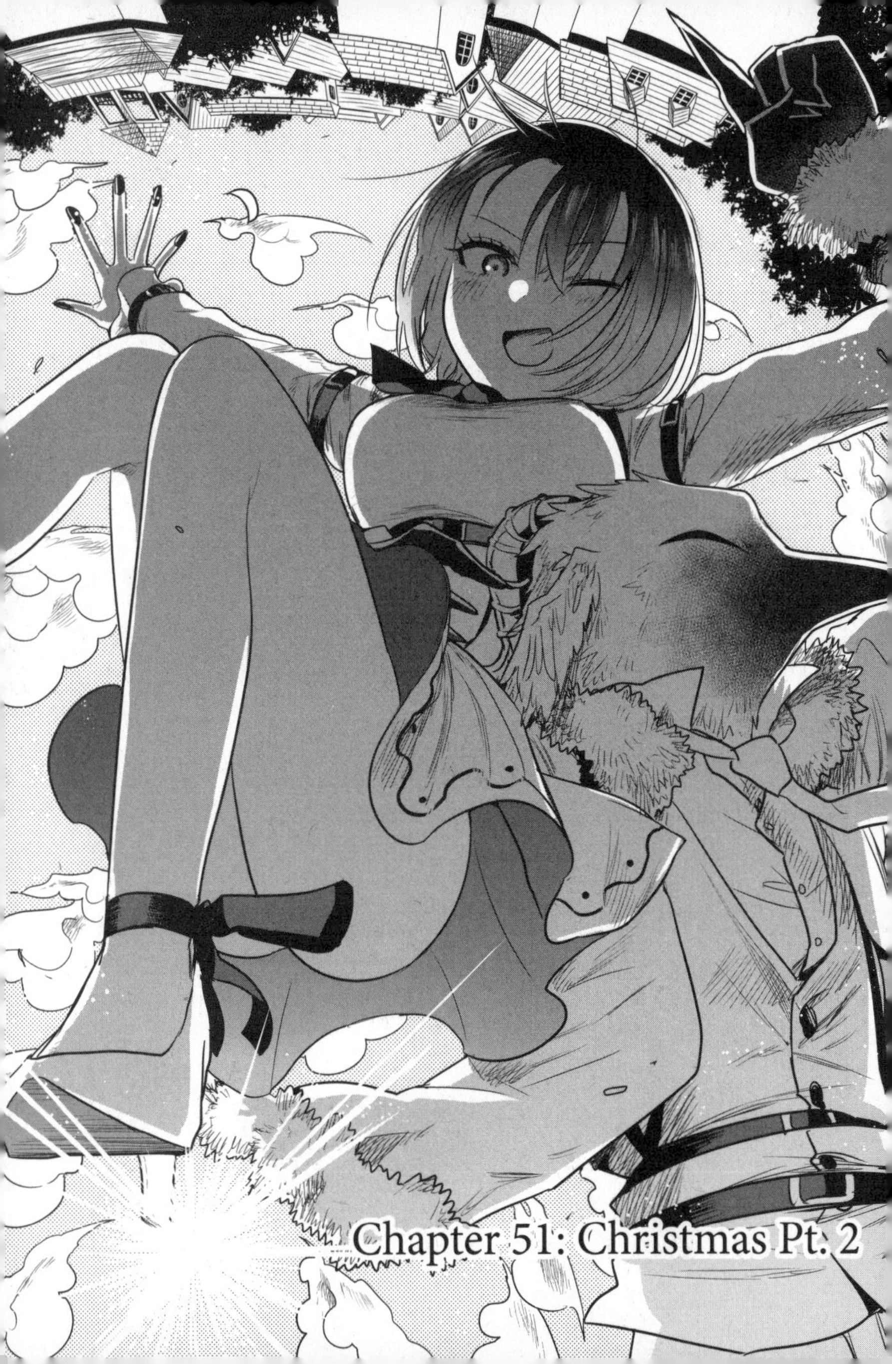

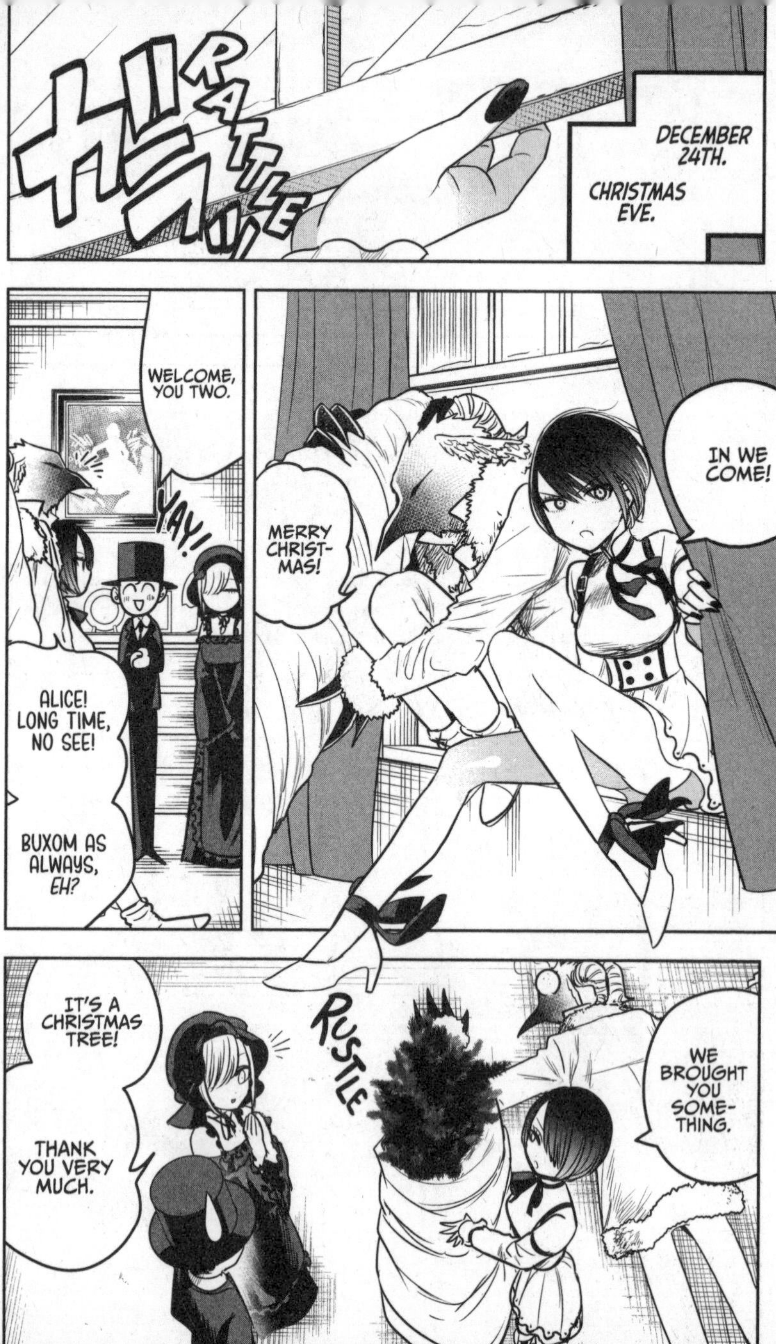
RATTLE
DECEMBER 24TH.
CHRISTMAS EVE.
IN WE COME!
MERRY CHRIST-MAS!
WELCOME, YOU TWO.
YAY!
ALICE! LONG TIME, NO SEE!
BUXOM AS ALWAYS, EH?
WE BROUGHT YOU SOME-THING.
RUSTLE
IT'S A CHRISTMAS TREE!
THANK YOU VERY MUCH.

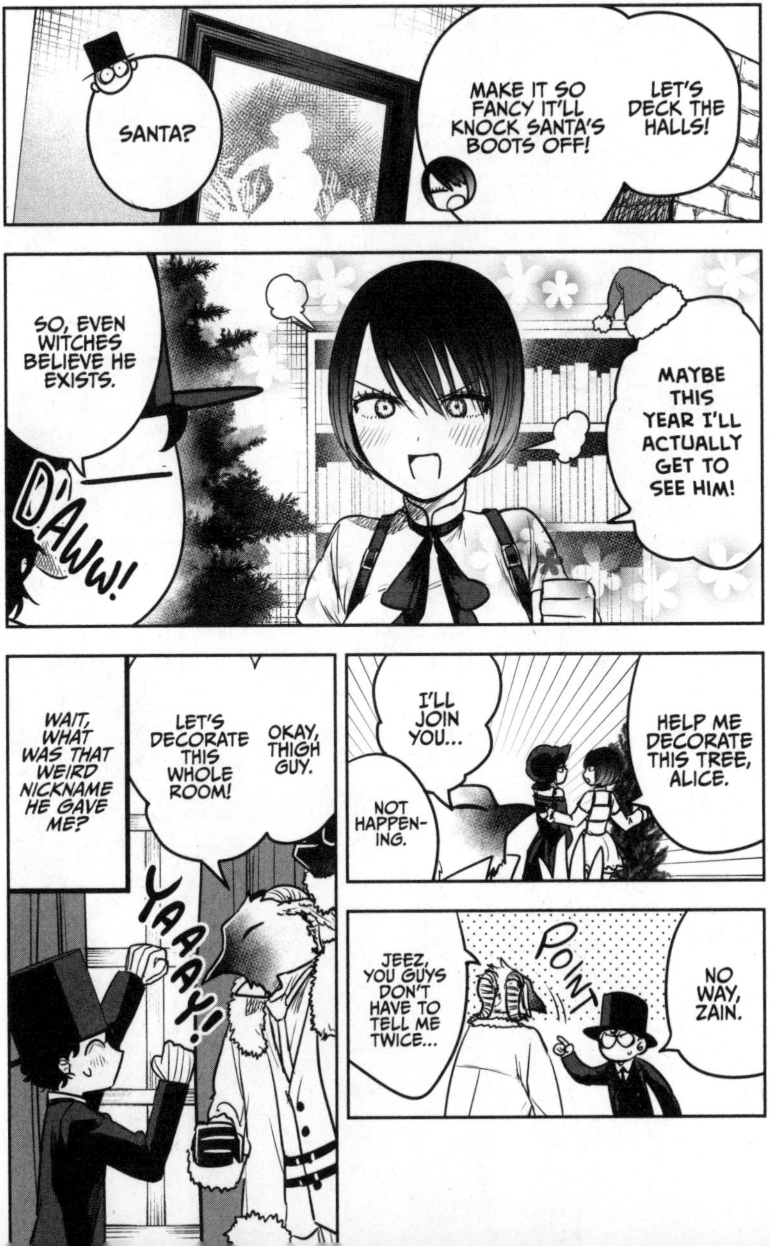
LET'S DECK THE HALLS!
MAKE IT SO FANCY IT'LL KNOCK SANTA'S BOOTS OFF!
SANTA?
MAYBE THIS YEAR I'LL ACTUALLY GET TO SEE HIM!
SO, EVEN WITCHES BELIEVE HE EXISTS.
D'AWW!
HELP ME DECORATE THIS TREE, ALICE.
I'LL JOIN YOU...
NOT HAPPENING.
NO WAY, ZAIN.
POINT
JEEZ, YOU GUYS DON'T HAVE TO TELL ME TWICE...
OKAY, THIGH GUY.
LET'S DECORATE THIS WHOLE ROOM!
WAIT, WHAT WAS THAT WEIRD NICKNAME HE GAVE ME?
YAAAY!

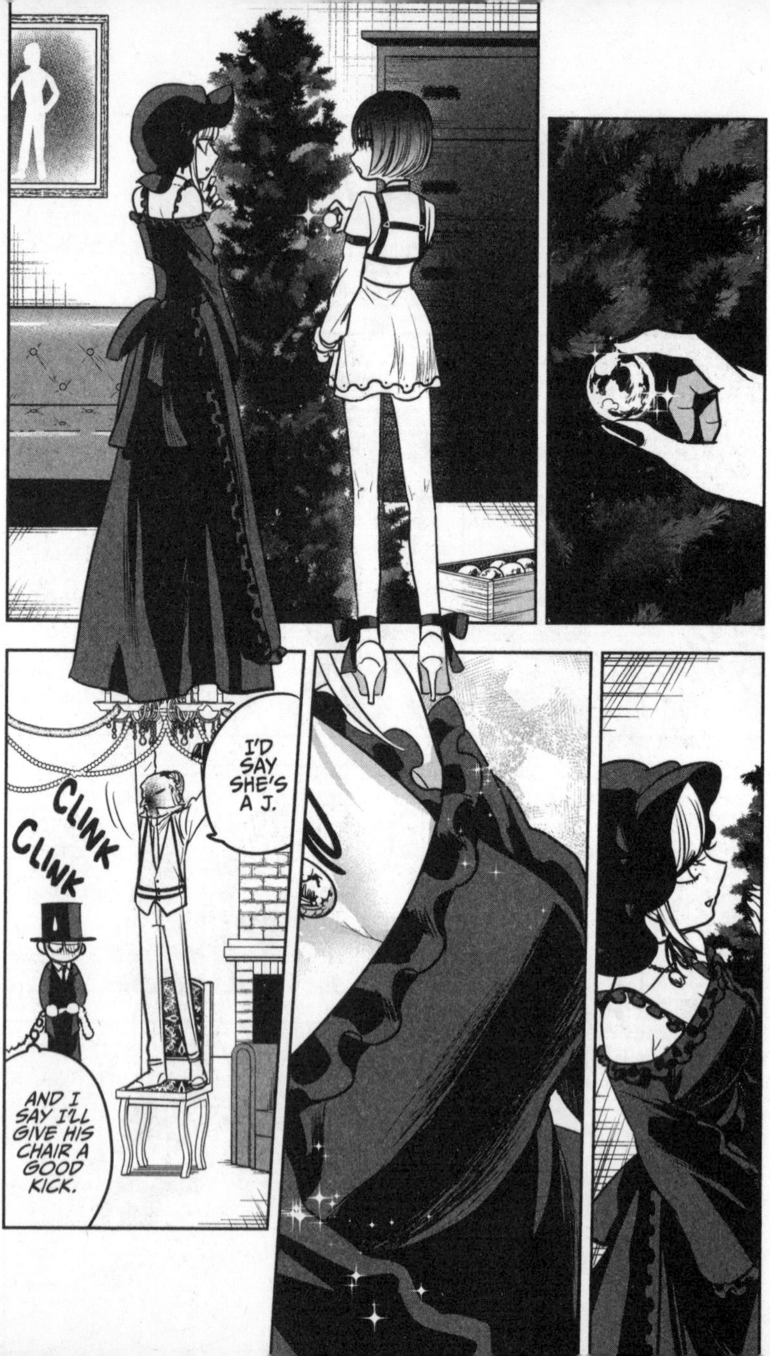
I'D SAY SHE'S A J.
CLINK CLINK
AND I SAY I'LL GIVE HIS CHAIR A GOOD KICK.

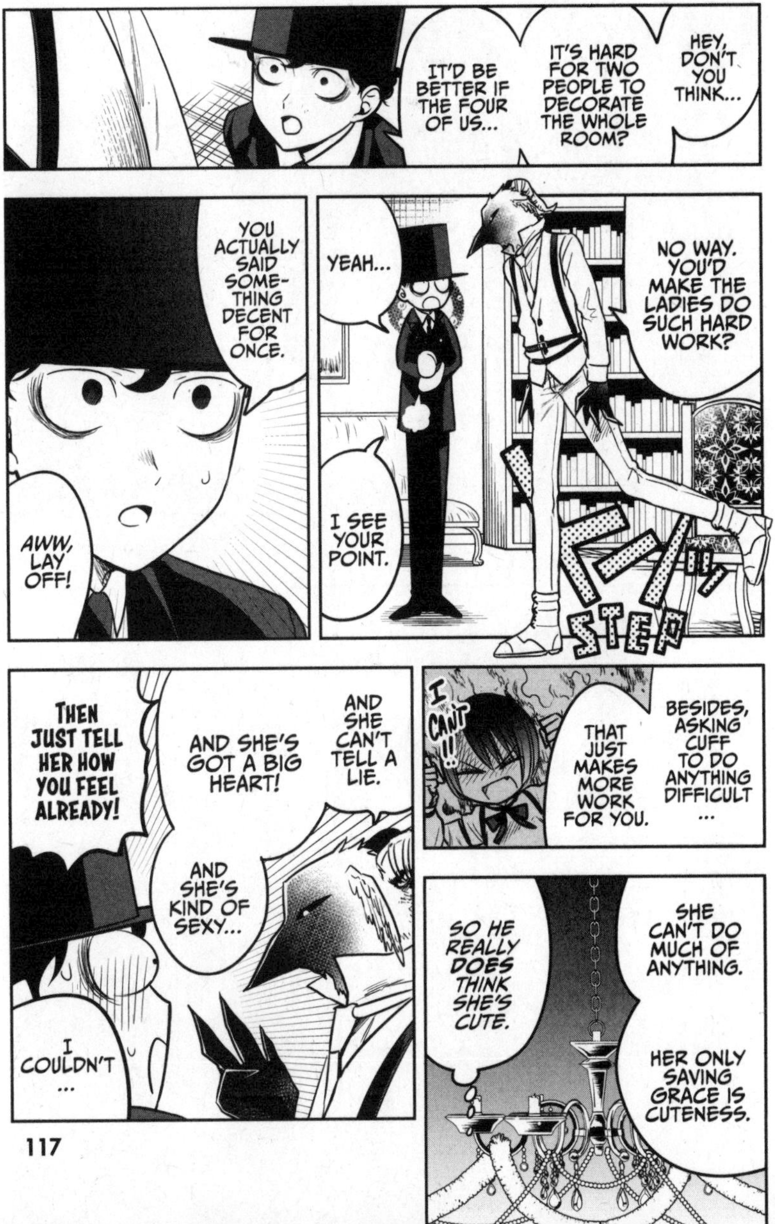
HEY, DON'T YOU THINK...
IT'S HARD FOR TWO PEOPLE TO DECORATE THE WHOLE ROOM?
IT'D BE BETTER IF THE FOUR OF US...
NO WAY. YOU'D MAKE THE LADIES DO SUCH HARD WORK?
YEAH...
I SEE YOUR POINT.
STEP
YOU ACTUALLY SAID SOME-THING DECENT FOR ONCE.
AWW, LAY OFF!
BESIDES, ASKING CUFF TO DO ANYTHING DIFFICULT ...
THAT JUST MAKES MORE WORK FOR YOU.
I CAN'T!!
SHE CAN'T DO MUCH OF ANYTHING.
HER ONLY SAVING GRACE IS CUTENESS.
SO HE REALLY DOES THINK SHE'S CUTE.
AND SHE CAN'T TELL A LIE.
AND SHE'S GOT A BIG HEART!
AND SHE'S KIND OF SEXY...
THEN JUST TELL HER HOW YOU FEEL ALREADY!
I COULDN'T ...

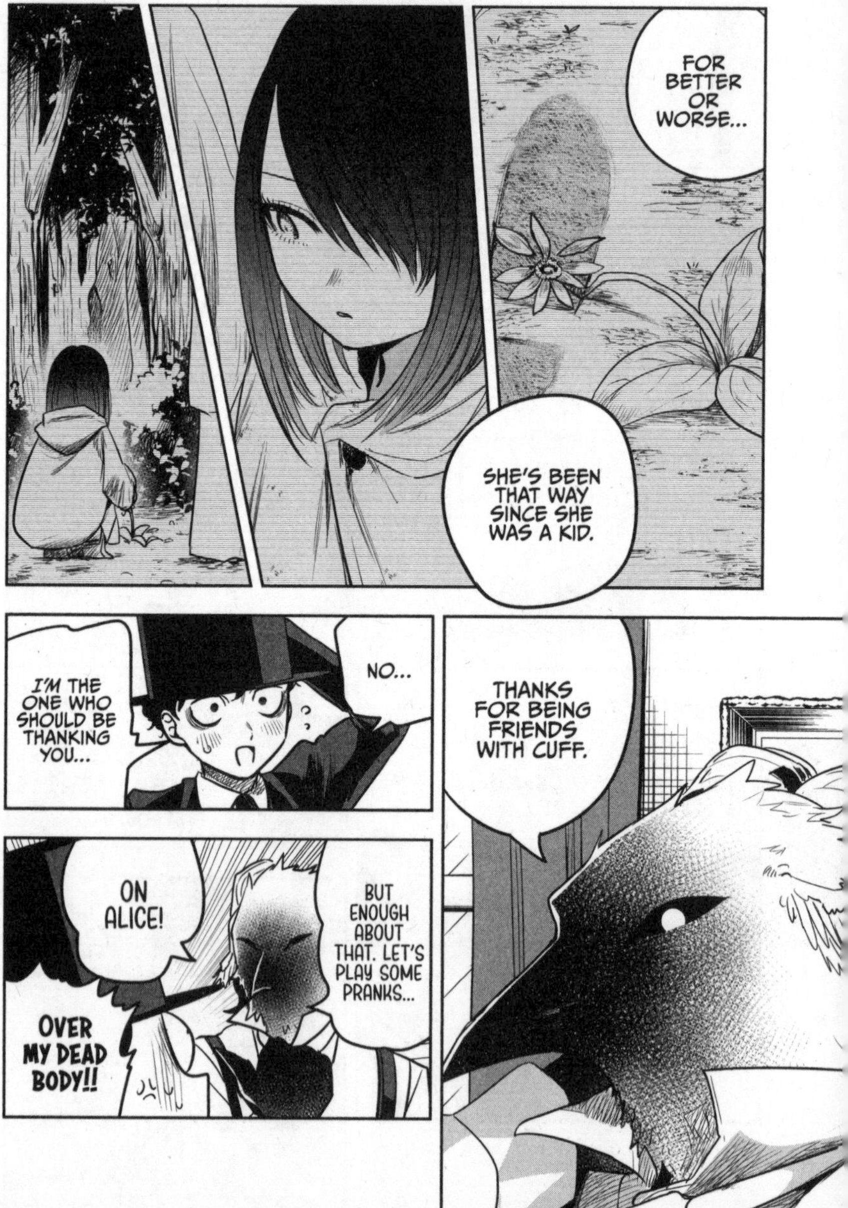
FOR BETTER OR WORSE...
SHE'S BEEN THAT WAY SINCE SHE WAS A KID.
THANKS FOR BEING FRIENDS WITH CUFF.
NO...
I'M THE ONE WHO SHOULD BE THANKING YOU...
BUT ENOUGH ABOUT THAT. LET'S PLAY SOME PRANKS...
ON ALICE!
OVER MY DEAD BODY!!

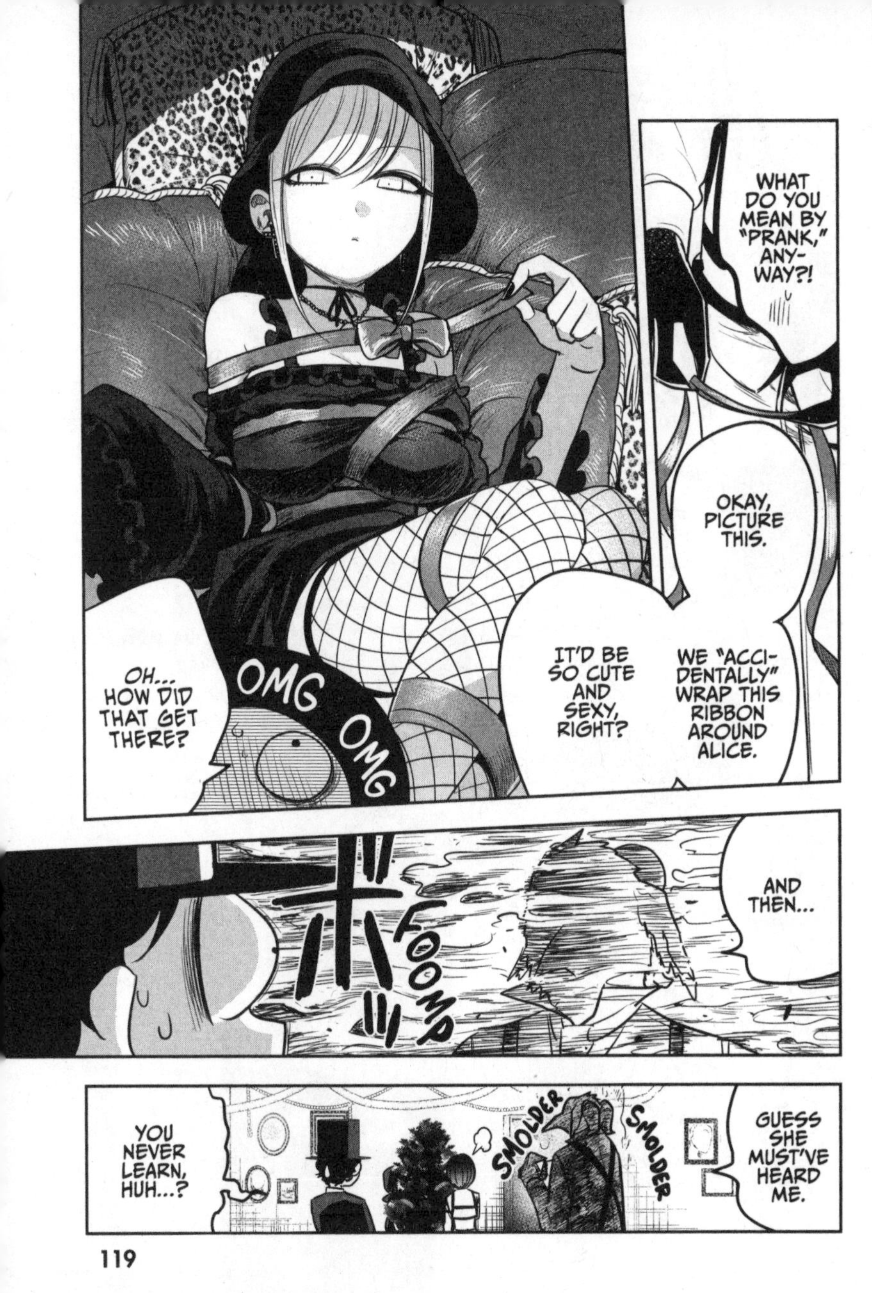
WHAT DO YOU MEAN BY "PRANK," ANYWAY?!
OKAY, PICTURE THIS.
WE "ACCIDENTALLY" WRAP THIS RIBBON AROUND ALICE.
IT'D BE SO CUTE AND SEXY, RIGHT?
OMG OMG OMG
OH... HOW DID THAT GET THERE?
AND THEN...
FOOMP
GUESS SHE MUST'VE HEARD ME.
SMOLDER SMOLDER
YOU NEVER LEARN, HUH...?

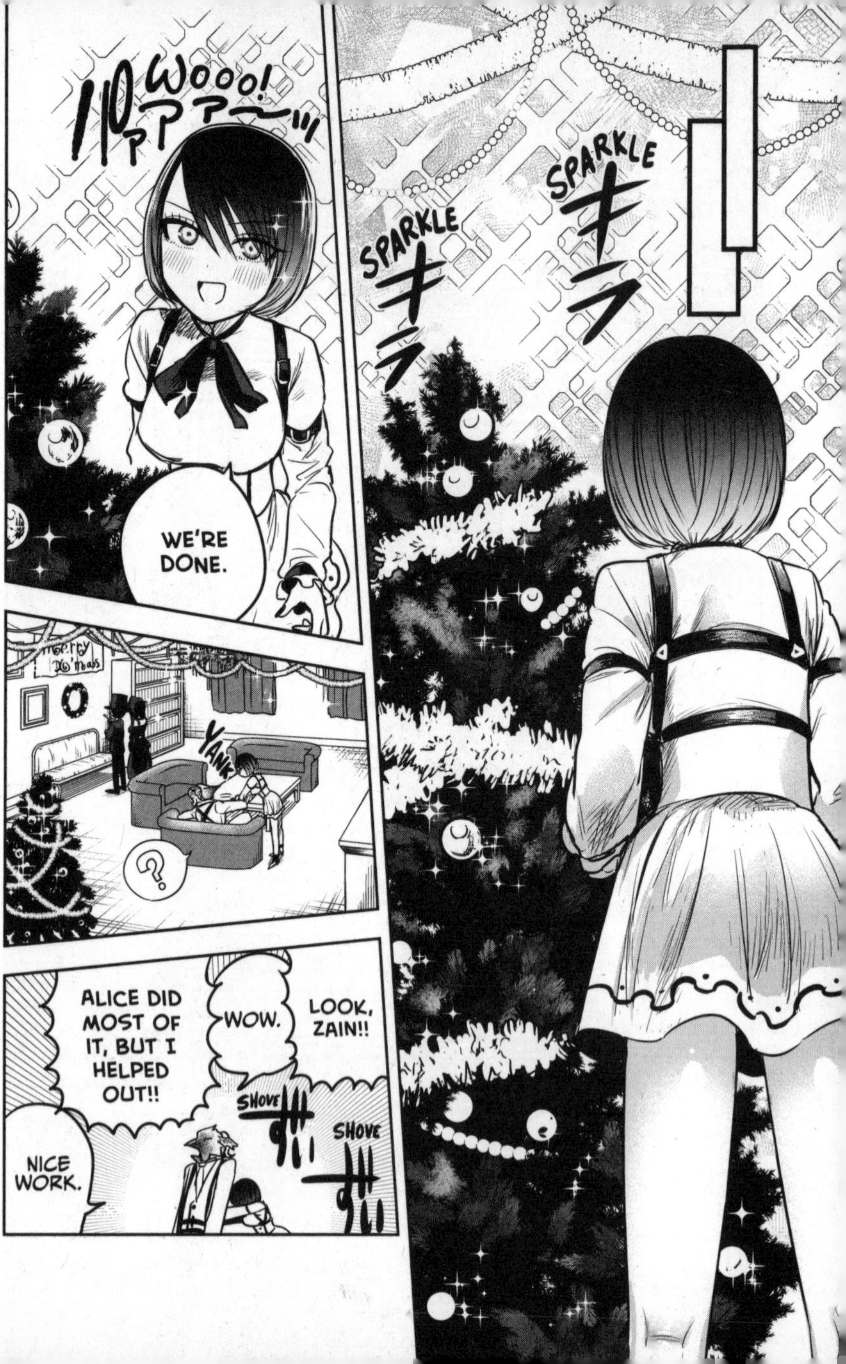
SPARKLE
SPARKLE
Wooo!
WE'RE DONE.
YANK
?
LOOK, ZAIN!!
WOW.
ALICE DID MOST OF IT, BUT I HELPED OUT!!
SHOVE
SHOVE
NICE WORK.

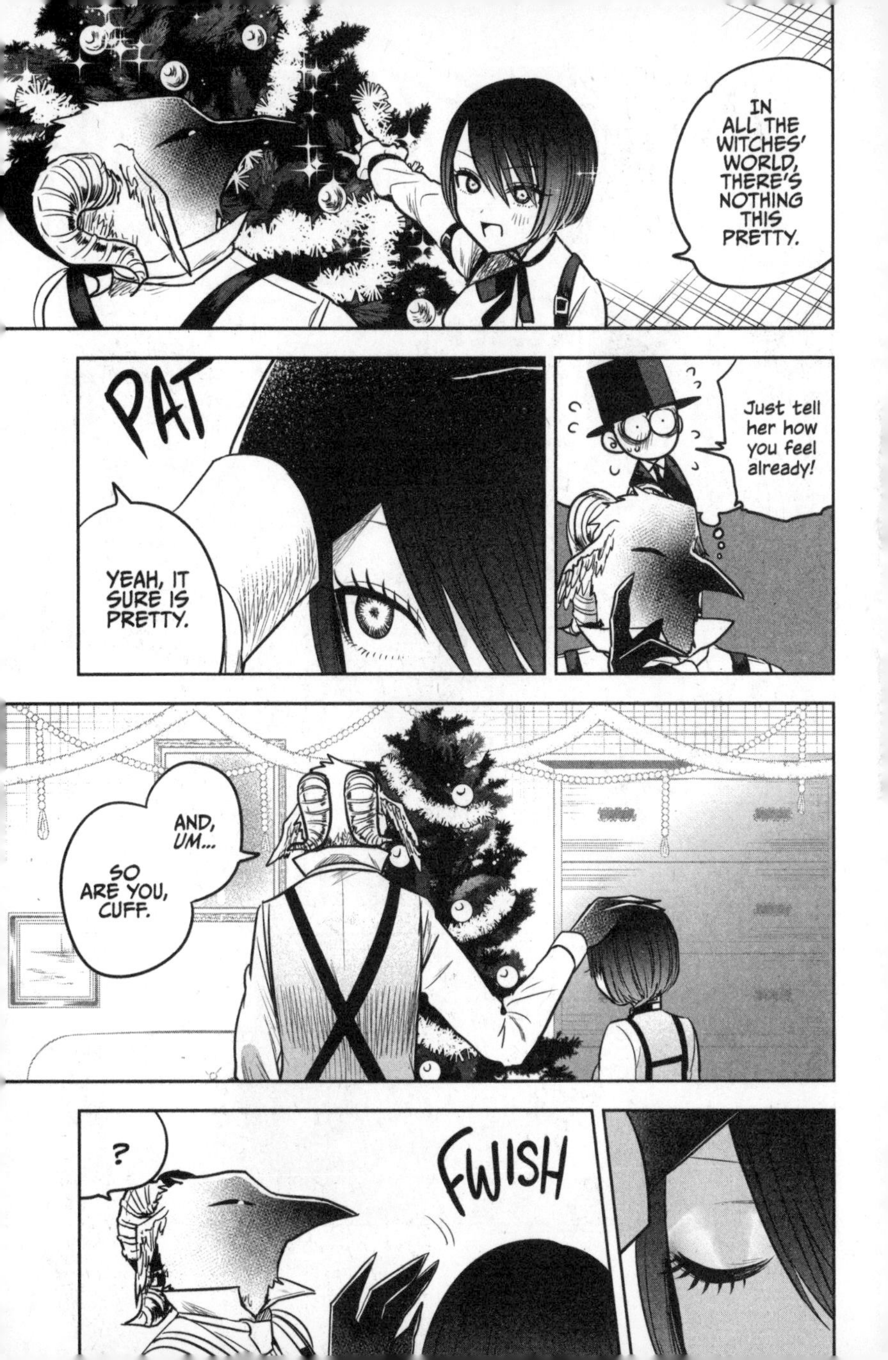
IN ALL THE WITCHES' WORLD, THERE'S NOTHING THIS PRETTY.
Just tell her how you feel already!
PAT
YEAH, IT SURE IS PRETTY.
AND, UM...
SO ARE YOU, CUFF.
FWISH
?

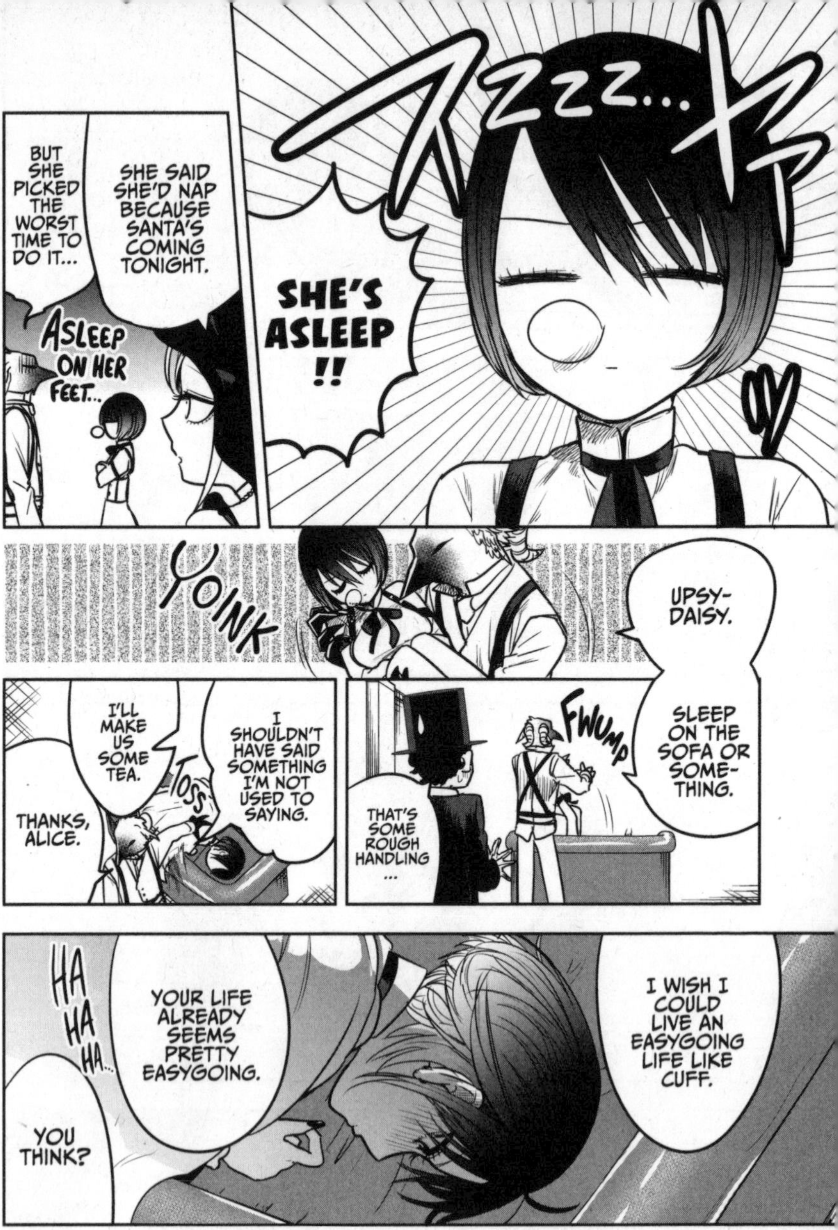
ZZZZ...
SHE'S ASLEEP!!
SHE SAID SHE'D NAP BECAUSE SANTA'S COMING TONIGHT.
BUT SHE PICKED THE WORST TIME TO DO IT...
ASLEEP ON HER FEET...
UPSY-DAISY.
YOINK
SLEEP ON THE SOFA OR SOME-THING.
FWUMP
THAT'S SOME ROUGH HANDLING...
I SHOULDN'T HAVE SAID SOMETHING I'M NOT USED TO SAYING.
TOSS
I'LL MAKE US SOME TEA.
THANKS, ALICE.
I WISH I COULD LIVE AN EASYGOING LIFE LIKE CUFF.
YOUR LIFE ALREADY SEEMS PRETTY EASYGOING.
HA HA HA...
YOU THINK?

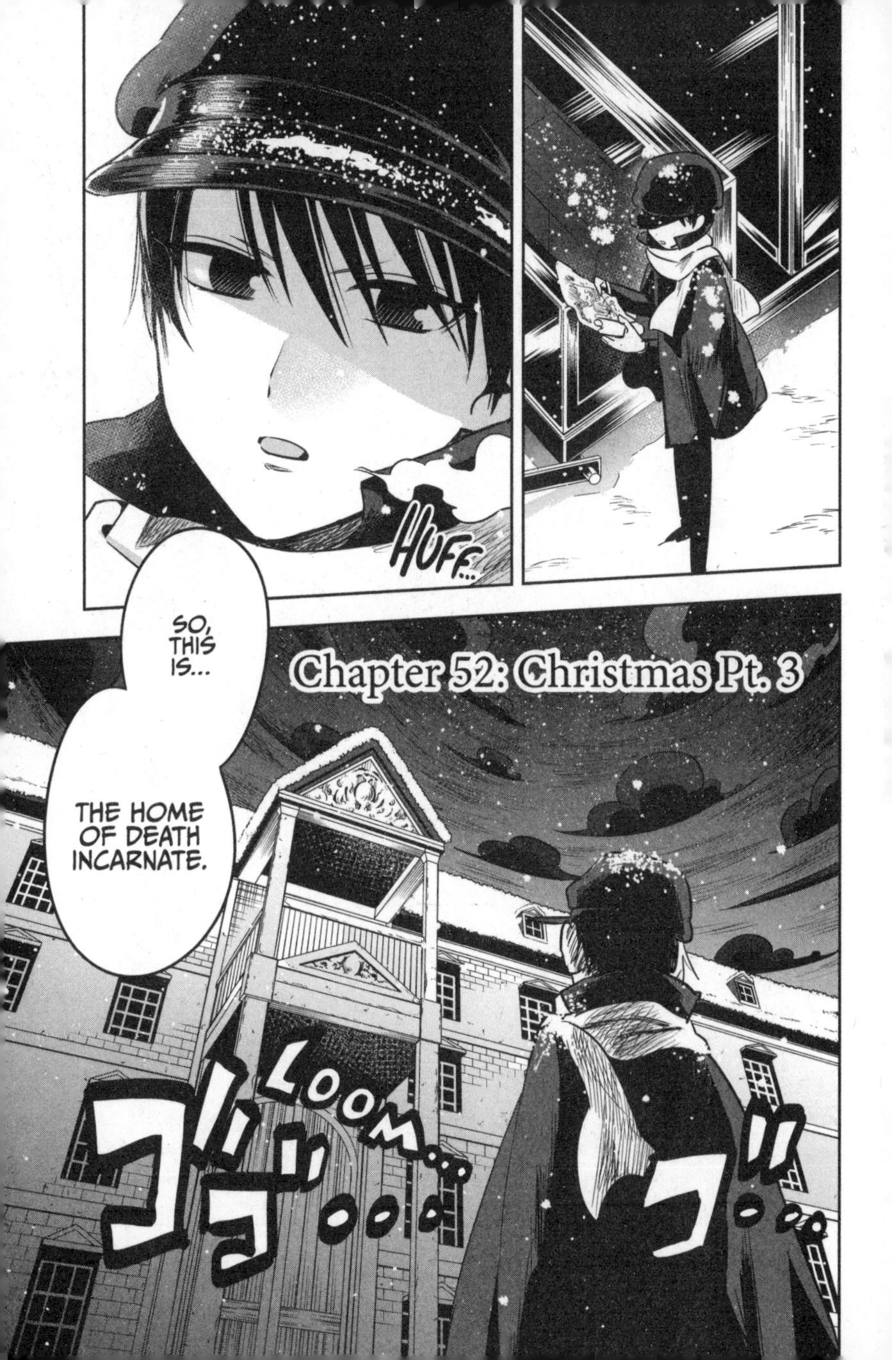
HUFF...
SO, THIS IS...
THE HOME OF DEATH INCARNATE.
Chapter 52: Christmas Pt. 3
LOOM...

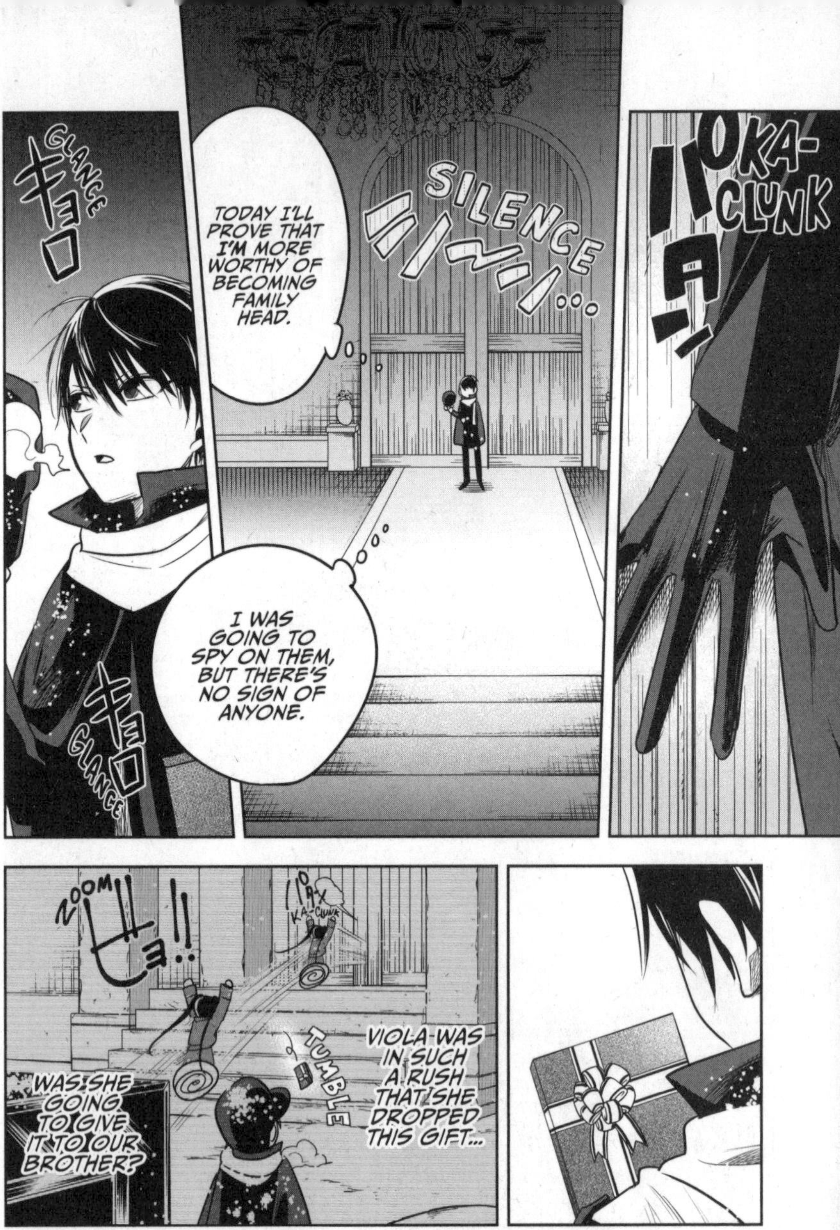
KA-CLUNK
TODAY I'LL PROVE THAT I'M MORE WORTHY OF BECOMING FAMILY HEAD.
SILENCE...
I WAS GOING TO SPY ON THEM, BUT THERE'S NO SIGN OF ANYONE.
GLANCE
GLANCE
KA-CLUNK
ZOOM
TUMBLE
VIOLA WAS IN SUCH A RUSH THAT SHE DROPPED THIS GIFT...
WAS SHE GOING TO GIVE IT TO OUR BROTHER?

Chapter 52: Christmas Pt. 3

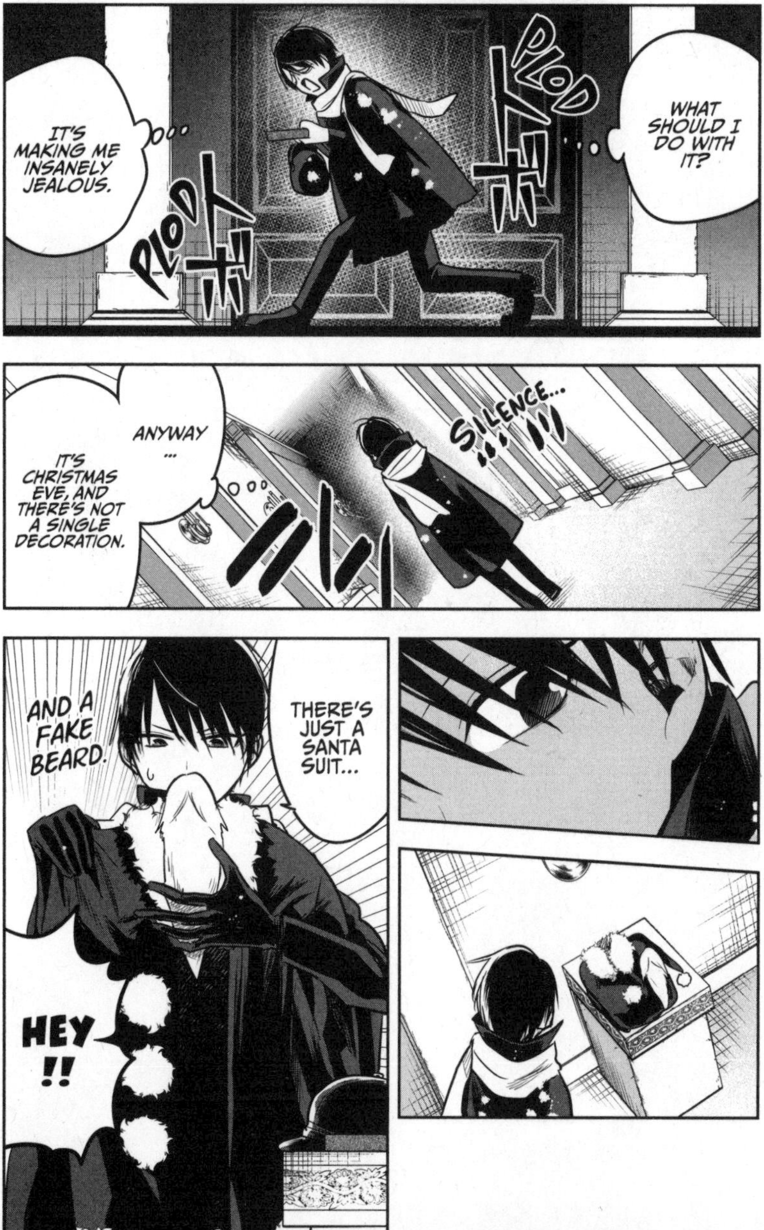
WHAT SHOULD I DO WITH IT?
PLOD
IT'S MAKING ME INSANELY JEALOUS.
PLOD
SILENCE...
ANYWAY...
IT'S CHRISTMAS EVE, AND THERE'S NOT A SINGLE DECORATION.
THERE'S JUST A SANTA SUIT...
AND A FAKE BEARD.
HEY!!

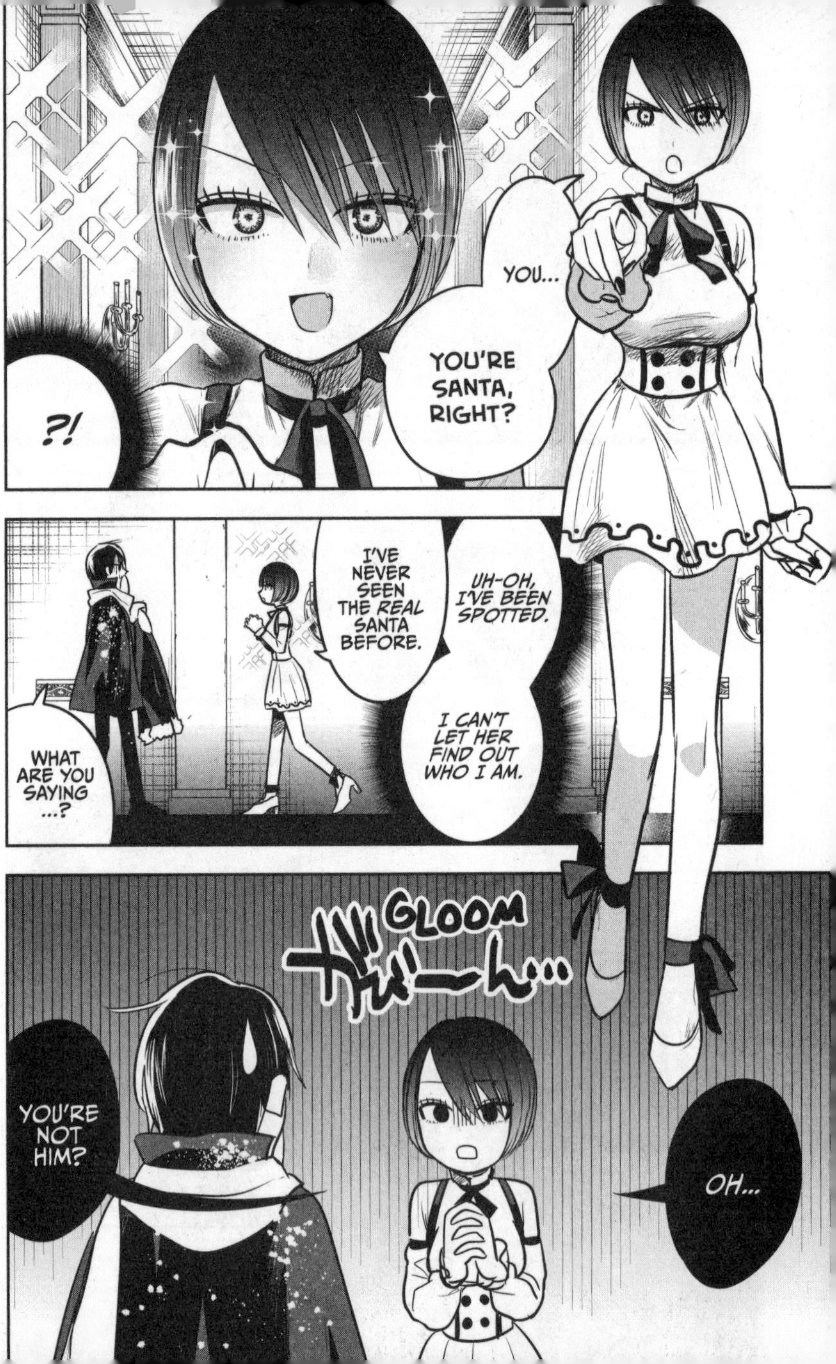
YOU...
YOU'RE SANTA, RIGHT?
?!
UH-OH, I'VE BEEN SPOTTED.
I CAN'T LET HER FIND OUT WHO I AM.
I'VE NEVER SEEN THE REAL SANTA BEFORE.
WHAT ARE YOU SAYING ...?
GLOOM
OH...
YOU'RE NOT HIM?

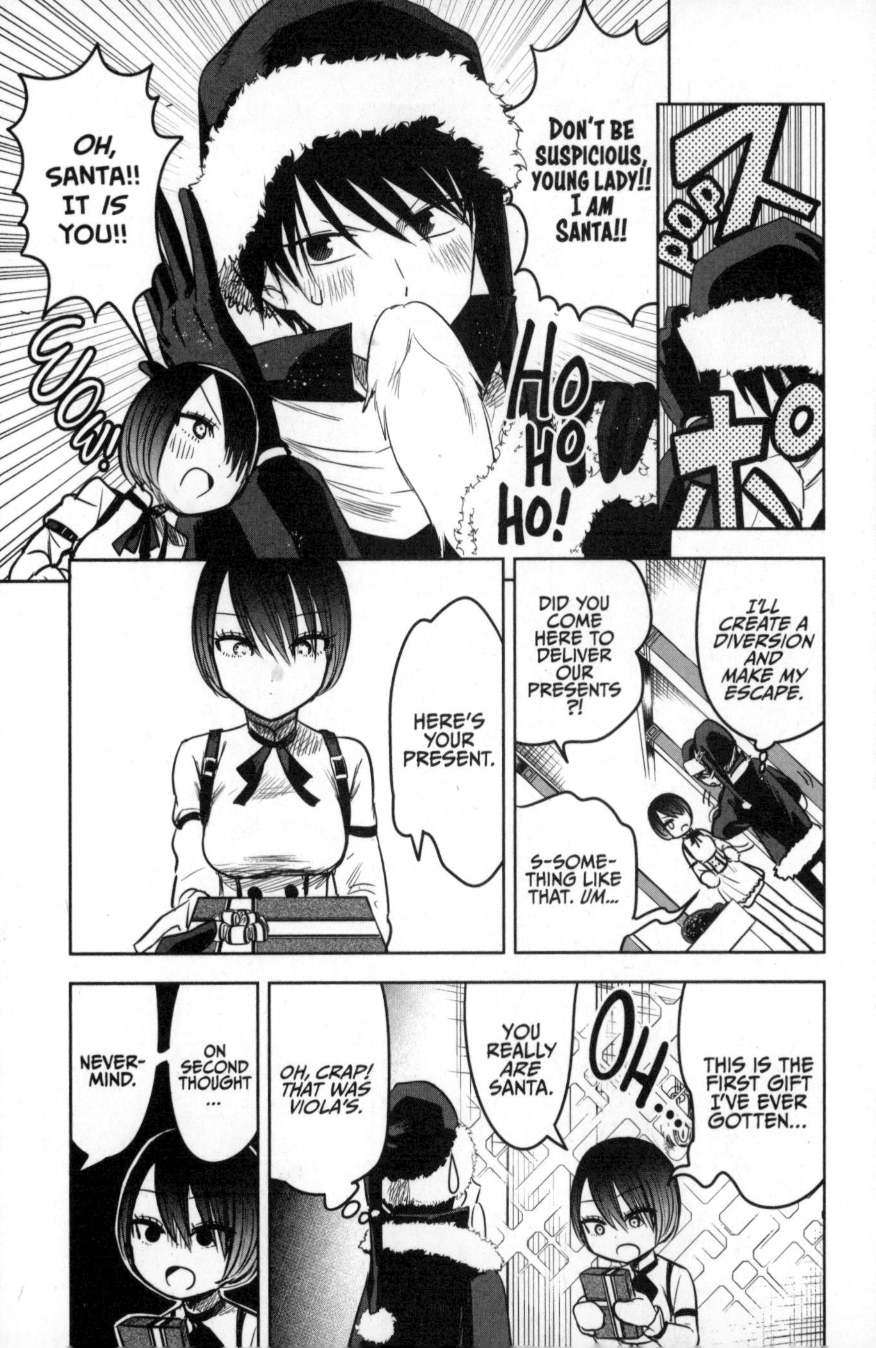
POP
DON'T BE SUSPICIOUS, YOUNG LADY!! I AM SANTA!!
HO HO HO HO!
OH, SANTA!! IT *IS* YOU!!
WOW!
I'LL CREATE A DIVERSION AND MAKE MY ESCAPE.
DID YOU COME HERE TO DELIVER OUR PRESENTS?!
S-SOMETHING LIKE THAT. *UM...*
HERE'S YOUR PRESENT.
THIS IS THE FIRST GIFT I'VE EVER GOTTEN...
OH...
YOU REALLY *ARE* SANTA.
OH, CRAP! THAT WAS VIOLA'S.
ON SECOND THOUGHT...
NEVER-MIND.

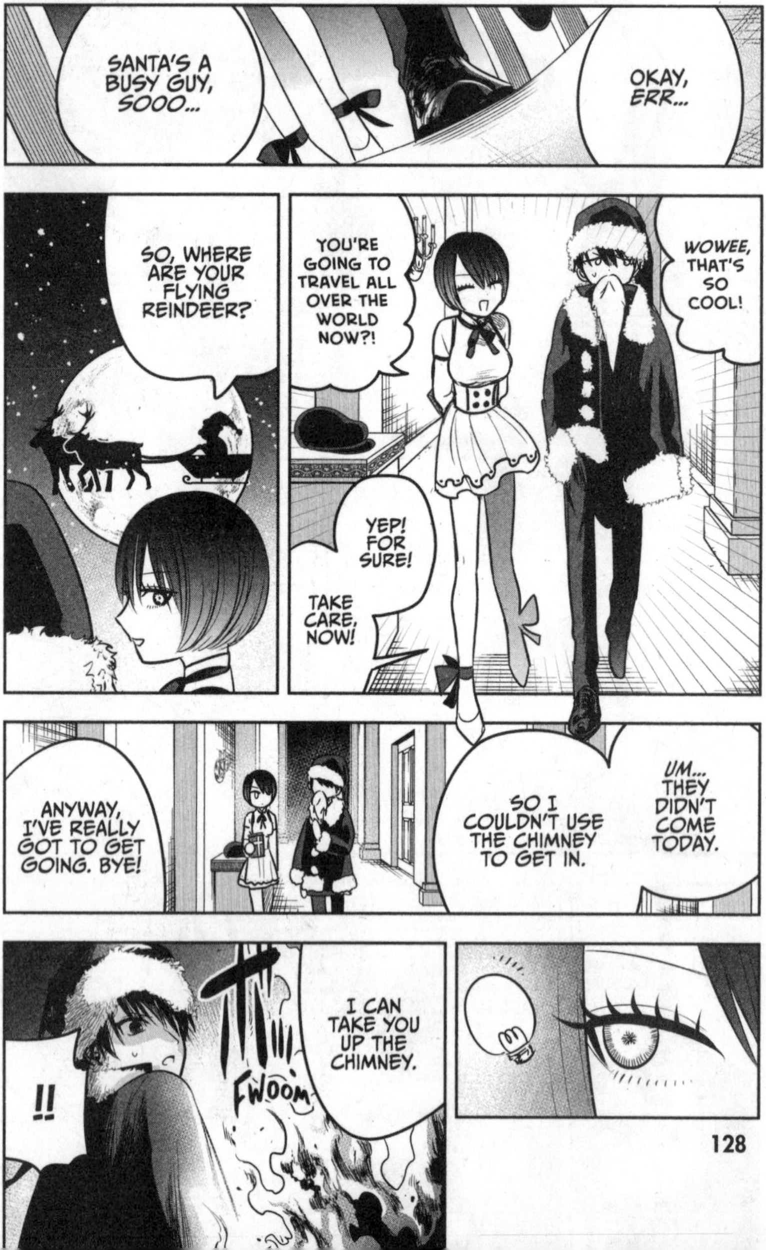
OKAY, ERR...
SANTA'S A BUSY GUY, SOOO...
WOWEE, THAT'S SO COOL!
YOU'RE GOING TO TRAVEL ALL OVER THE WORLD NOW?!
YEP! FOR SURE!
TAKE CARE, NOW!
SO, WHERE ARE YOUR FLYING REINDEER?
UM... THEY DIDN'T COME TODAY.
SO I COULDN'T USE THE CHIMNEY TO GET IN.
ANYWAY, I'VE REALLY GOT TO GET GOING. BYE!
I CAN TAKE YOU UP THE CHIMNEY.
FWOOM
!!

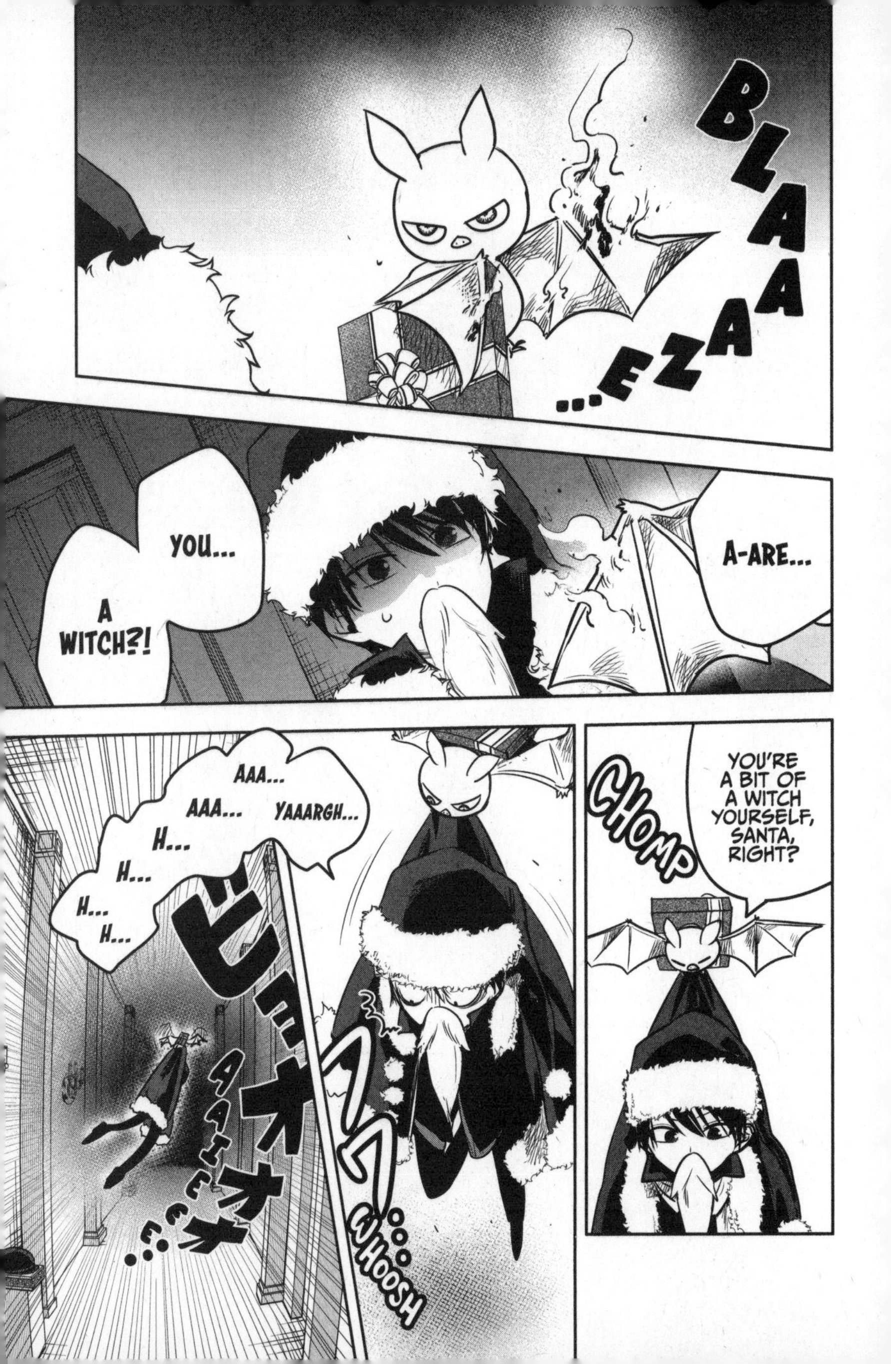
BLAAAAZE...
A-ARE...
YOU... A WITCH?!
YOU'RE A BIT OF A WITCH YOURSELF, SANTA, RIGHT?
CHOMP
AAA... AAA... YAAARGH... H... H... H... H...
AAAIEEE...
WHOOSH...

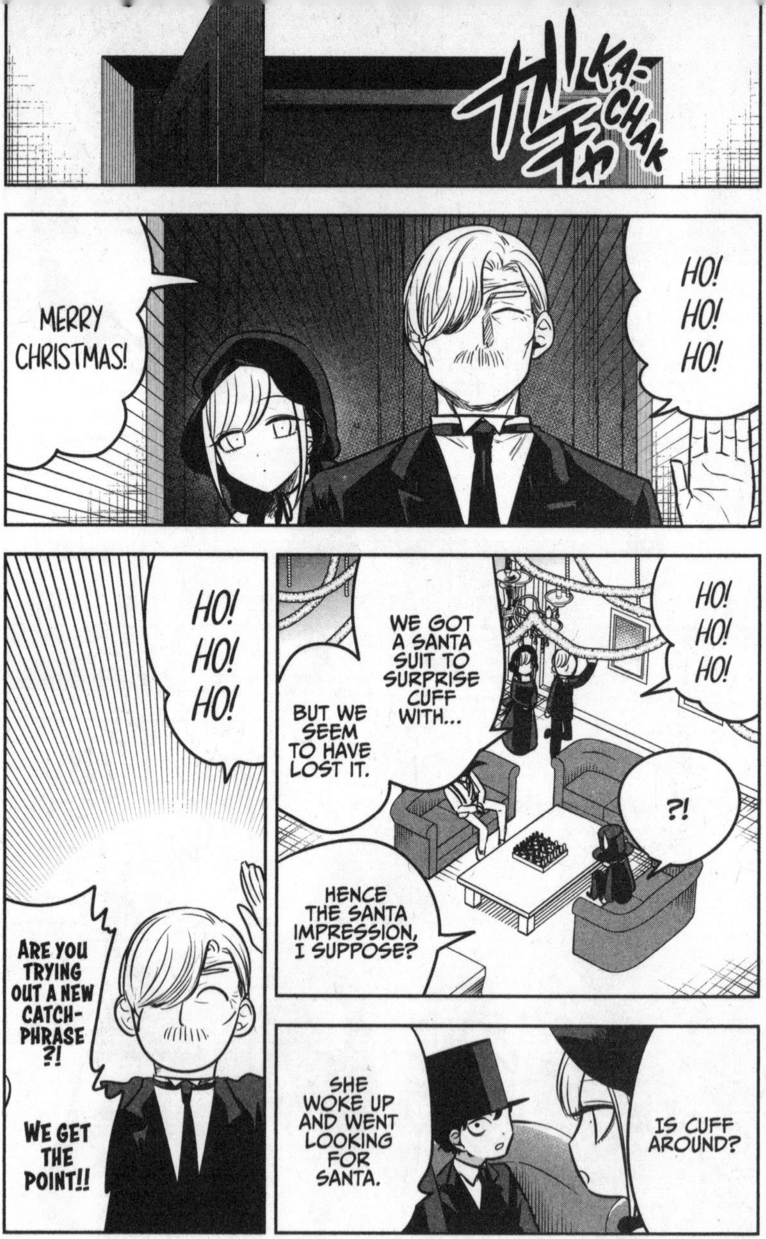
KA-CHAK
HO! HO! HO!
MERRY CHRISTMAS!
HO! HO! HO!
WE GOT A SANTA SUIT TO SURPRISE CUFF WITH...
BUT WE SEEM TO HAVE LOST IT.
?!
HENCE THE SANTA IMPRESSION, I SUPPOSE?
IS CUFF AROUND?
SHE WOKE UP AND WENT LOOKING FOR SANTA.
HO! HO! HO!
ARE YOU TRYING OUT A NEW CATCH-PHRASE?!
WE GET THE POINT!!

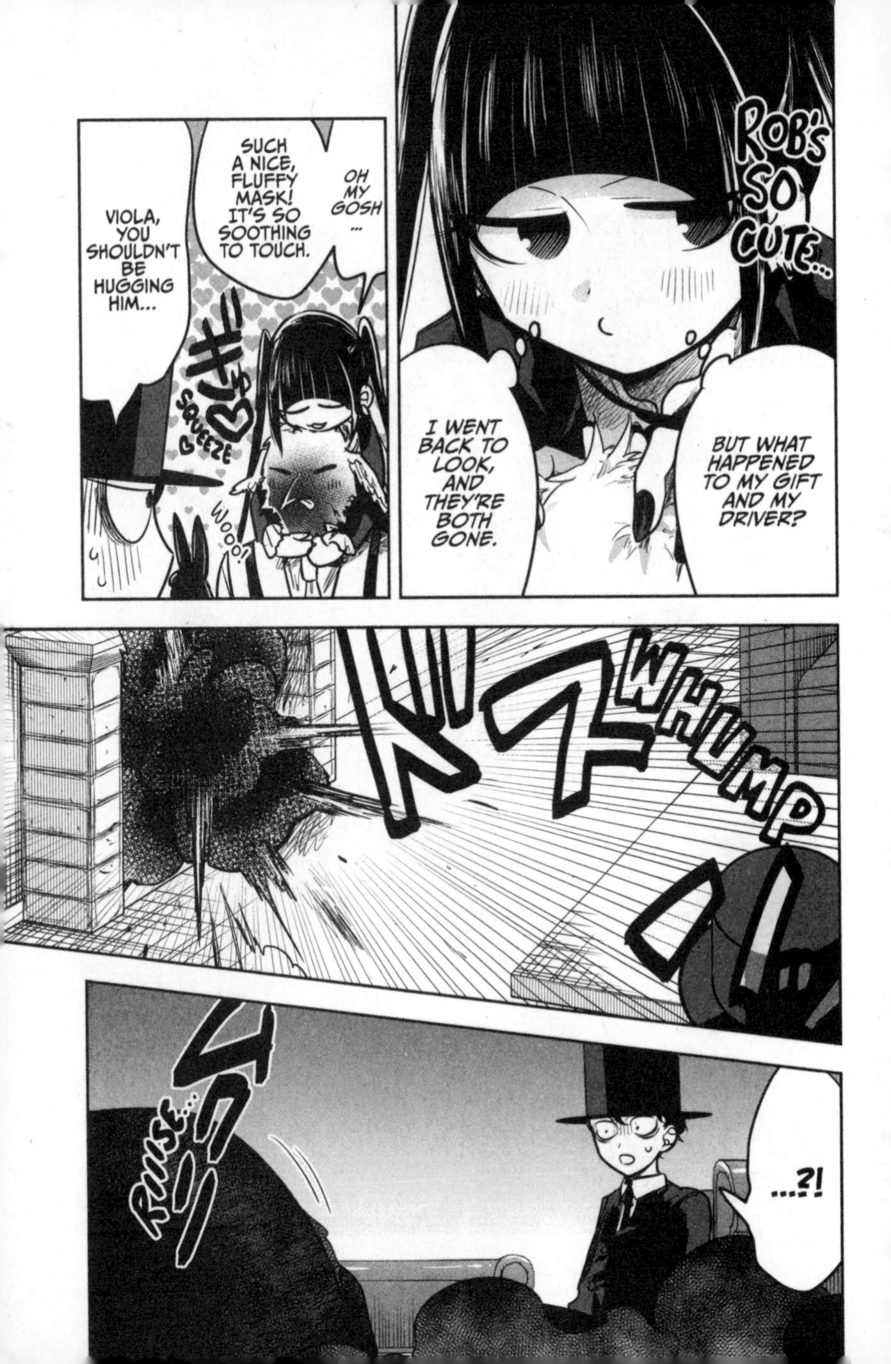
ROB'S SO CUTE...
BUT WHAT HAPPENED TO MY GIFT AND MY DRIVER?
I WENT BACK TO LOOK, AND THEY'RE BOTH GONE.
OH MY GOSH...
SUCH A NICE, FLUFFY MASK! IT'S SO SOOTHING TO TOUCH.
VIOLA, YOU SHOULDN'T BE HUGGING HIM...
SQUEEZE
WOOO?!
WHUMP
RIIISE...
...?!

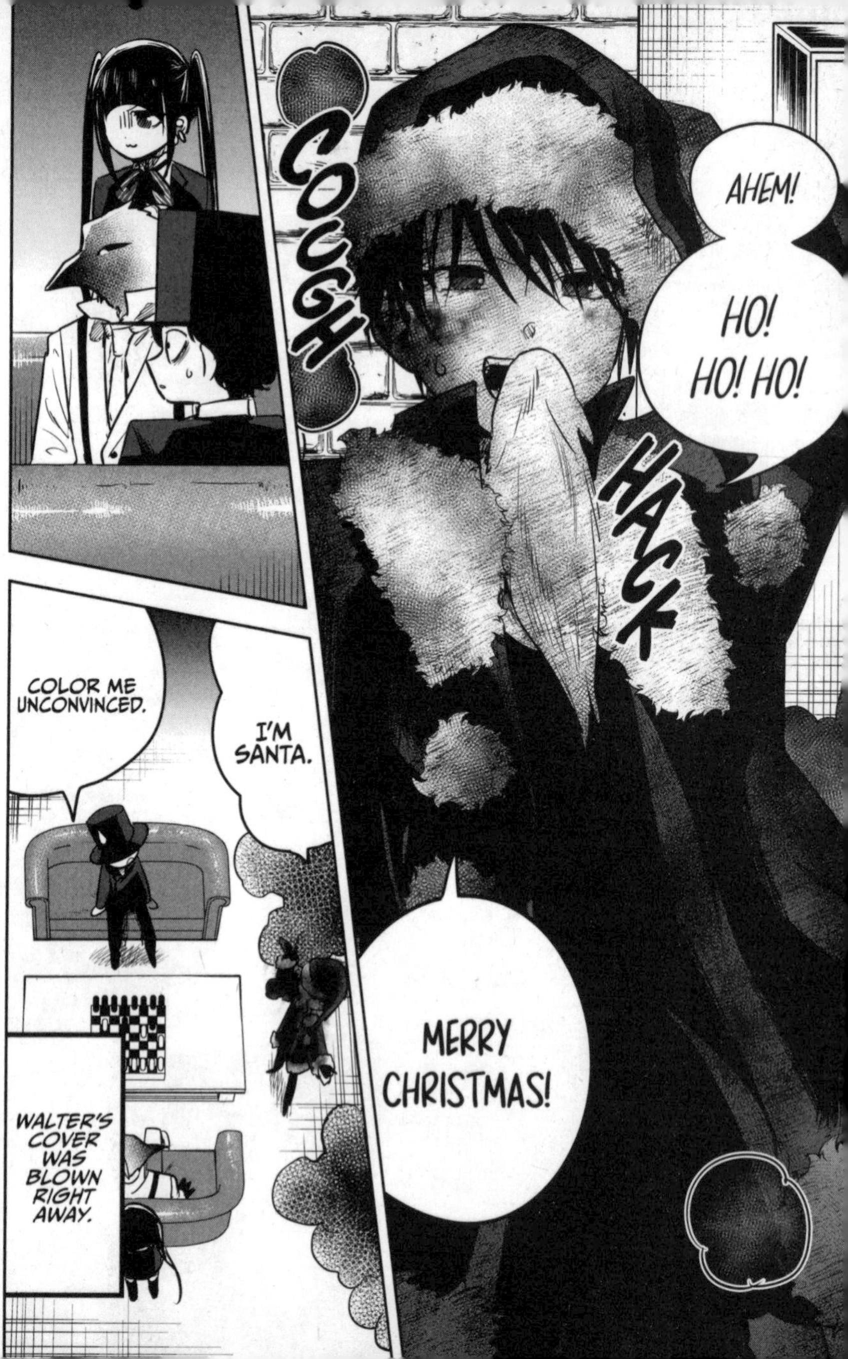
AHEM!
HO! HO! HO!
COUGH
HACK
MERRY CHRISTMAS!
I'M SANTA.
COLOR ME UNCONVINCED.
WALTER'S COVER WAS BLOWN RIGHT AWAY.

Chapter 53: Christmas Pt. 4

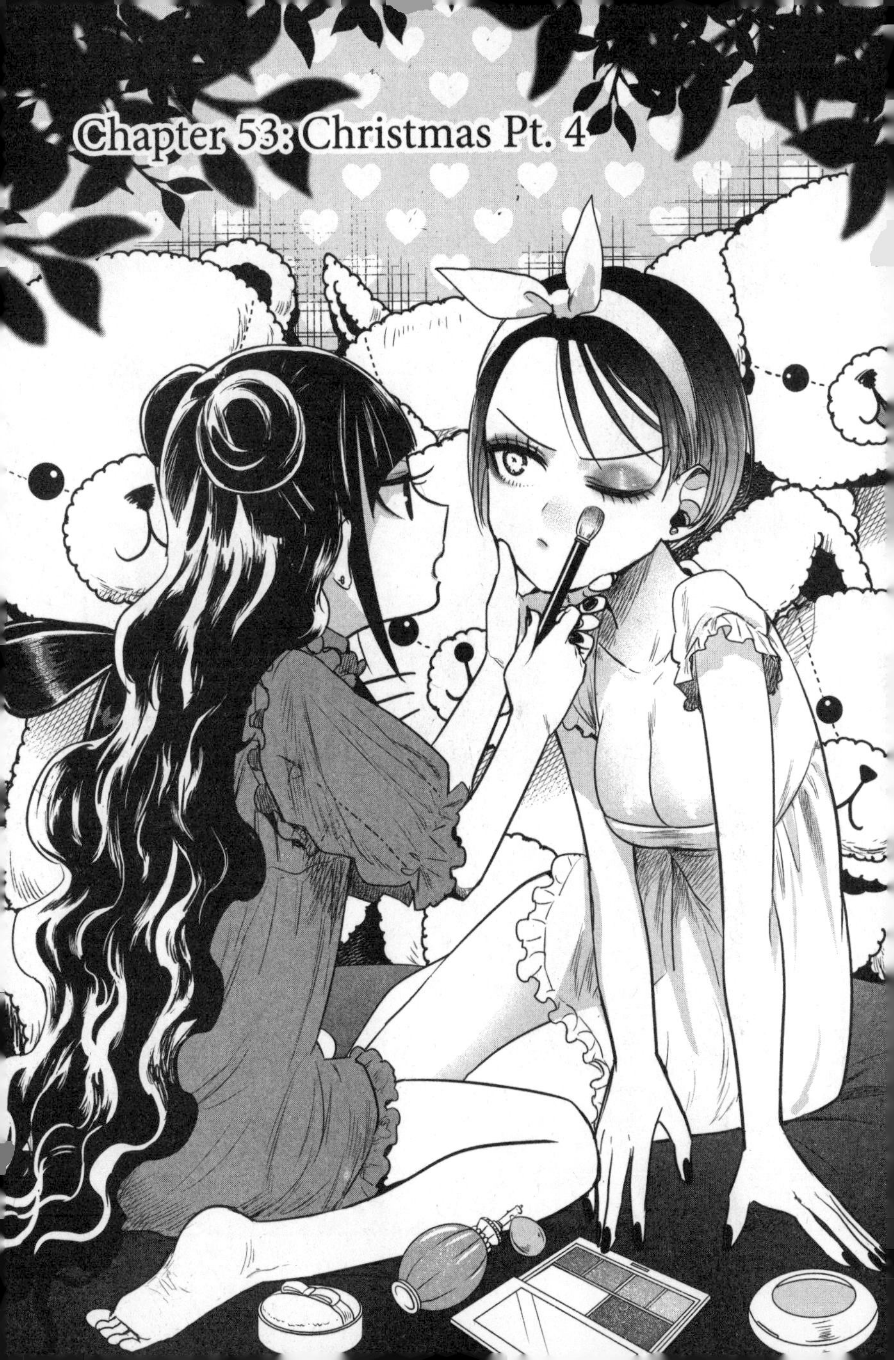

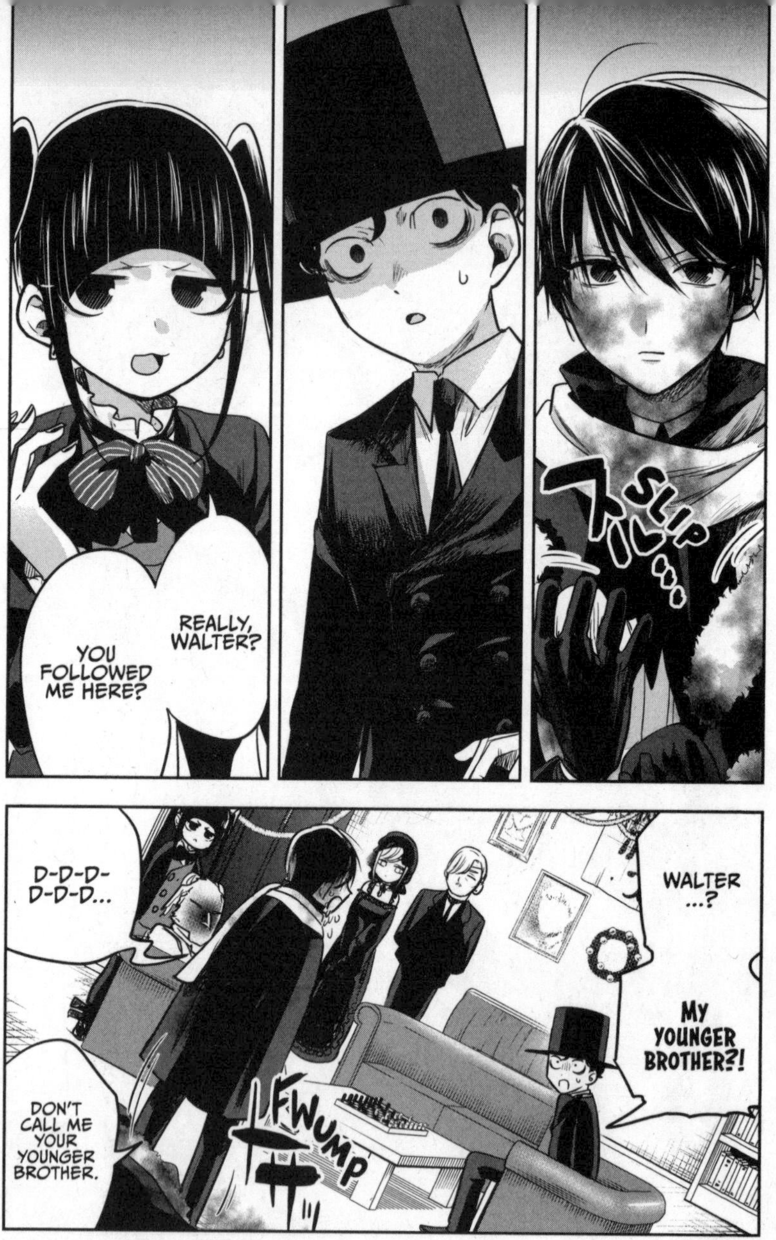
SLIP
REALLY, WALTER? YOU FOLLOWED ME HERE?
WALTER ...?
My YOUNGER BROTHER?!
D-D-D- D-D-D...
FWUMP
DON'T CALL ME YOUR YOUNGER BROTHER.

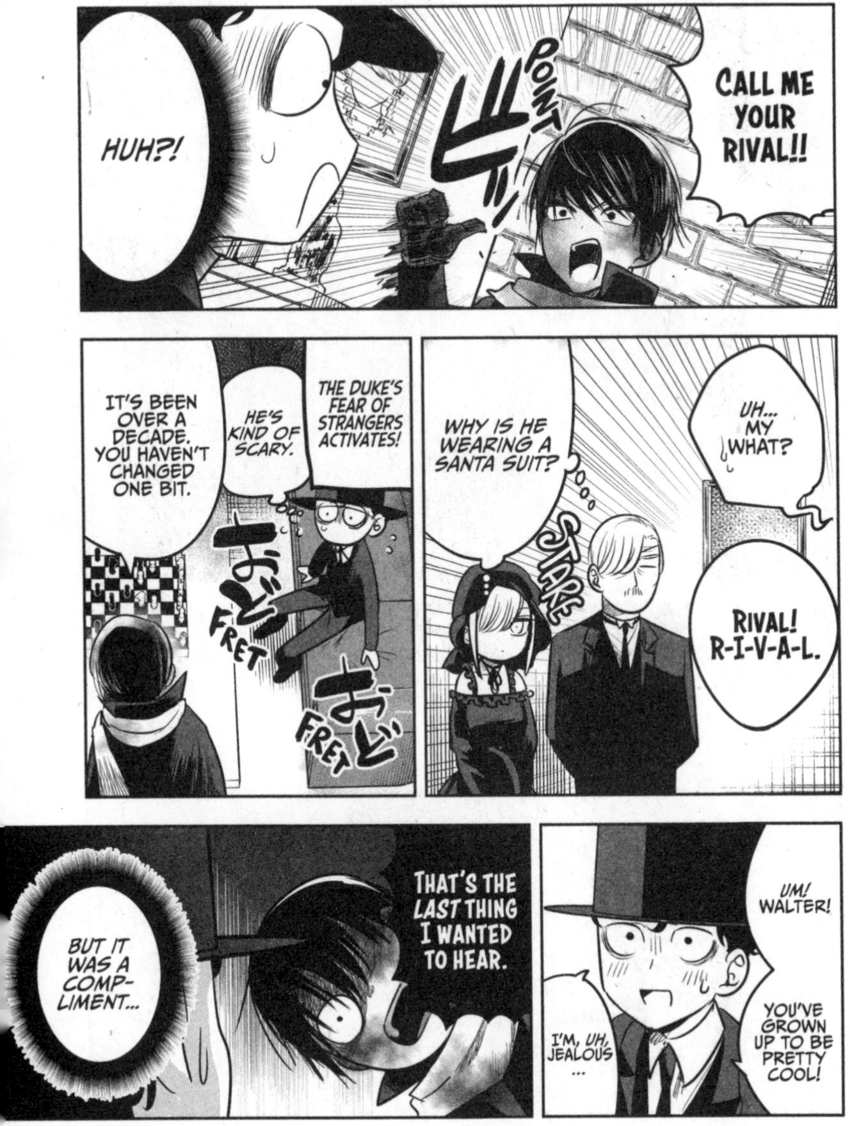
CALL ME YOUR RIVAL!!
POINT
HUH?!
UH... MY WHAT?
RIVAL! R-I-V-A-L.
WHY IS HE WEARING A SANTA SUIT?
STARE
THE DUKE'S FEAR OF STRANGERS ACTIVATES!
HE'S KIND OF SCARY.
IT'S BEEN OVER A DECADE. YOU HAVEN'T CHANGED ONE BIT.
おど FRET
おど FRET
UM! WALTER!
YOU'VE GROWN UP TO BE PRETTY COOL!
I'M, UH, JEALOUS...
THAT'S THE LAST THING I WANTED TO HEAR.
BUT IT WAS A COMPLIMENT...

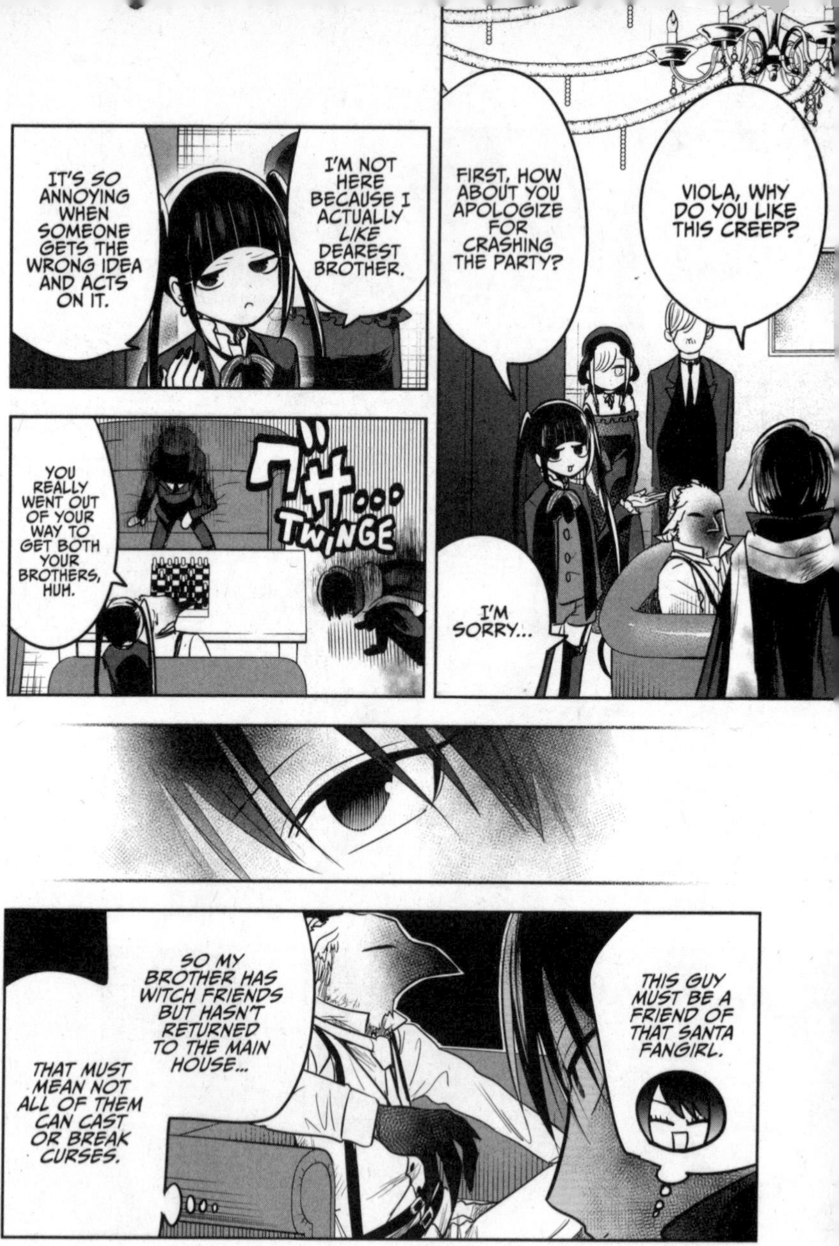
VIOLA, WHY DO YOU LIKE THIS CREEP?
FIRST, HOW ABOUT YOU APOLOGIZE FOR CRASHING THE PARTY?
I'M SORRY...
I'M NOT HERE BECAUSE I ACTUALLY *LIKE* DEAREST BROTHER.
IT'S SO ANNOYING WHEN SOMEONE GETS THE WRONG IDEA AND ACTS ON IT.
グサ
TWINGE
YOU REALLY WENT OUT OF YOUR WAY TO GET BOTH YOUR BROTHERS, HUH.
THIS GUY MUST BE A FRIEND OF THAT SANTA FANGIRL.
SO MY BROTHER HAS WITCH FRIENDS BUT HASN'T RETURNED TO THE MAIN HOUSE...
THAT MUST MEAN NOT ALL OF THEM CAN CAST OR BREAK CURSES.

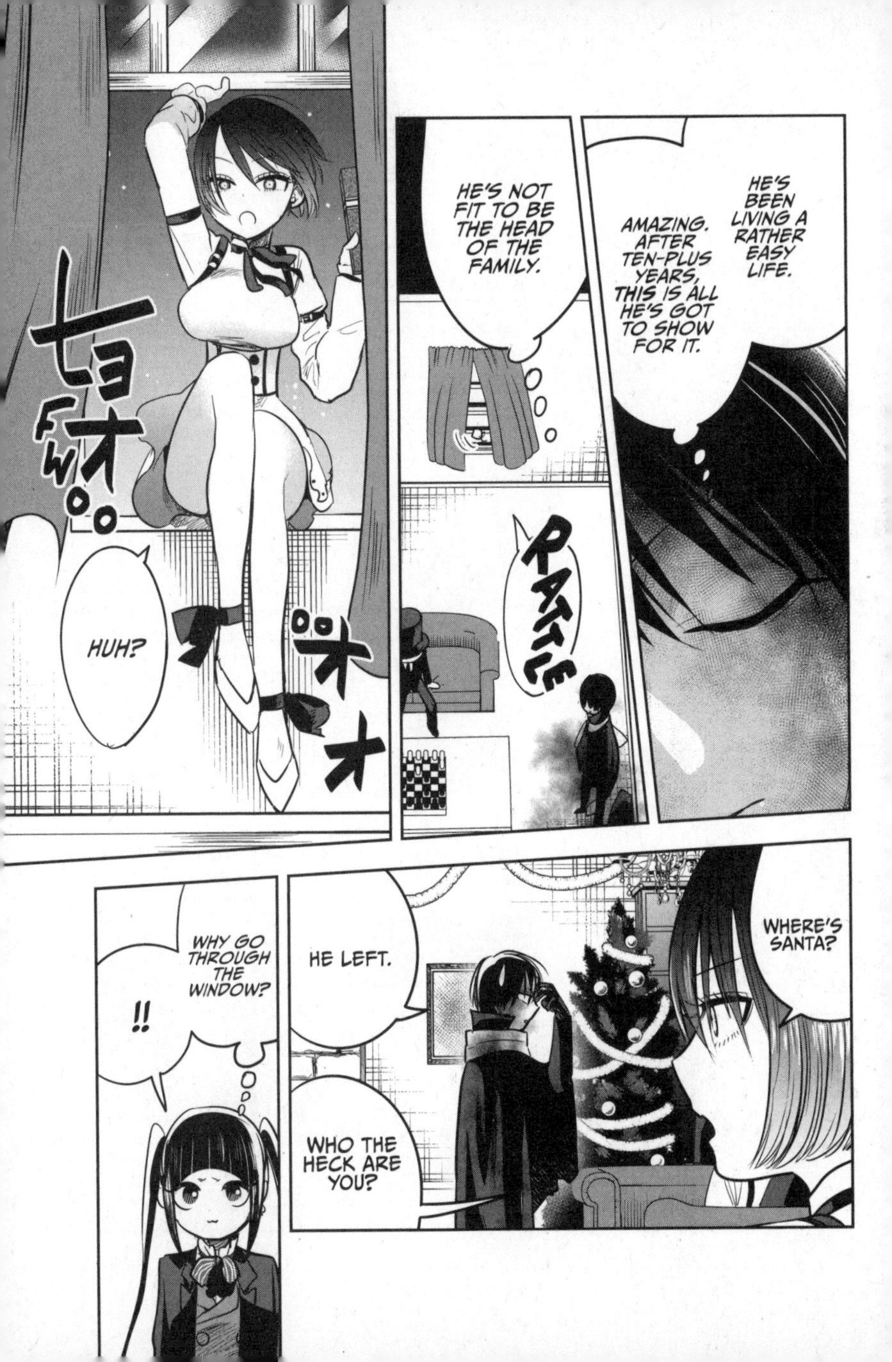
HE'S BEEN LIVING A RATHER EASY LIFE.
AMAZING. AFTER TEN-PLUS YEARS, THIS IS ALL HE'S GOT TO SHOW FOR IT.
HE'S NOT FIT TO BE THE HEAD OF THE FAMILY.
RATTLE
FWOO
HUH?
WHERE'S SANTA?
HE LEFT.
WHO THE HECK ARE YOU?
WHY GO THROUGH THE WINDOW?
!!

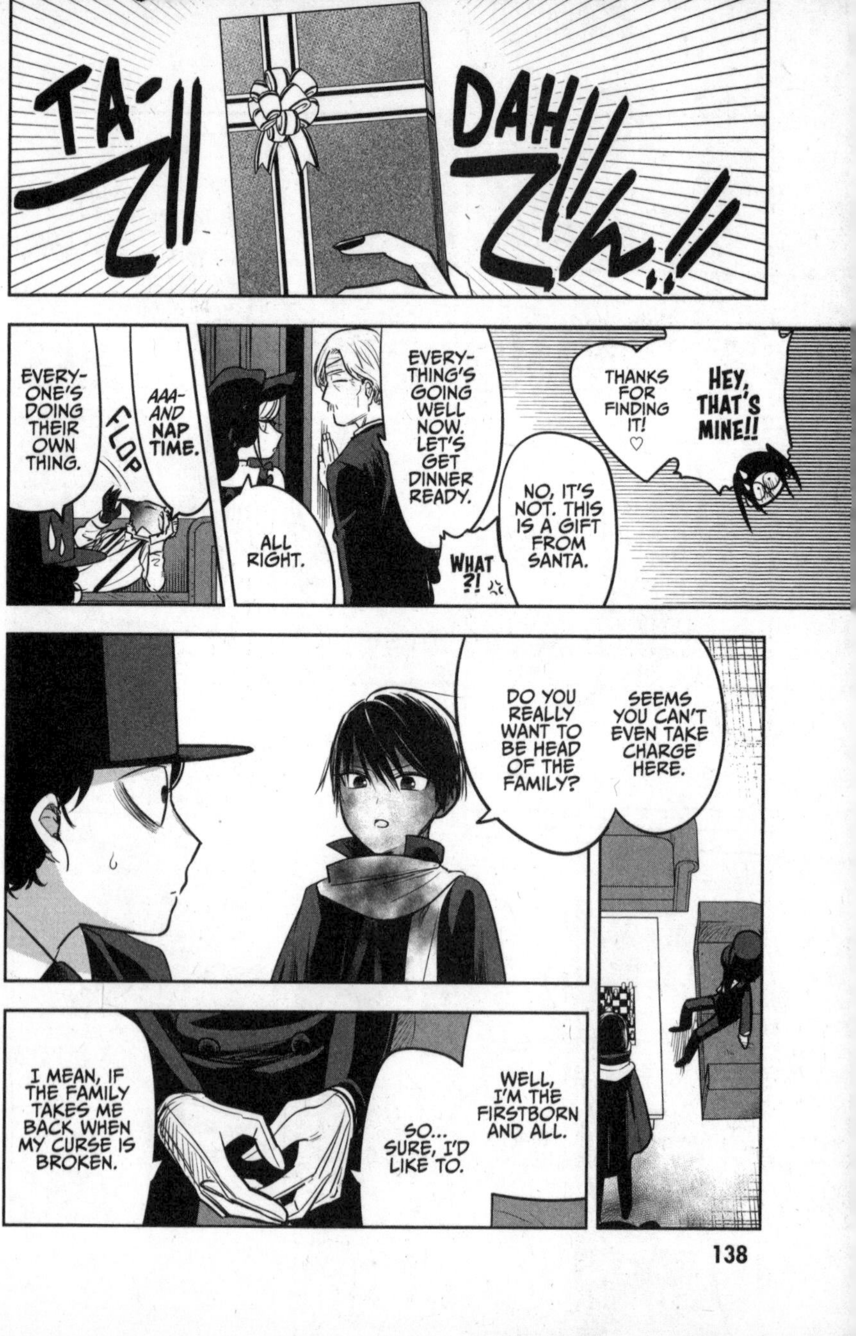
TA-DAH!!
HEY, THAT'S MINE!!
THANKS FOR FINDING IT! ♡
NO, IT'S NOT. THIS IS A GIFT FROM SANTA.
WHAT?!
EVERYTHING'S GOING WELL NOW. LET'S GET DINNER READY.
ALL RIGHT.
AAA-AND NAP TIME.
FLOP
EVERYONE'S DOING THEIR OWN THING.
SEEMS YOU CAN'T EVEN TAKE CHARGE HERE.
DO YOU REALLY WANT TO BE HEAD OF THE FAMILY?
WELL, I'M THE FIRSTBORN AND ALL.
SO... SURE, I'D LIKE TO.
I MEAN, IF THE FAMILY TAKES ME BACK WHEN MY CURSE IS BROKEN.

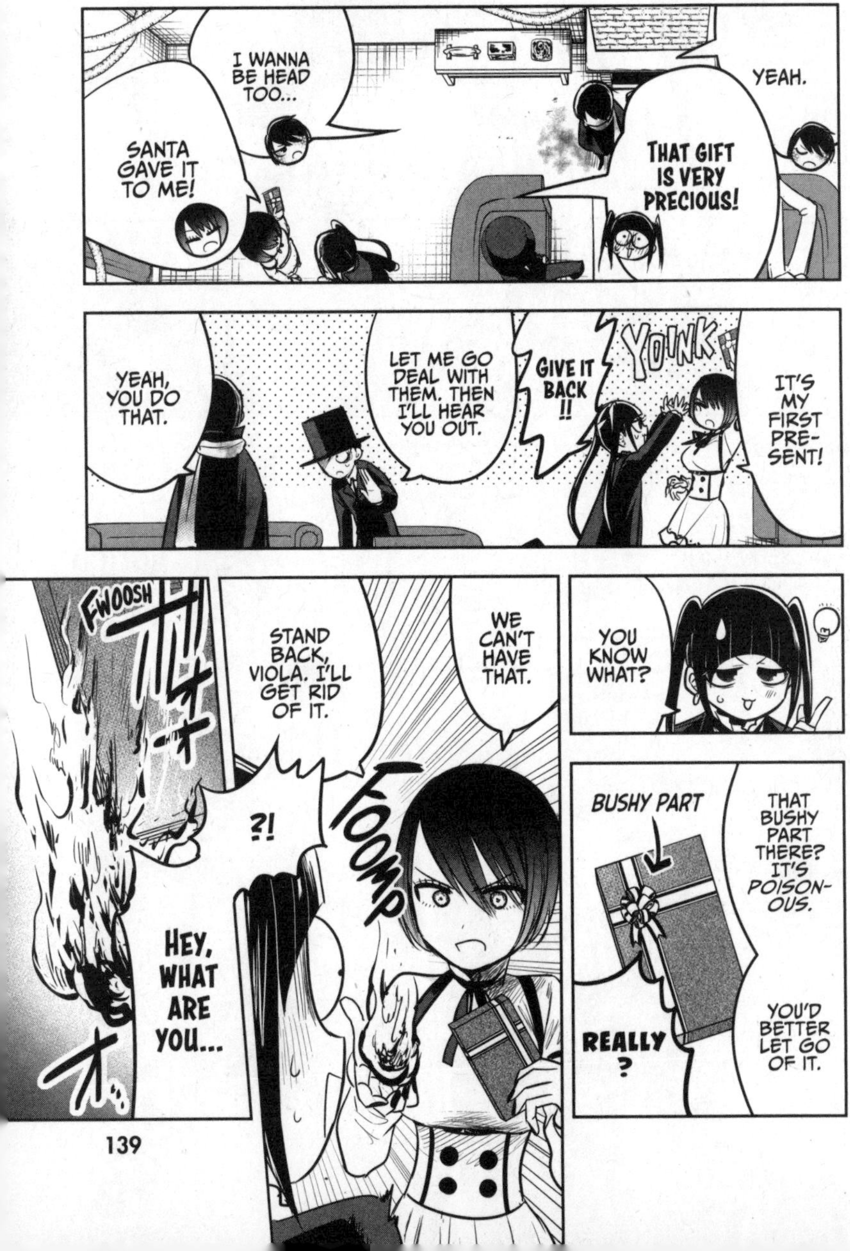
YEAH.
THAT GIFT IS VERY PRECIOUS!
I WANNA BE HEAD TOO...
SANTA GAVE IT TO ME!
IT'S MY FIRST PRE-SENT!
YOINK
GIVE IT BACK!!
LET ME GO DEAL WITH THEM. THEN I'LL HEAR YOU OUT.
YEAH, YOU DO THAT.
YOU KNOW WHAT?
THAT BUSHY PART THERE? IT'S POISON-OUS.
BUSHY PART
YOU'D BETTER LET GO OF IT.
REALLY?
WE CAN'T HAVE THAT.
STAND BACK, VIOLA. I'LL GET RID OF IT.
FOOMP
?!
FWOOSH
HEY, WHAT ARE YOU...

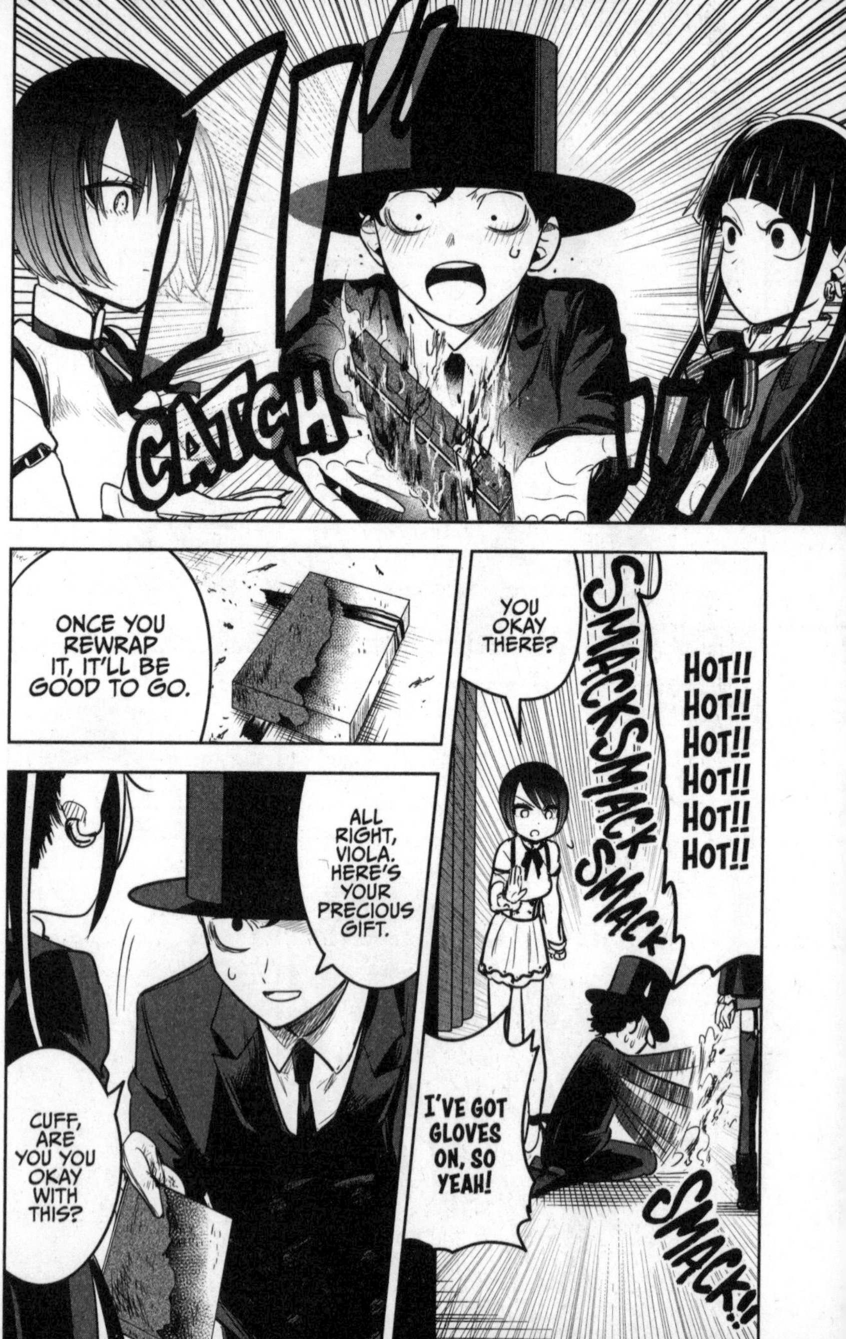
CATCH
HOT!! HOT!! HOT!! HOT!! HOT!! HOT!!
SMACKSMACK SMACK
YOU OKAY THERE?
SMACK!!
I'VE GOT GLOVES ON, SO YEAH!
ONCE YOU REWRAP IT, IT'LL BE GOOD TO GO.
ALL RIGHT, VIOLA. HERE'S YOUR PRECIOUS GIFT.
CUFF, ARE YOU YOU OKAY WITH THIS?

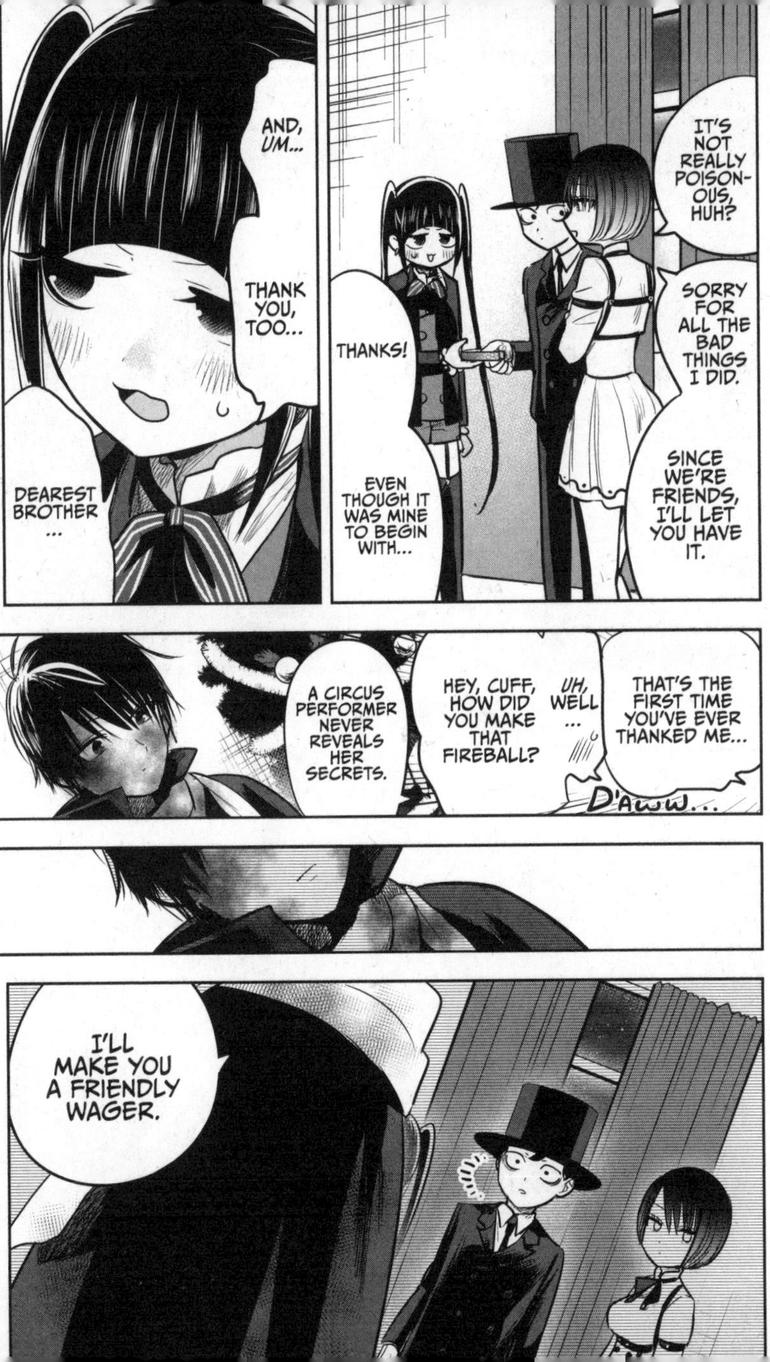
IT'S NOT REALLY POISON-OUS, HUH?
SORRY FOR ALL THE BAD THINGS I DID.
SINCE WE'RE FRIENDS, I'LL LET YOU HAVE IT.
THANKS!
EVEN THOUGH IT WAS MINE TO BEGIN WITH...
AND, UM...
THANK YOU, TOO...
DEAREST BROTHER ...
THAT'S THE FIRST TIME YOU'VE EVER THANKED ME...
D'AWW...
UH, WELL ...
HEY, CUFF, HOW DID YOU MAKE THAT FIREBALL?
A CIRCUS PERFORMER NEVER REVEALS HER SECRETS.
I'LL MAKE YOU A FRIENDLY WAGER.

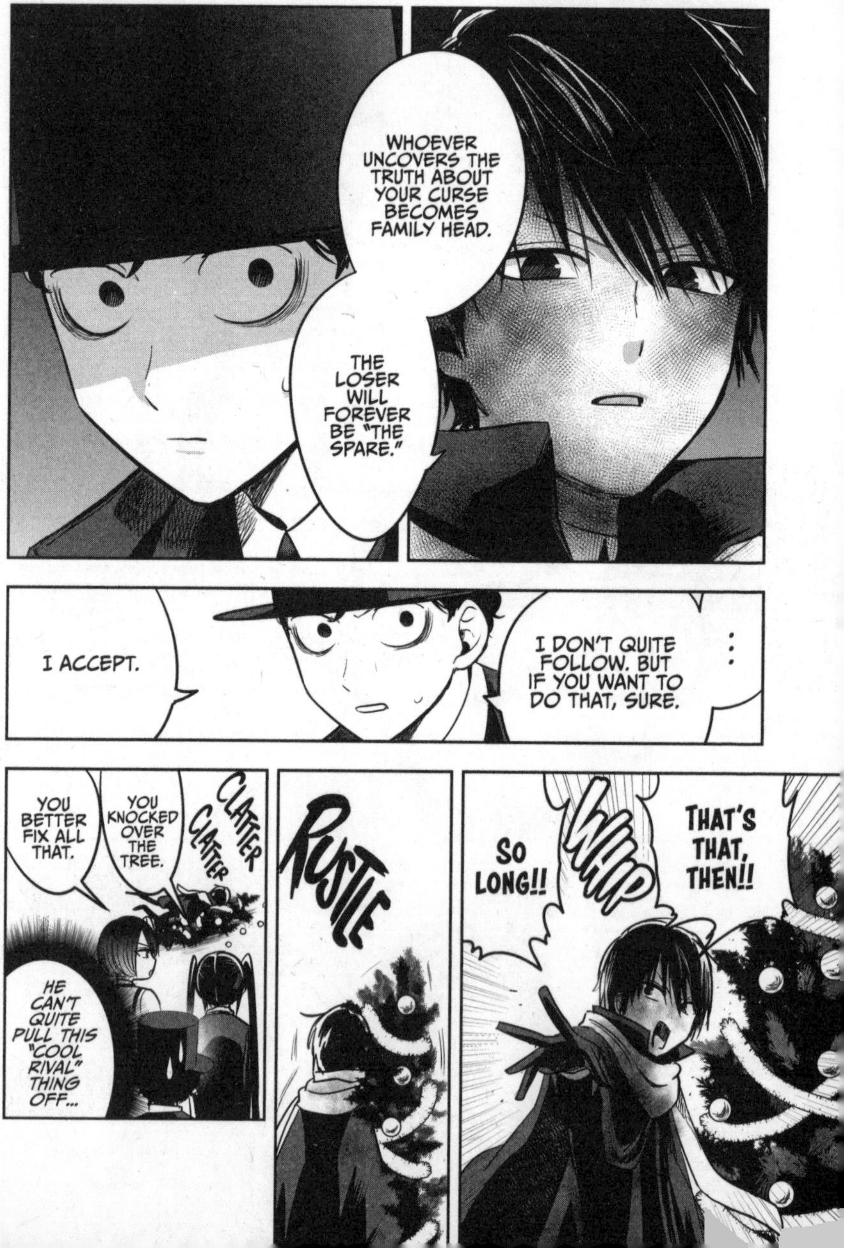
WHOEVER UNCOVERS THE TRUTH ABOUT YOUR CURSE BECOMES FAMILY HEAD.
THE LOSER WILL FOREVER BE "THE SPARE."
...
I DON'T QUITE FOLLOW. BUT IF YOU WANT TO DO THAT, SURE.
I ACCEPT.
THAT'S THAT, THEN!!
WHIP
SO LONG!!
RUSTLE
CLATTER CLATTER
YOU KNOCKED OVER THE TREE.
YOU BETTER FIX ALL THAT.
HE CAN'T QUITE PULL THIS "COOL RIVAL" THING OFF...

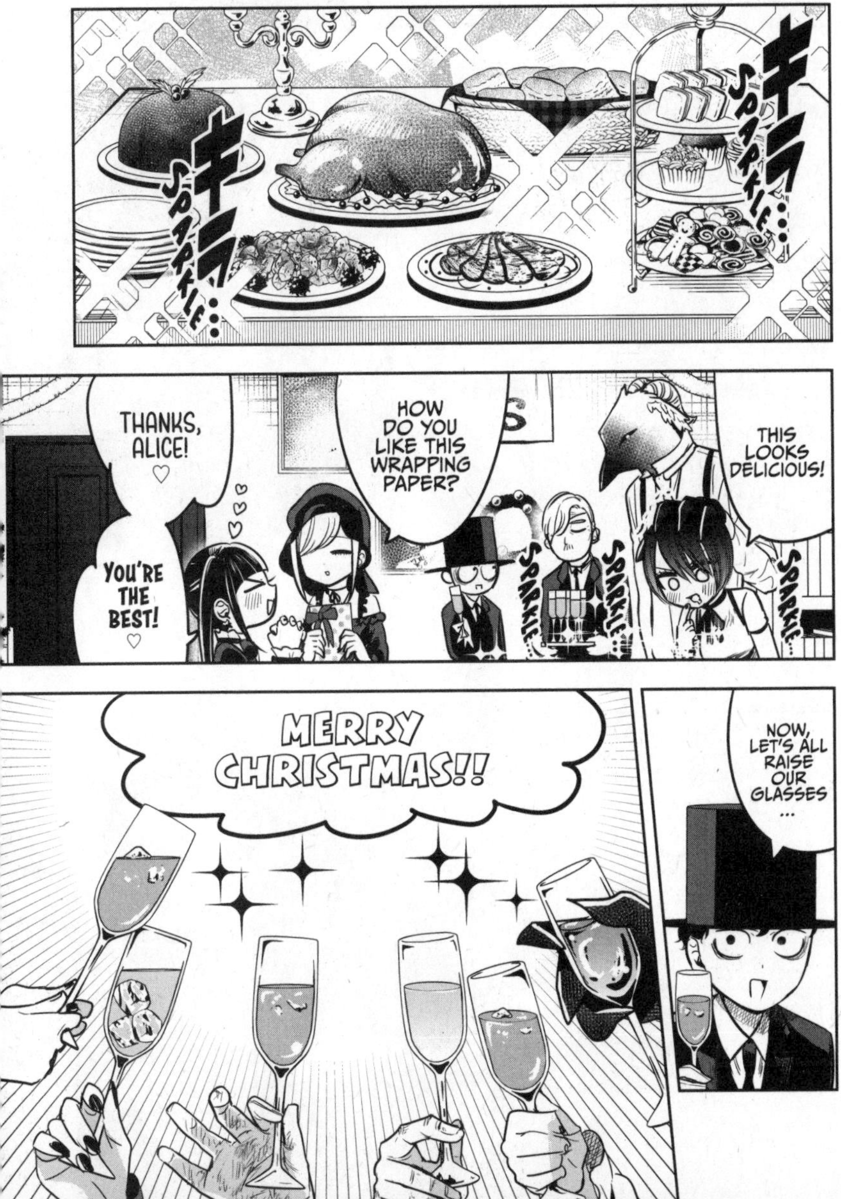
キラ
SPARKLE...
キラ
SPARKLE...
THIS LOOKS DELICIOUS!
SPARKLE...
SPARKLE...
SPARKLE...
HOW DO YOU LIKE THIS WRAPPING PAPER?
THANKS, ALICE! ♡
YOU'RE THE BEST! ♡
NOW, LET'S ALL RAISE OUR GLASSES...
MERRY CHRISTMAS!!

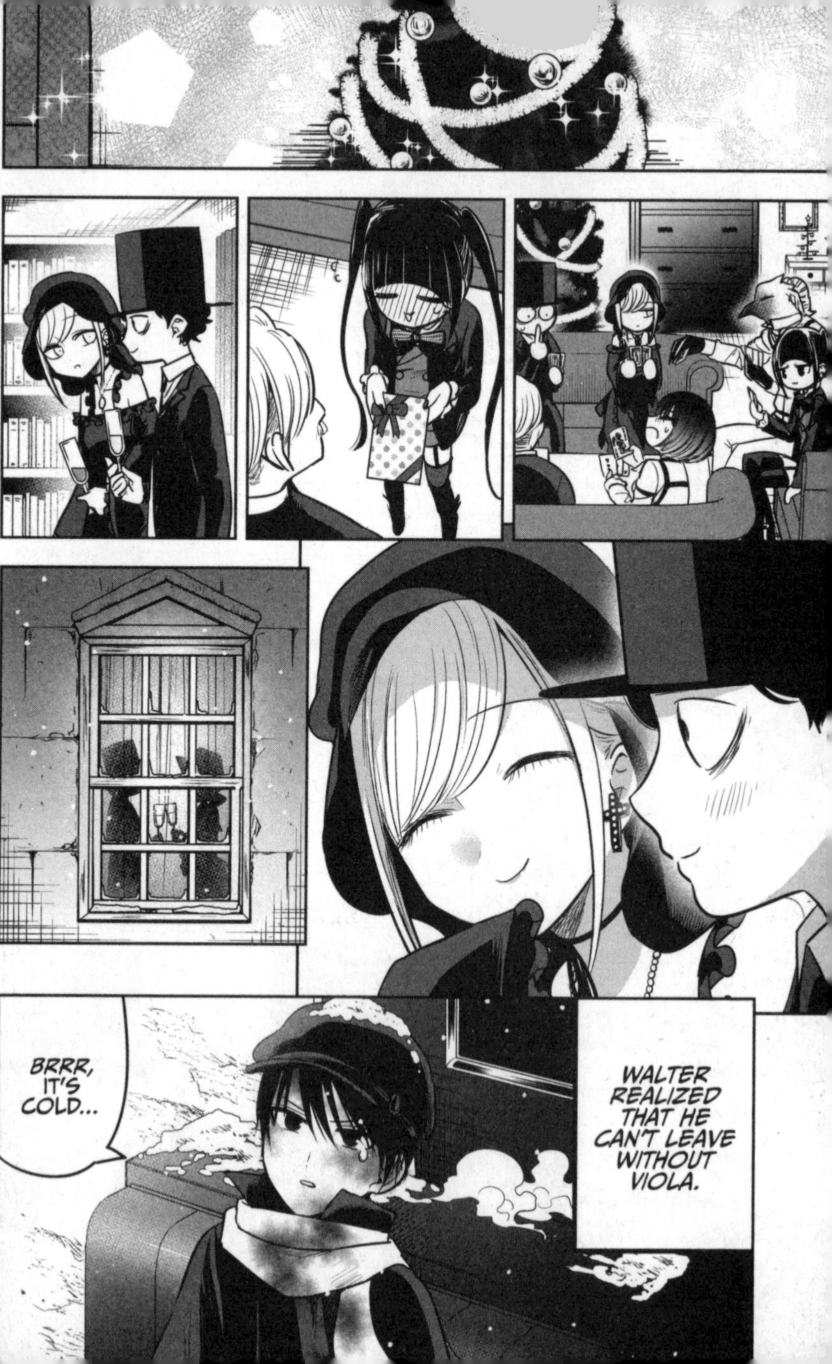
WALTER REALIZED THAT HE CAN'T LEAVE WITHOUT VIOLA.
BRRR, IT'S COLD...

Chapter 54: Christmas Pt. 5

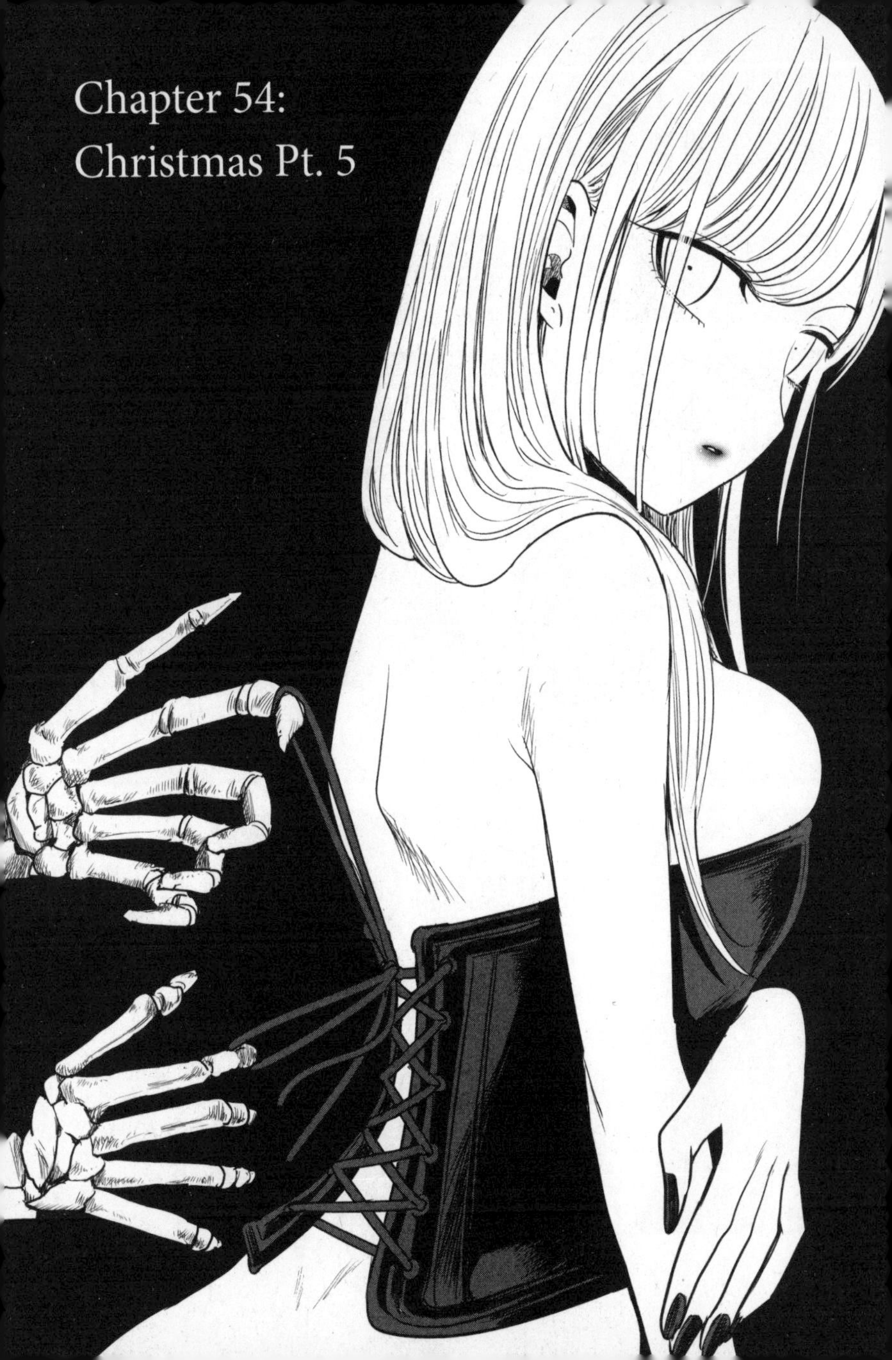

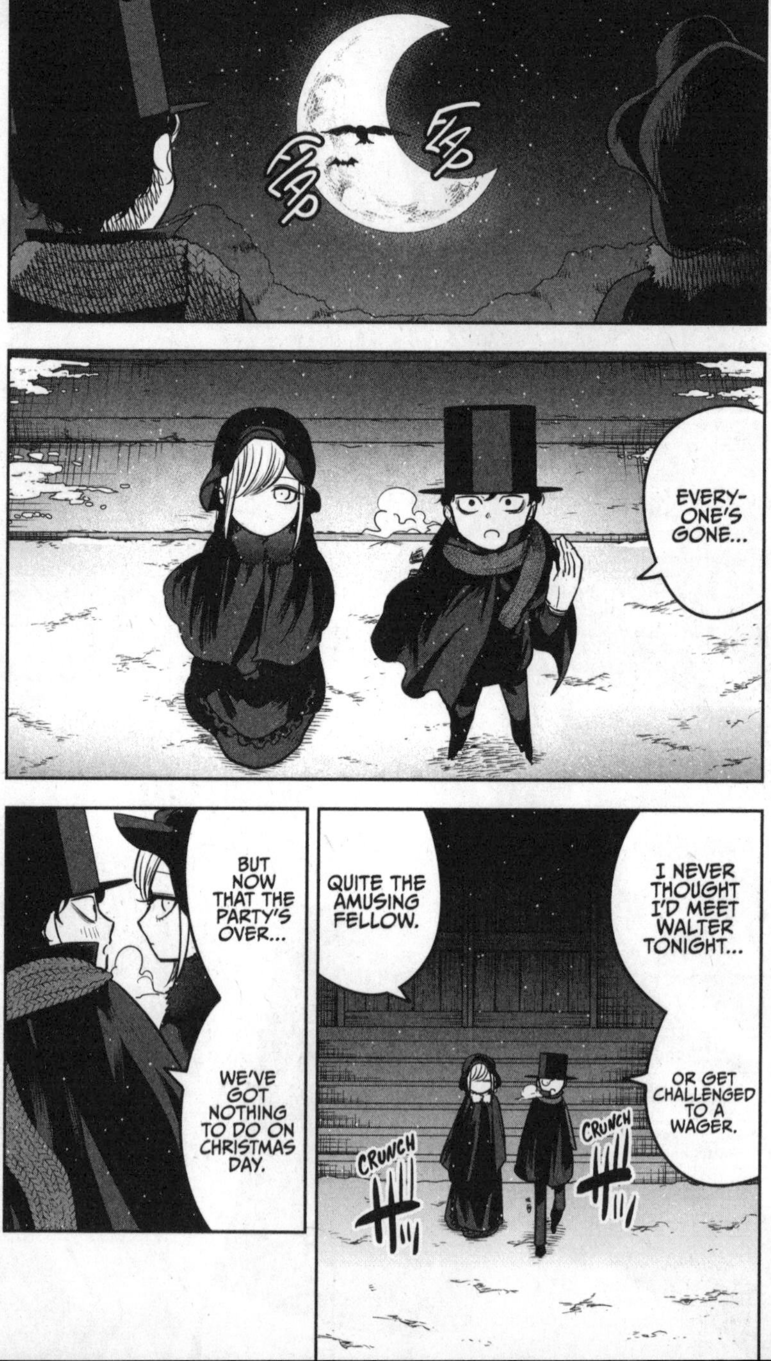
FLAP
FLAP
EVERY-ONE'S GONE...
I NEVER THOUGHT I'D MEET WALTER TONIGHT...
OR GET CHALLENGED TO A WAGER.
QUITE THE AMUSING FELLOW.
CRUNCH
CRUNCH
BUT NOW THAT THE PARTY'S OVER...
WE'VE GOT NOTHING TO DO ON CHRISTMAS DAY.

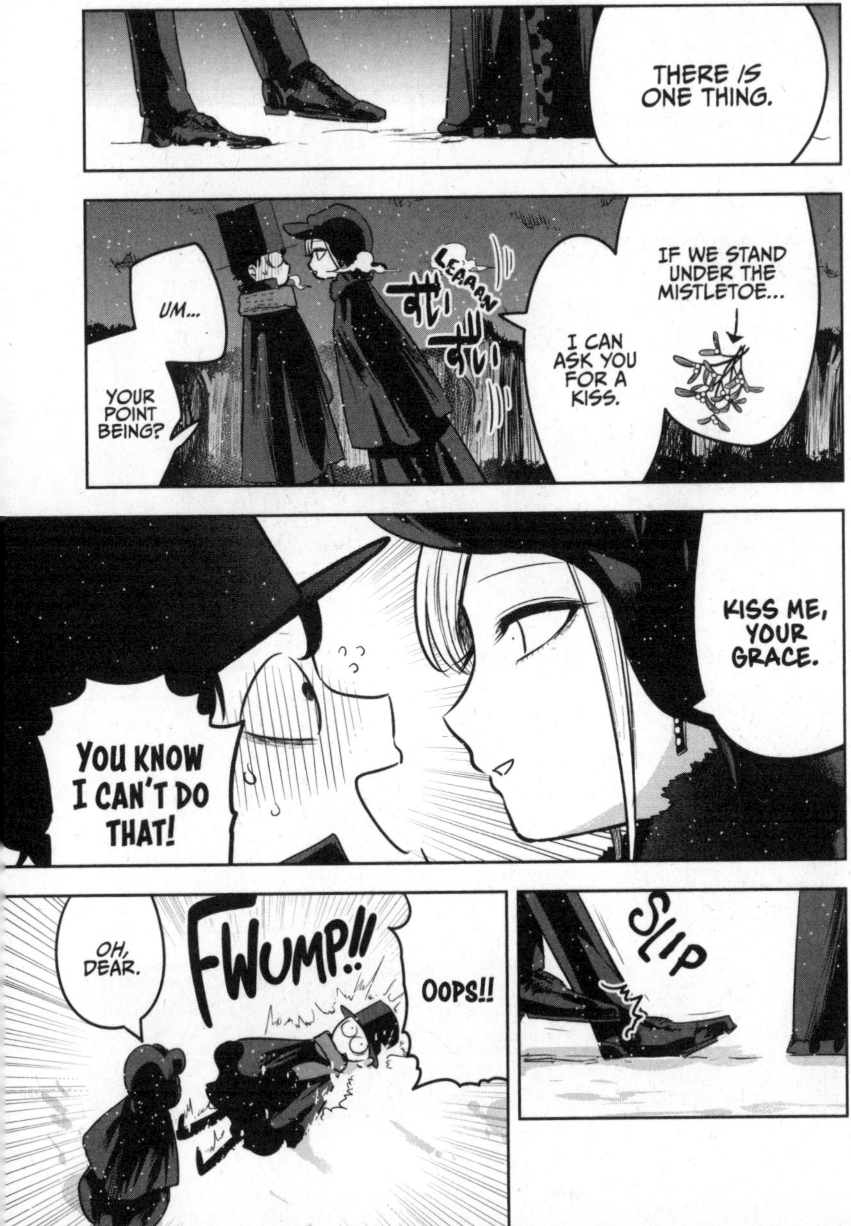
THERE IS ONE THING.
IF WE STAND UNDER THE MISTLETOE...
I CAN ASK YOU FOR A KISS.
LEAAAN
UM...
YOUR POINT BEING?
KISS ME, YOUR GRACE.
YOU KNOW I CAN'T DO THAT!
SLIP
OOPS!!
FWUMP!!
OH, DEAR.

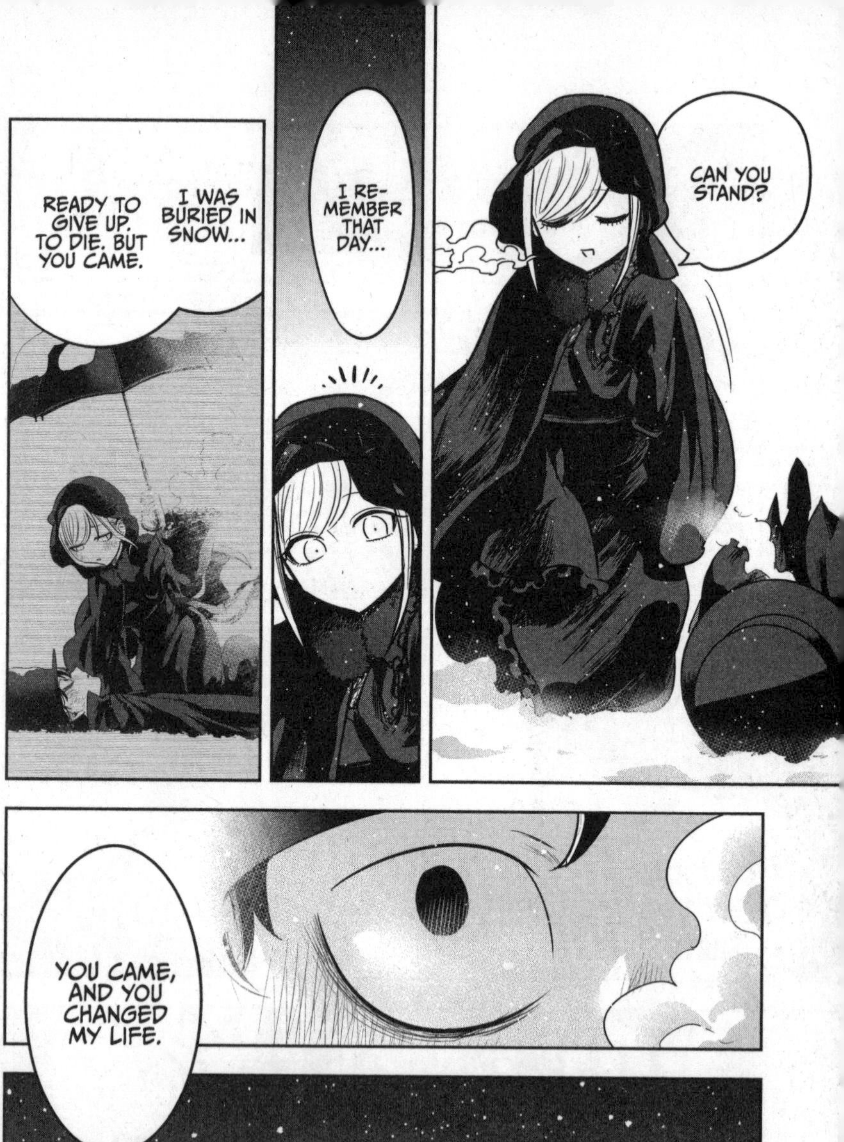
CAN YOU STAND?
I RE-MEMBER THAT DAY...
I WAS BURIED IN SNOW...
READY TO GIVE UP. TO DIE. BUT YOU CAME.
YOU CAME, AND YOU CHANGED MY LIFE.

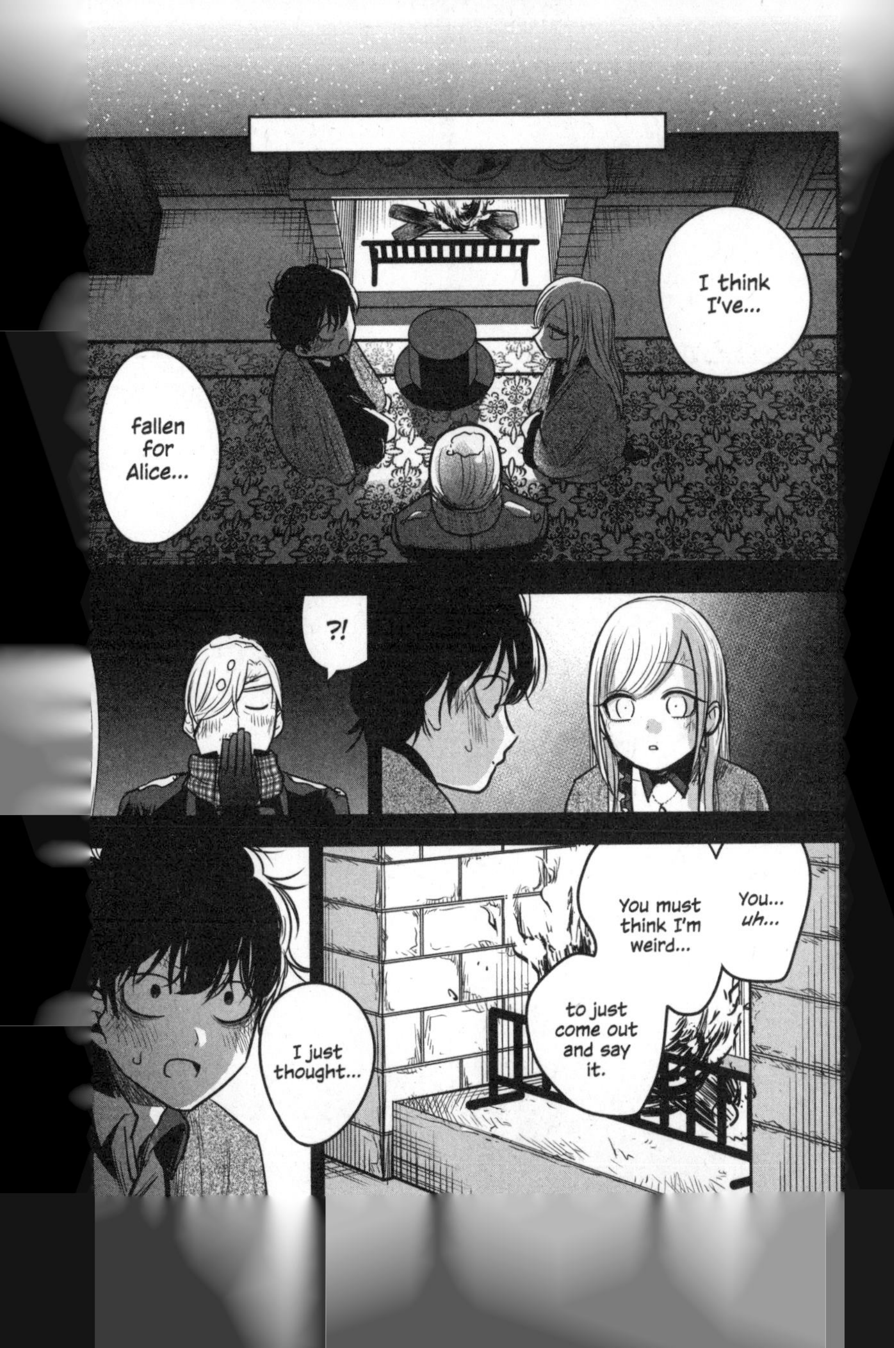
I think I've...
fallen for Alice...
?!
You... uh...
You must think I'm weird...
to just come out and say it.
I just thought...

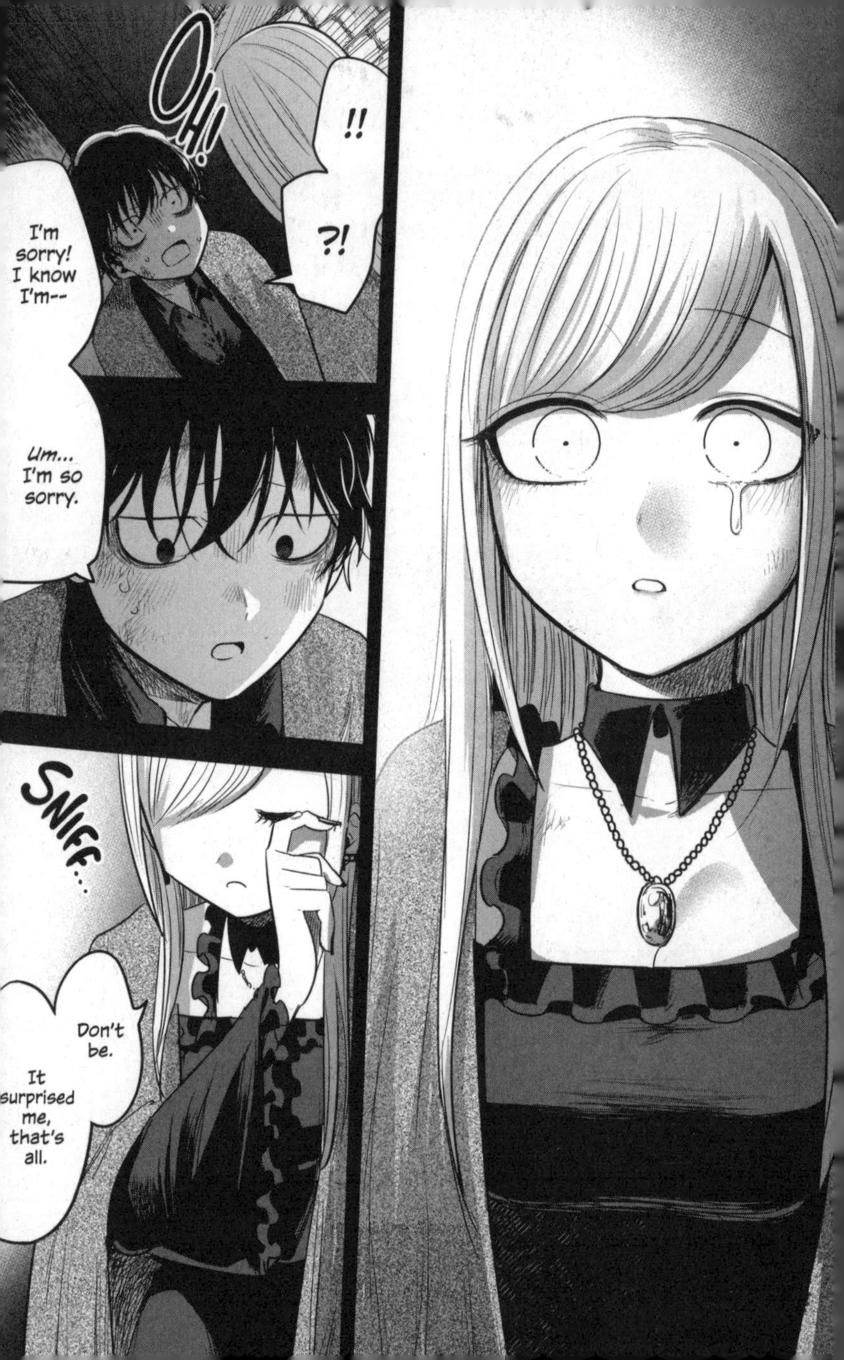
!!
OH!
?!
I'm sorry! I know I'm--
Um... I'm so sorry.
SNIFF...
Don't be.
It surprised me, that's all.

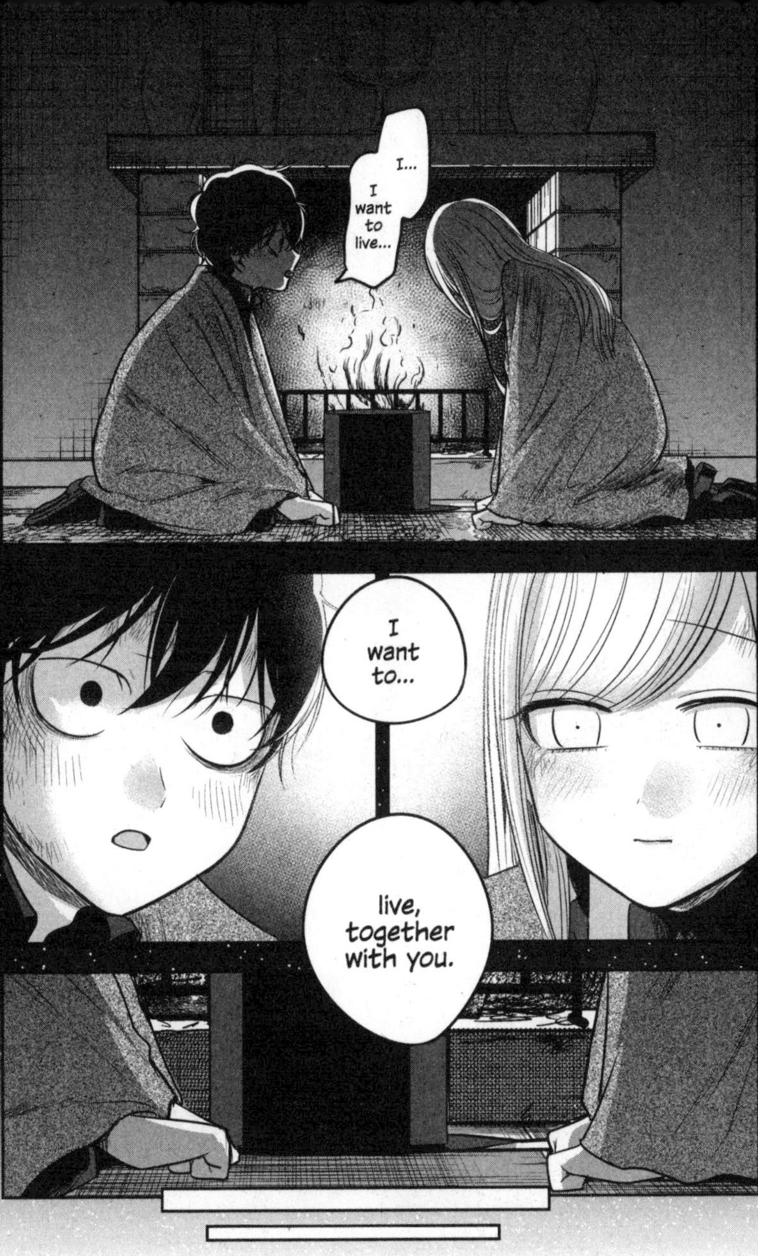
I...
I want to live...
I want to...
live, together with you.

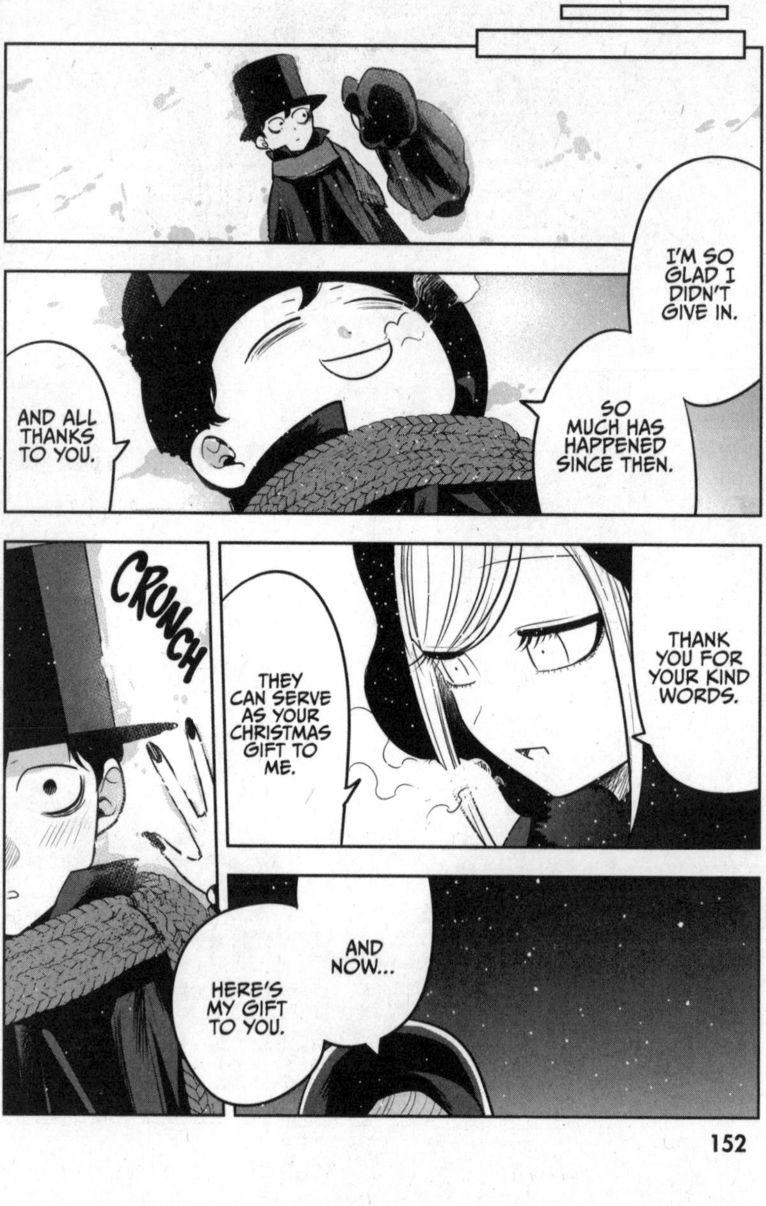
I'M SO GLAD I DIDN'T GIVE IN.
SO MUCH HAS HAPPENED SINCE THEN.
AND ALL THANKS TO YOU.
THANK YOU FOR YOUR KIND WORDS.
THEY CAN SERVE AS YOUR CHRISTMAS GIFT TO ME.
AND NOW...
HERE'S MY GIFT TO YOU.
CRUNCH

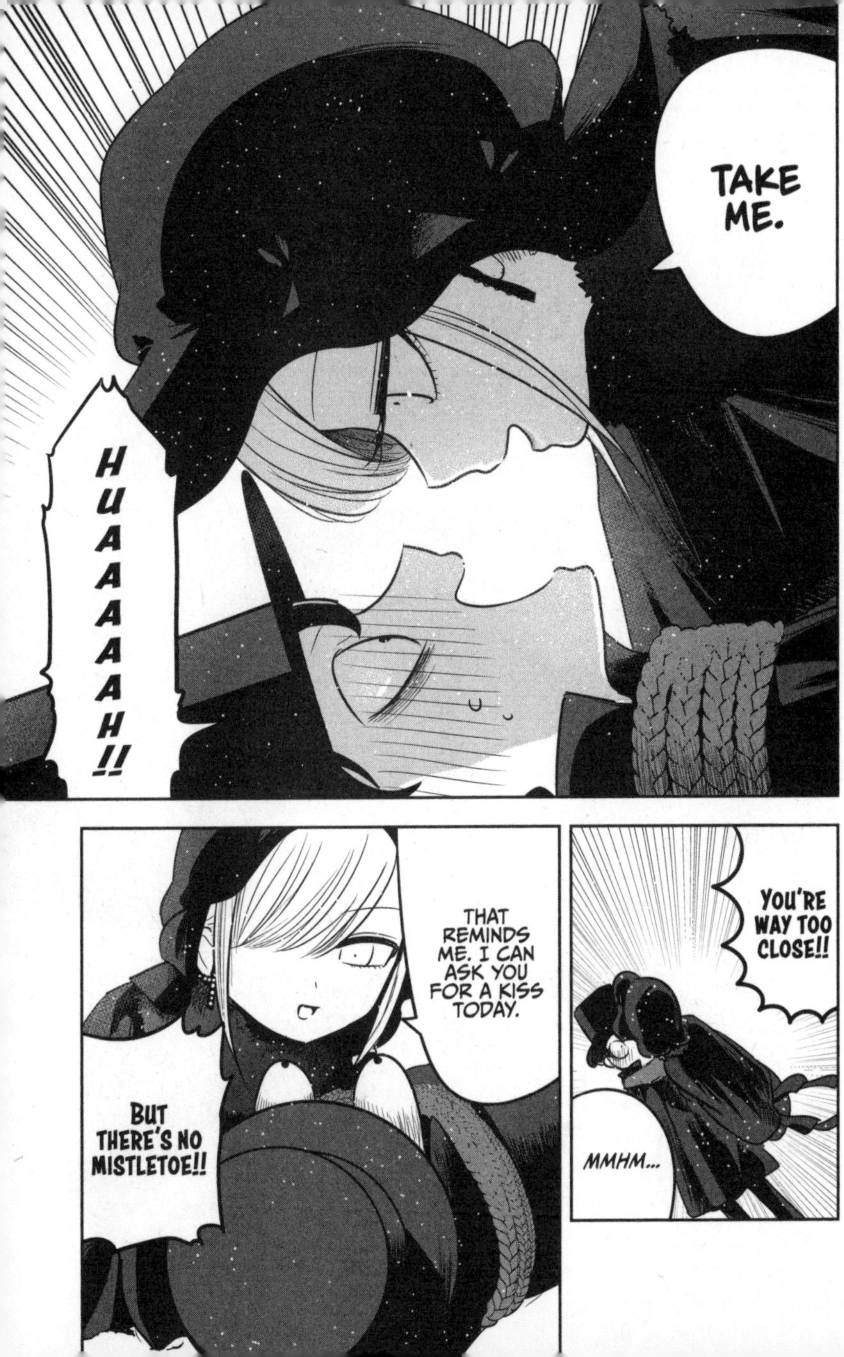
TAKE ME.
HUAAAAAAAAH!!
YOU'RE WAY TOO CLOSE!!
MMHM...
THAT REMINDS ME. I CAN ASK YOU FOR A KISS TODAY.
BUT THERE'S NO MISTLETOE!!

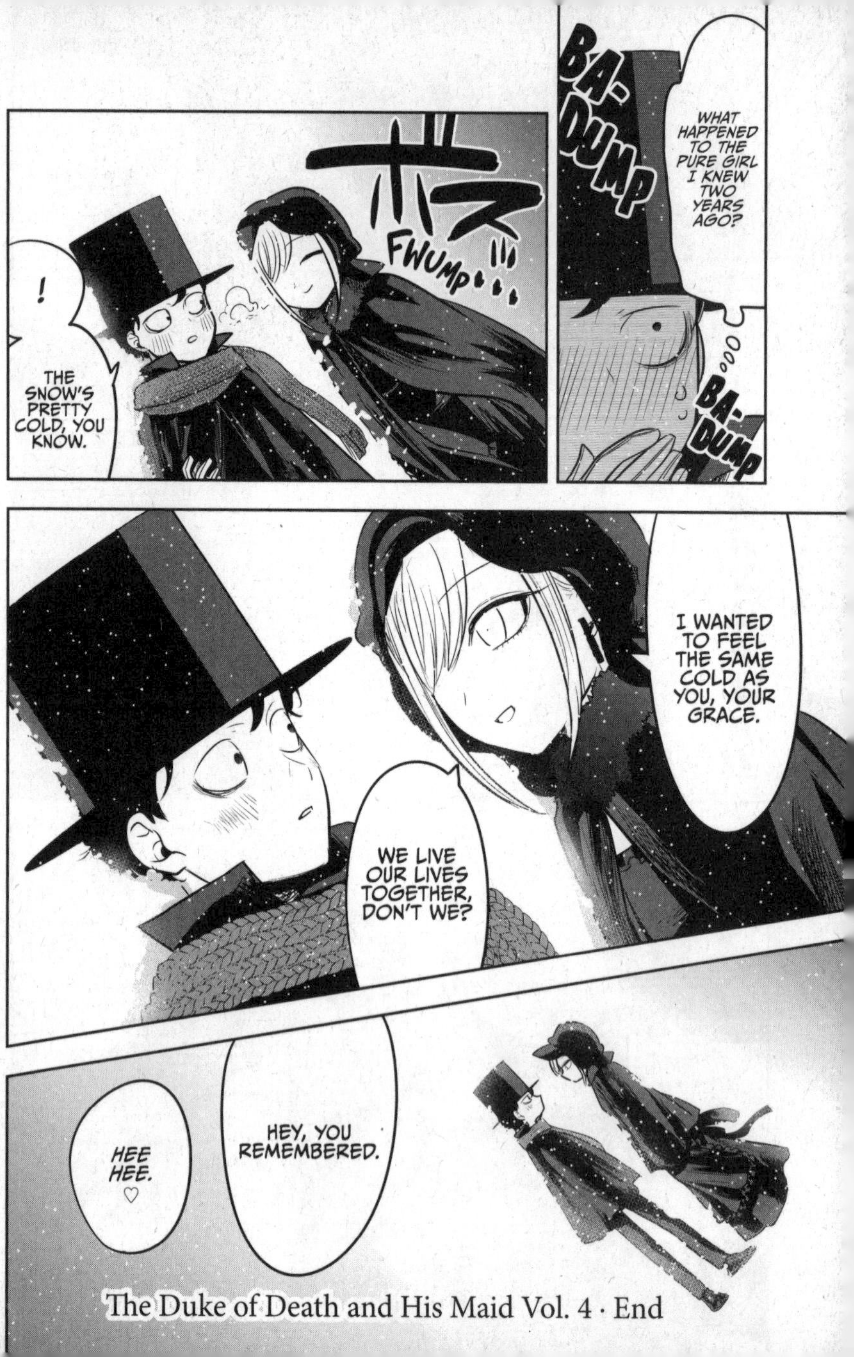
BA-DUMP
WHAT HAPPENED TO THE PURE GIRL I KNEW TWO YEARS AGO?
BA-DUMP
FWUMP
!
THE SNOW'S PRETTY COLD, YOU KNOW.
I WANTED TO FEEL THE SAME COLD AS YOU, YOUR GRACE.
WE LIVE OUR LIVES TOGETHER, DON'T WE?
HEY, YOU REMEMBERED.
HEE HEE. ♡
The Duke of Death and His Maid Vol. 4 · End

THE DUKE OF DEATH
AND HIS MAID

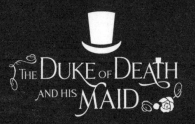

THE DUKE OF DEATH
AND HIS MAID

Extra Chapter: Watercolor

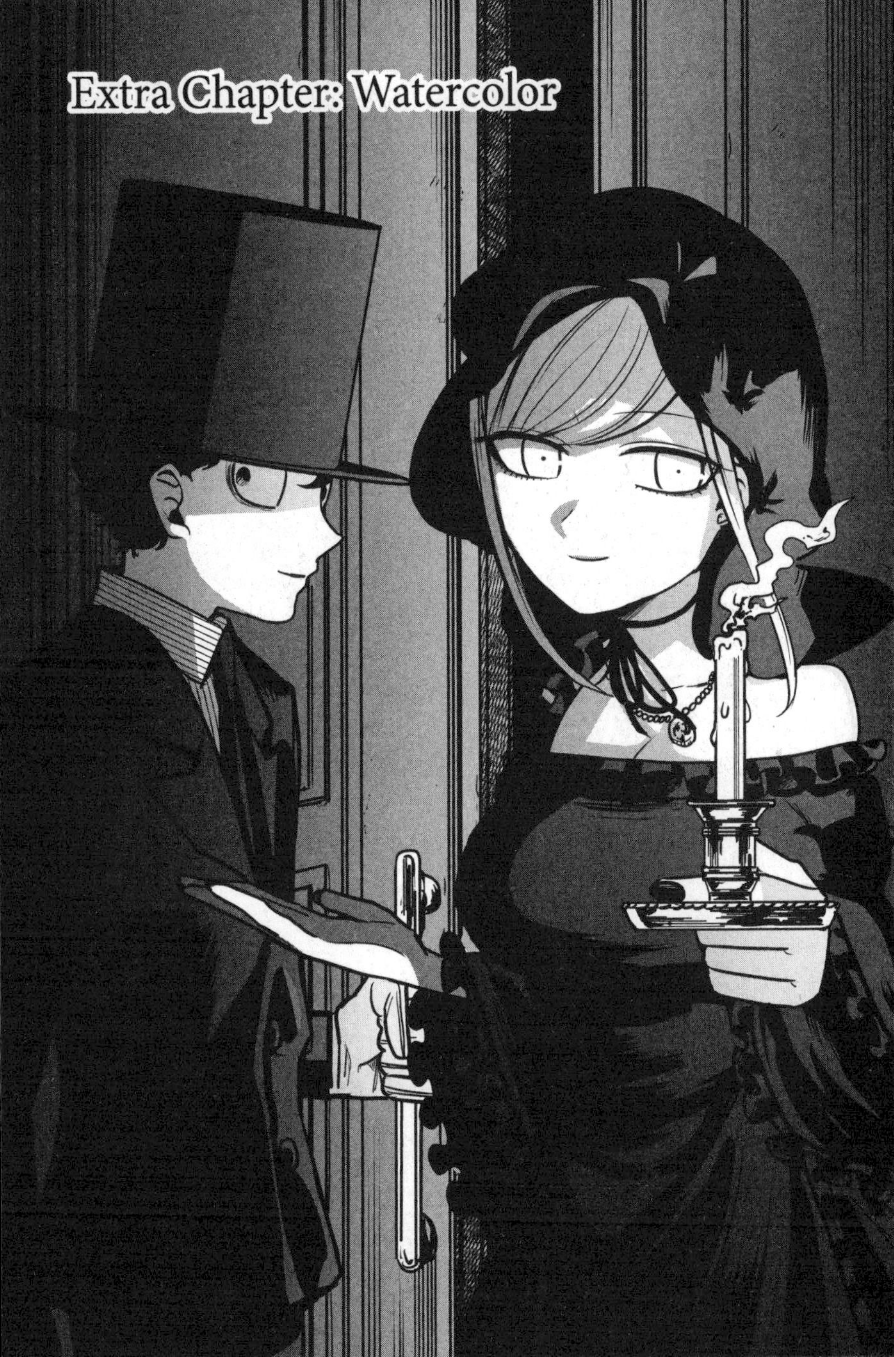

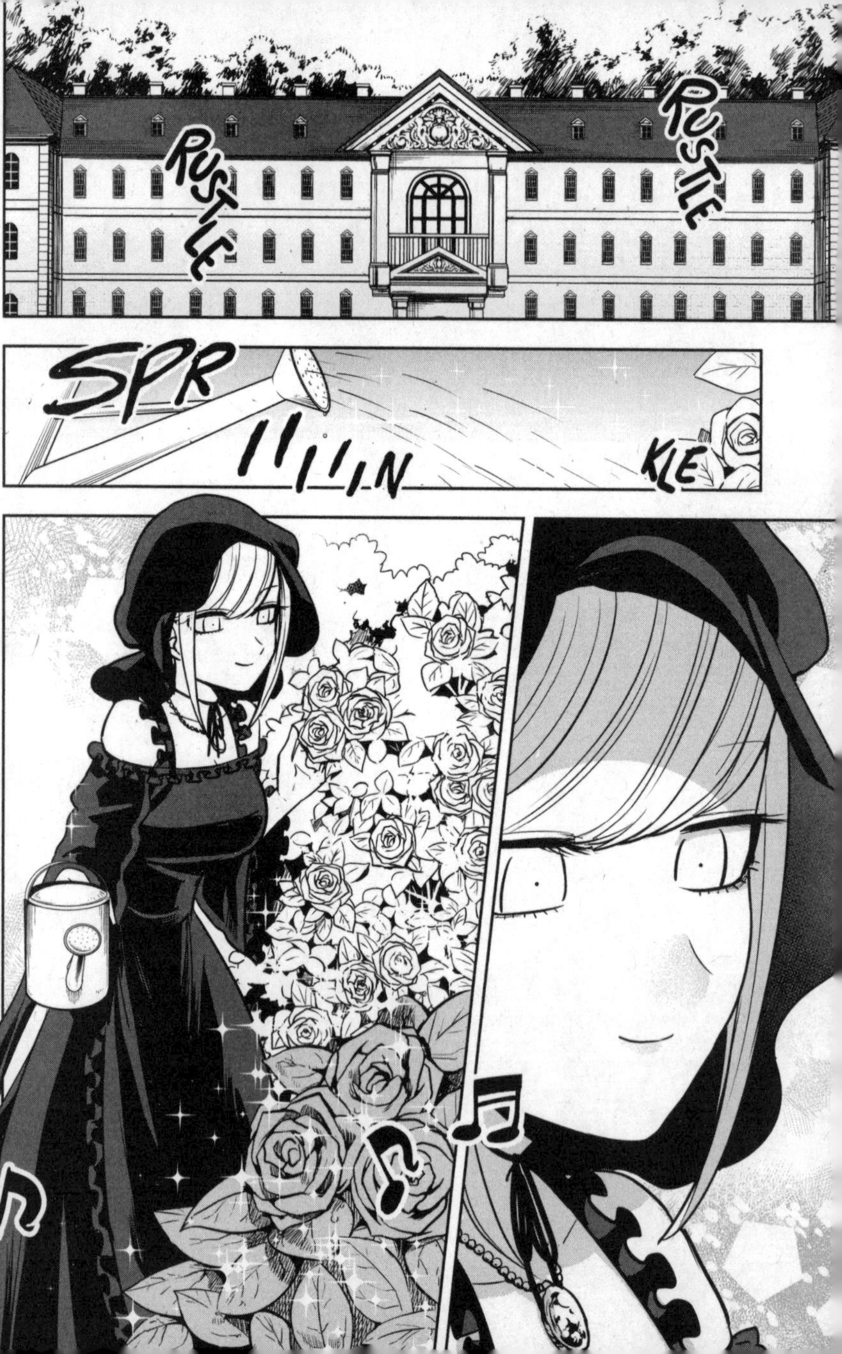
RUSTLE
RUSTLE
SPR
IIIIN
KLE

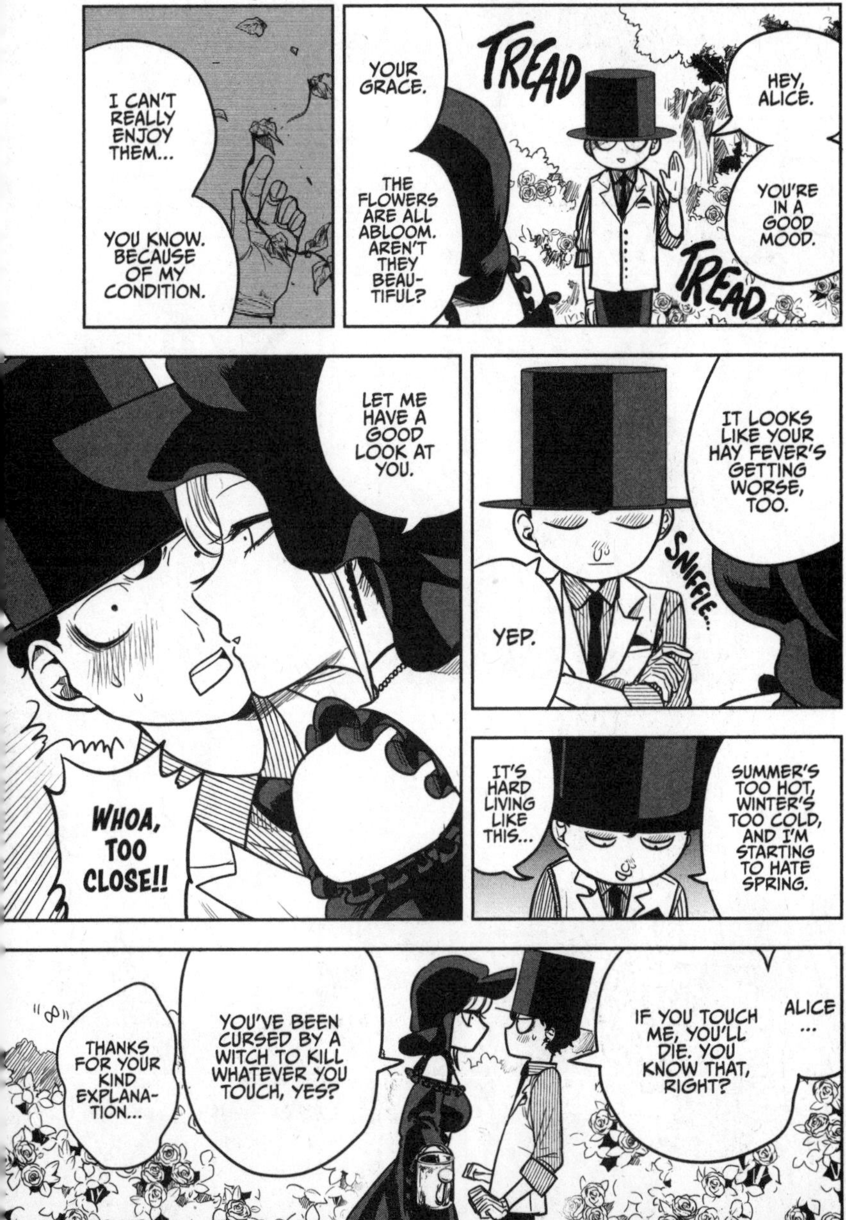
HEY, ALICE.
YOU'RE IN A GOOD MOOD.
TREAD
TREAD
YOUR GRACE.
THE FLOWERS ARE ALL ABLOOM. AREN'T THEY BEAUTIFUL?
I CAN'T REALLY ENJOY THEM...
YOU KNOW. BECAUSE OF MY CONDITION.
IT LOOKS LIKE YOUR HAY FEVER'S GETTING WORSE, TOO.
SNIFFLE...
YEP.
SUMMER'S TOO HOT, WINTER'S TOO COLD, AND I'M STARTING TO HATE SPRING.
IT'S HARD LIVING LIKE THIS...
LET ME HAVE A GOOD LOOK AT YOU.
WHOA, TOO CLOSE!!
ALICE...
IF YOU TOUCH ME, YOU'LL DIE. YOU KNOW THAT, RIGHT?
YOU'VE BEEN CURSED BY A WITCH TO KILL WHATEVER YOU TOUCH, YES?
THANKS FOR YOUR KIND EXPLANATION...

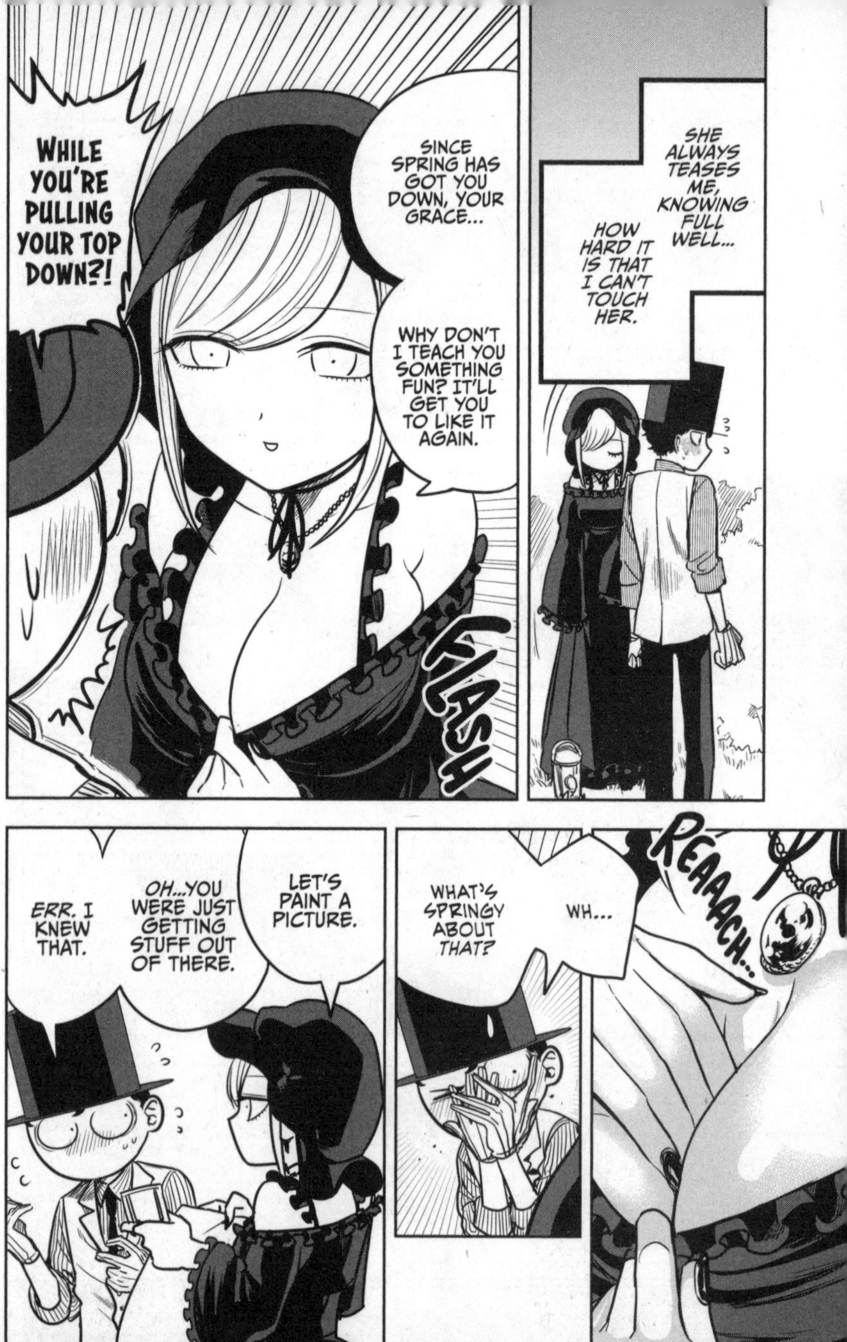
SHE ALWAYS TEASES ME, KNOWING FULL WELL...
HOW HARD IT IS THAT I CAN'T TOUCH HER.
SINCE SPRING HAS GOT YOU DOWN, YOUR GRACE...
WHY DON'T I TEACH YOU SOMETHING FUN? IT'LL GET YOU TO LIKE IT AGAIN.
FLASH
WHILE YOU'RE PULLING YOUR TOP DOWN?!
REAAAACH...
WH...
WHAT'S SPRINGY ABOUT *THAT?*
LET'S PAINT A PICTURE.
OH...YOU WERE JUST GETTING STUFF OUT OF THERE.
ERR. I KNEW THAT.

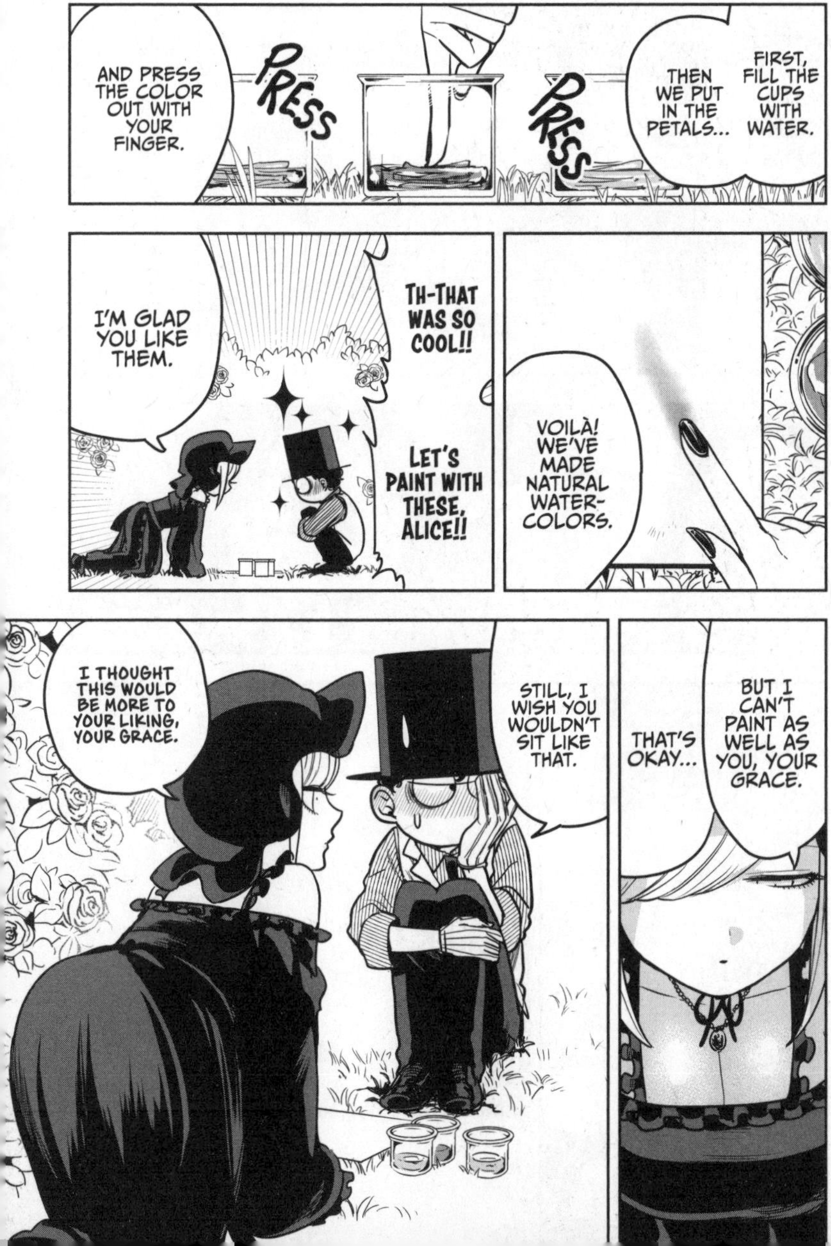
FIRST, FILL THE CUPS WITH WATER.
THEN WE PUT IN THE PETALS...
PRESS
PRESS
AND PRESS THE COLOR OUT WITH YOUR FINGER.
VOILÀ! WE'VE MADE NATURAL WATER-COLORS.
TH-THAT WAS SO COOL!!
LET'S PAINT WITH THESE, ALICE!!
I'M GLAD YOU LIKE THEM.
BUT I CAN'T PAINT AS WELL AS YOU, YOUR GRACE.
THAT'S OKAY...
STILL, I WISH YOU WOULDN'T SIT LIKE THAT.
I THOUGHT THIS WOULD BE MORE TO YOUR LIKING, YOUR GRACE.

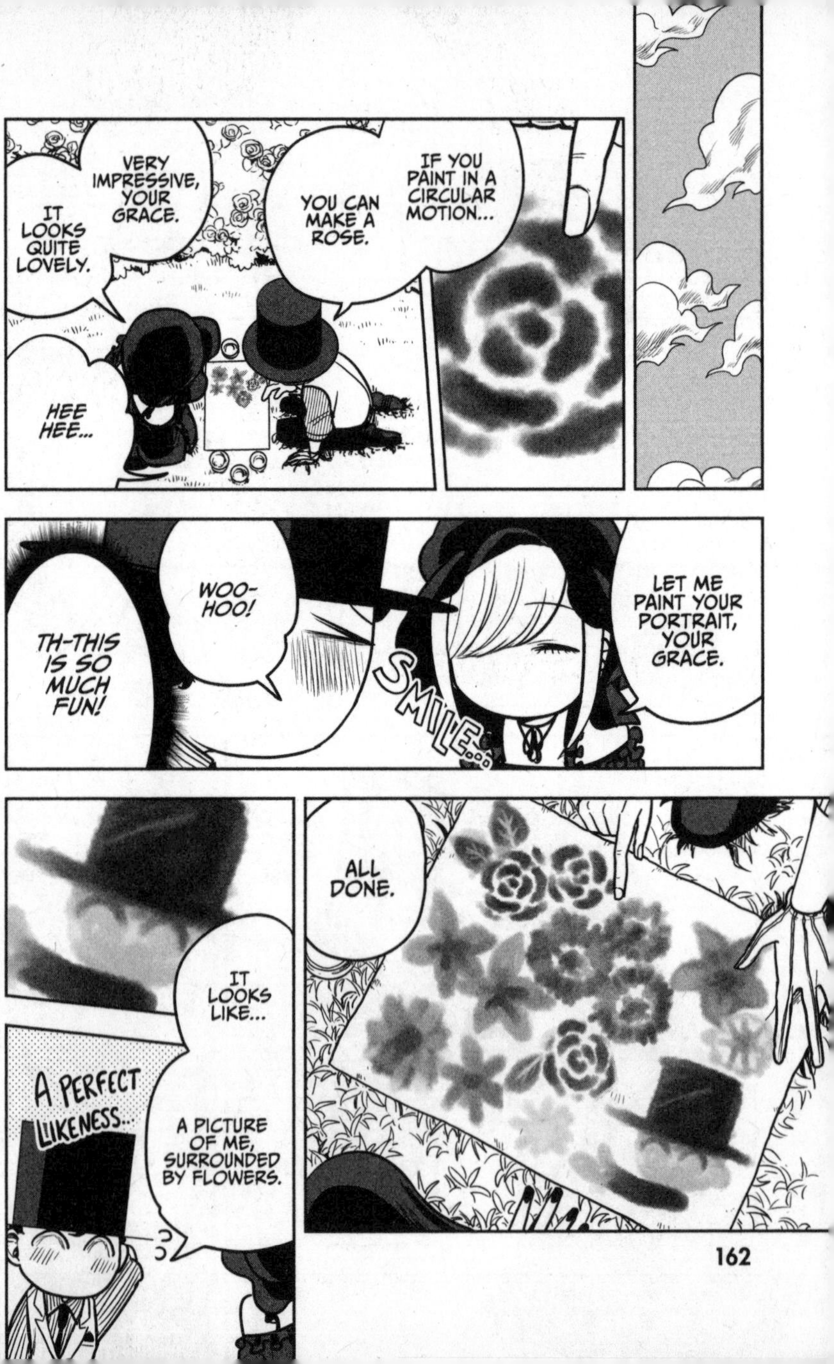
IF YOU PAINT IN A CIRCULAR MOTION...
YOU CAN MAKE A ROSE.
VERY IMPRESSIVE, YOUR GRACE.
IT LOOKS QUITE LOVELY.
HEE HEE...
LET ME PAINT YOUR PORTRAIT, YOUR GRACE.
SMILE...
WOO-HOO!
TH-THIS IS SO MUCH FUN!
ALL DONE.
IT LOOKS LIKE...
A PICTURE OF ME, SURROUNDED BY FLOWERS.
A PERFECT LIKENESS...

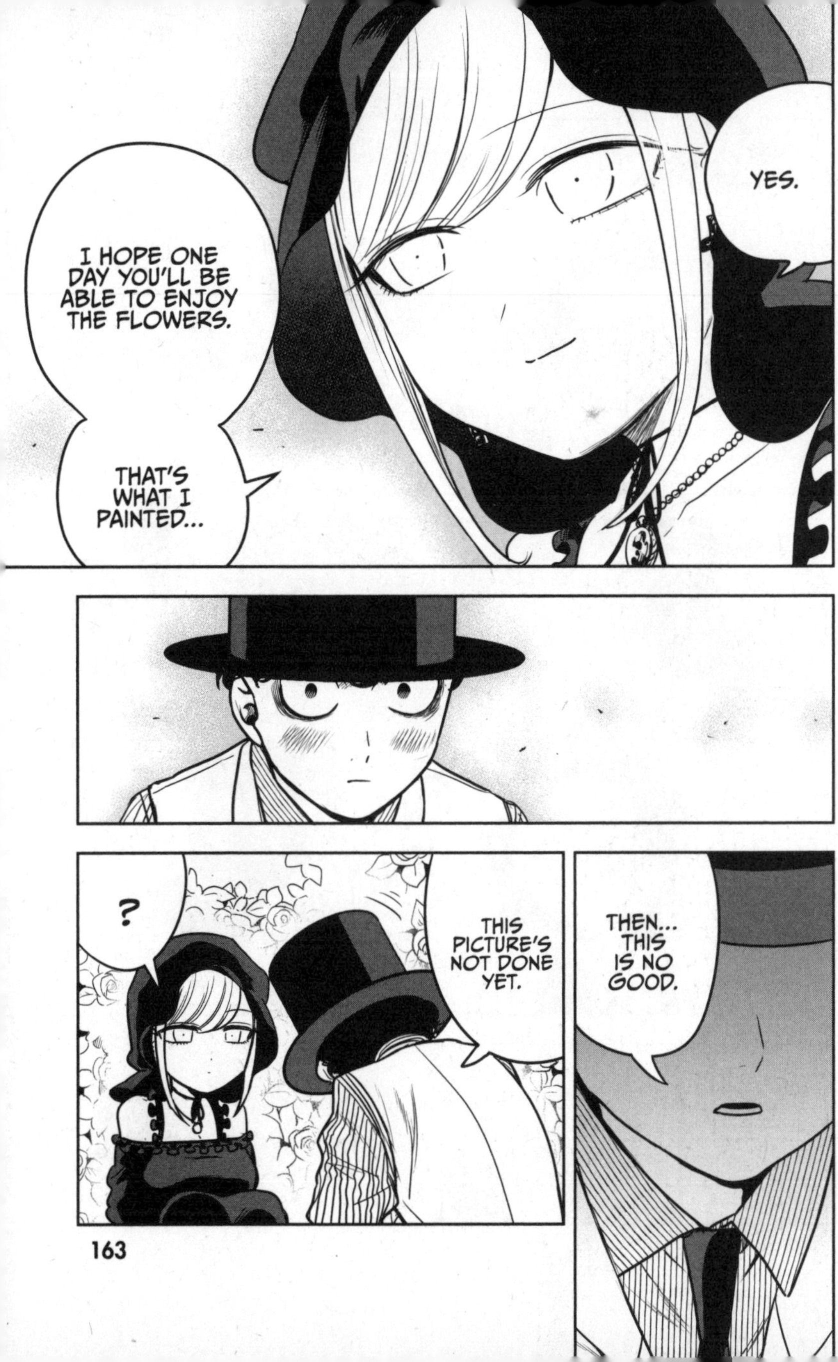
YES.
I HOPE ONE DAY YOU'LL BE ABLE TO ENJOY THE FLOWERS.
THAT'S WHAT I PAINTED...
THEN... THIS IS NO GOOD.
THIS PICTURE'S NOT DONE YET.
?

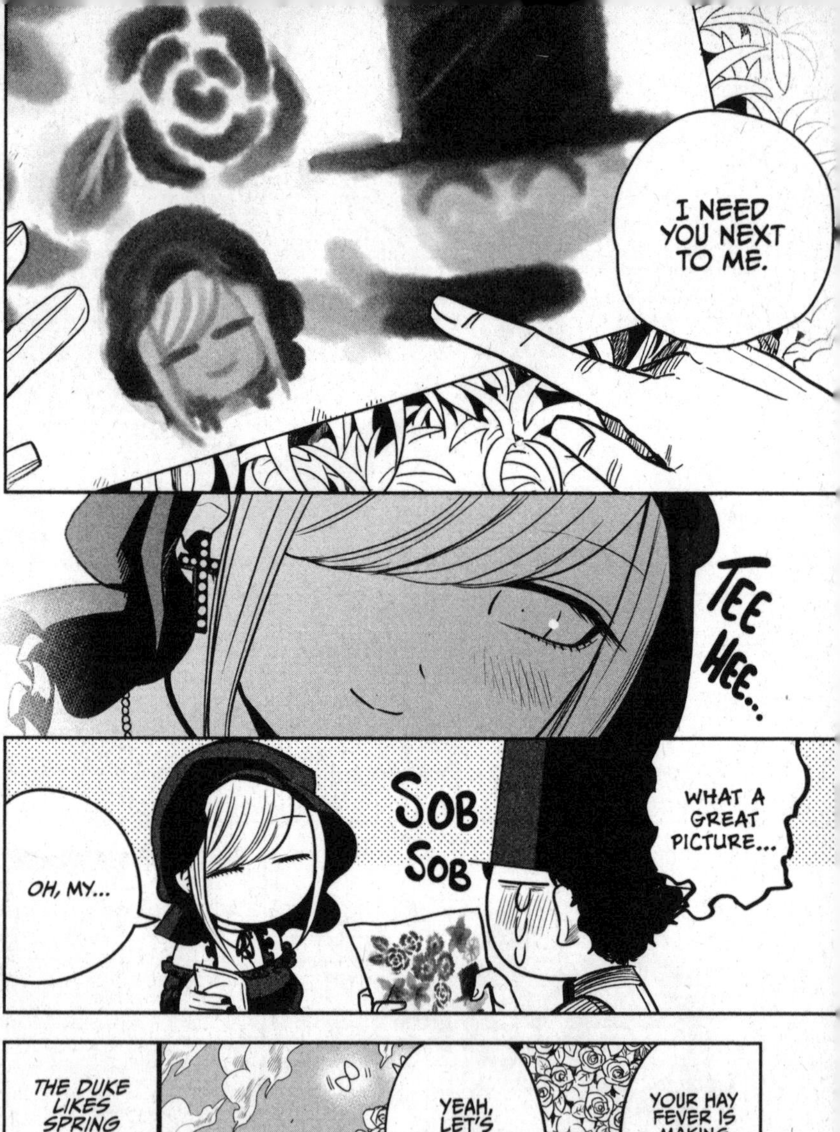
I NEED YOU NEXT TO ME.
TEE HEE...
WHAT A GREAT PICTURE...
SOB SOB
OH, MY...
YOUR HAY FEVER IS MAKING YOUR EYES WATER.
YEAH, LET'S GO WITH THAT...
THE DUKE LIKES SPRING A LITTLE MORE NOW.

THE DUKE OF DEATH AND HIS MAID

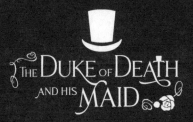

The Duke of Death and His Maid

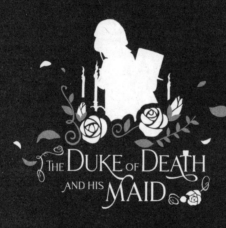

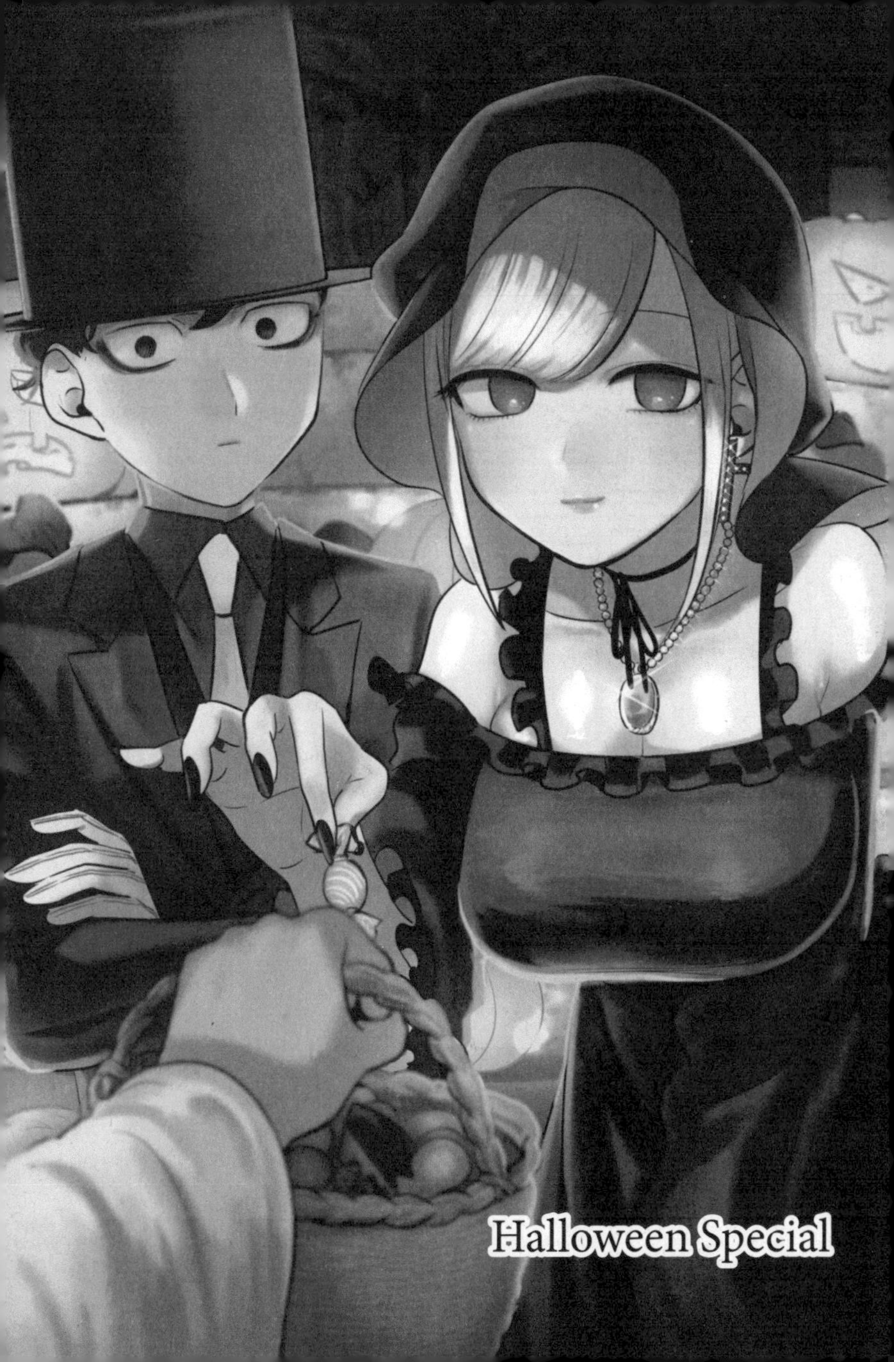
Halloween Special

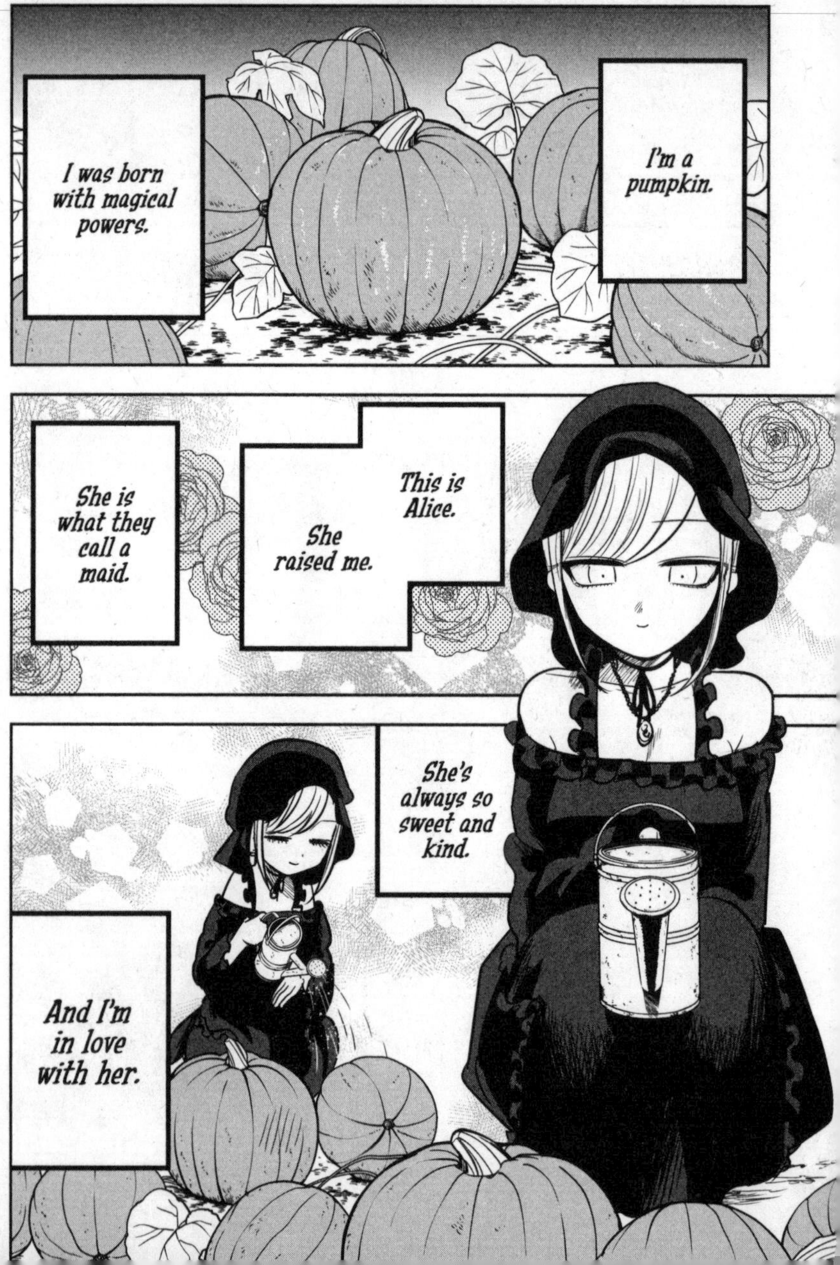
I'm a pumpkin.
I was born with magical powers.
This is Alice.
She raised me.
She is what they call a maid.
She's always so sweet and kind.
And I'm in love with her.

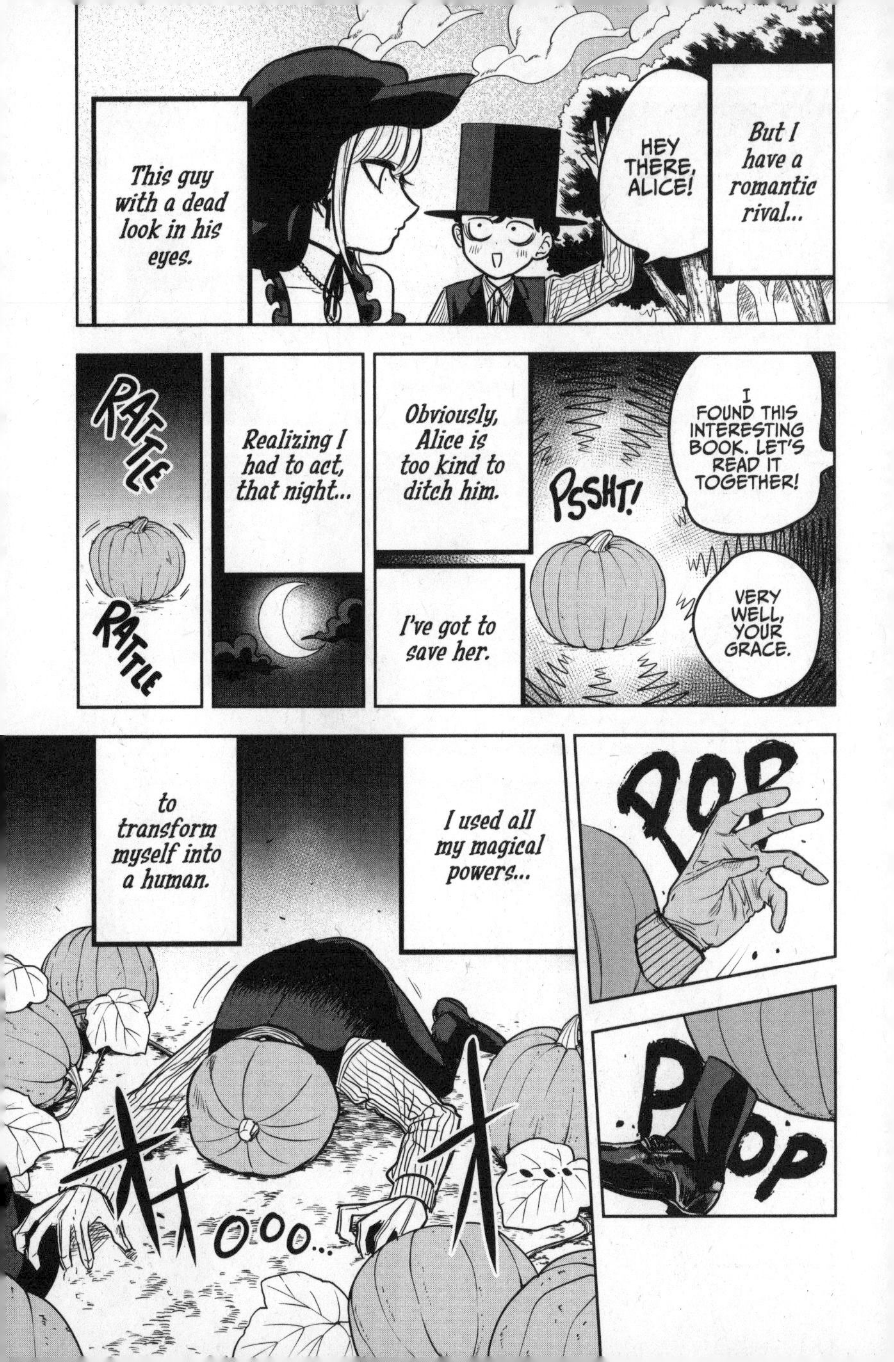
But I have a romantic rival...
HEY THERE, ALICE!
This guy with a dead look in his eyes.
I FOUND THIS INTERESTING BOOK. LET'S READ IT TOGETHER!
PSSHT!
VERY WELL, YOUR GRACE.
Obviously, Alice is too kind to ditch him.
I've got to save her.
Realizing I had to act, that night...
RATTLE
RATTLE
POP
POP
I used all my magical powers...
to transform myself into a human.
OOO...

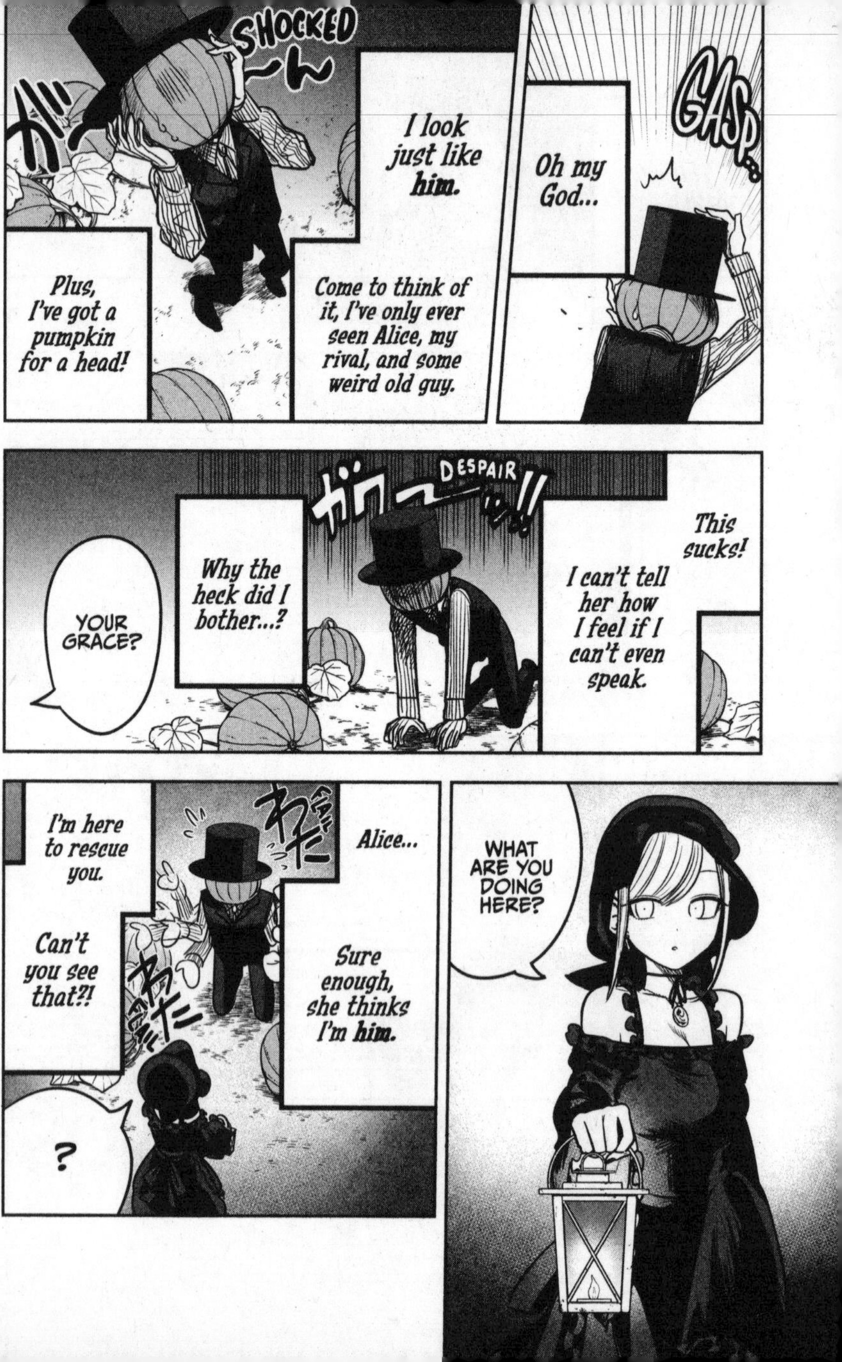
GASP...
Oh my God...
I look just like him.
Come to think of it, I've only ever seen Alice, my rival, and some weird old guy.
SHOCKED
Plus, I've got a pumpkin for a head!
This sucks!
I can't tell her how I feel if I can't even speak.
DESPAIR
Why the heck did I bother...?
YOUR GRACE?
WHAT ARE YOU DOING HERE?
Alice...
Sure enough, she thinks I'm him.
I'm here to rescue you.
Can't you see that?!
?

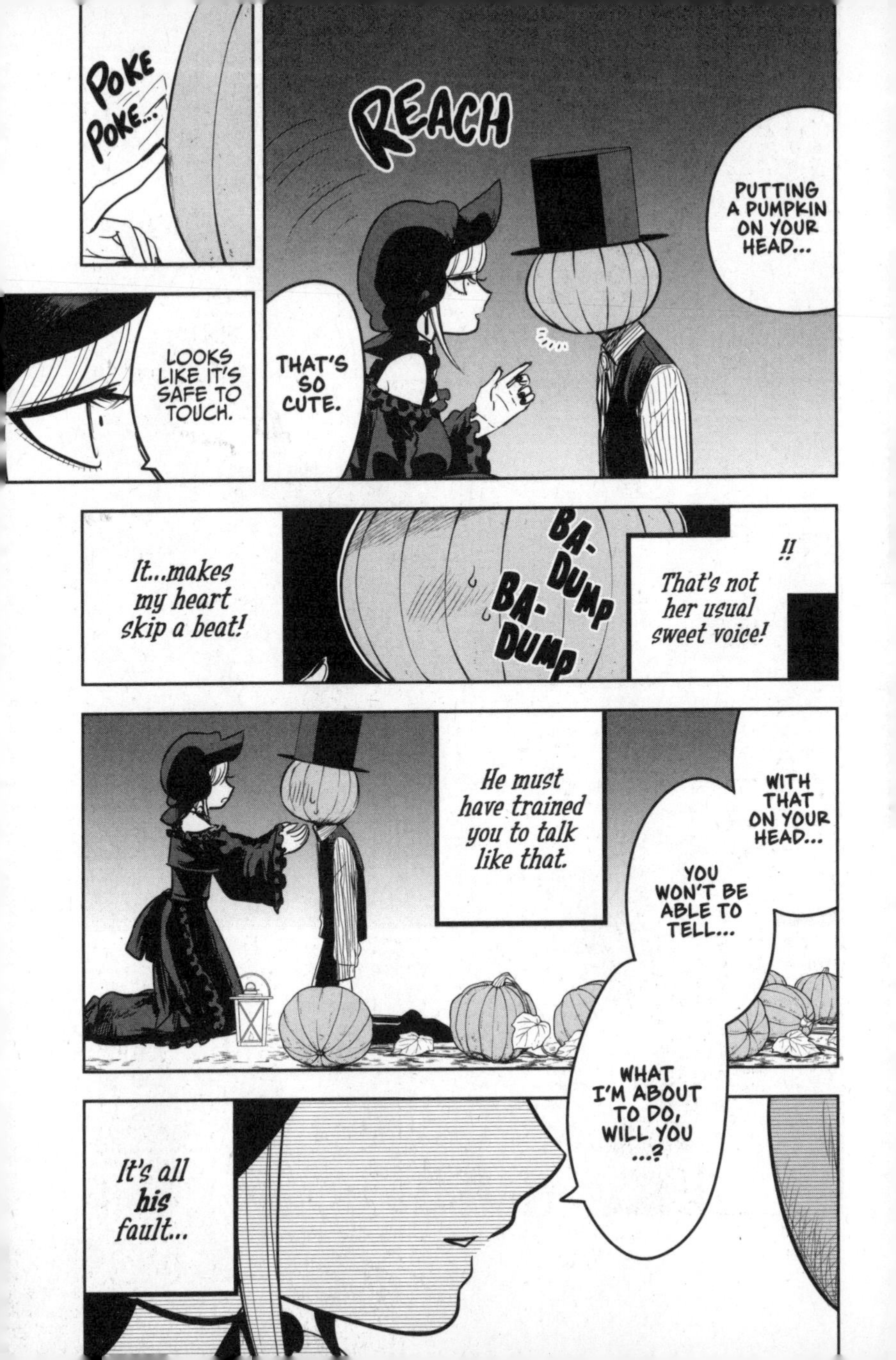
REACH
PUTTING A PUMPKIN ON YOUR HEAD...
THAT'S SO CUTE.
POKE POKE...
LOOKS LIKE IT'S SAFE TO TOUCH.
!!
That's not her usual sweet voice!
BA-DUMP BA-DUMP
It...makes my heart skip a beat!
WITH THAT ON YOUR HEAD...
YOU WON'T BE ABLE TO TELL...
WHAT I'M ABOUT TO DO, WILL YOU ...?
He must have trained you to talk like that.
It's all **his** fault...

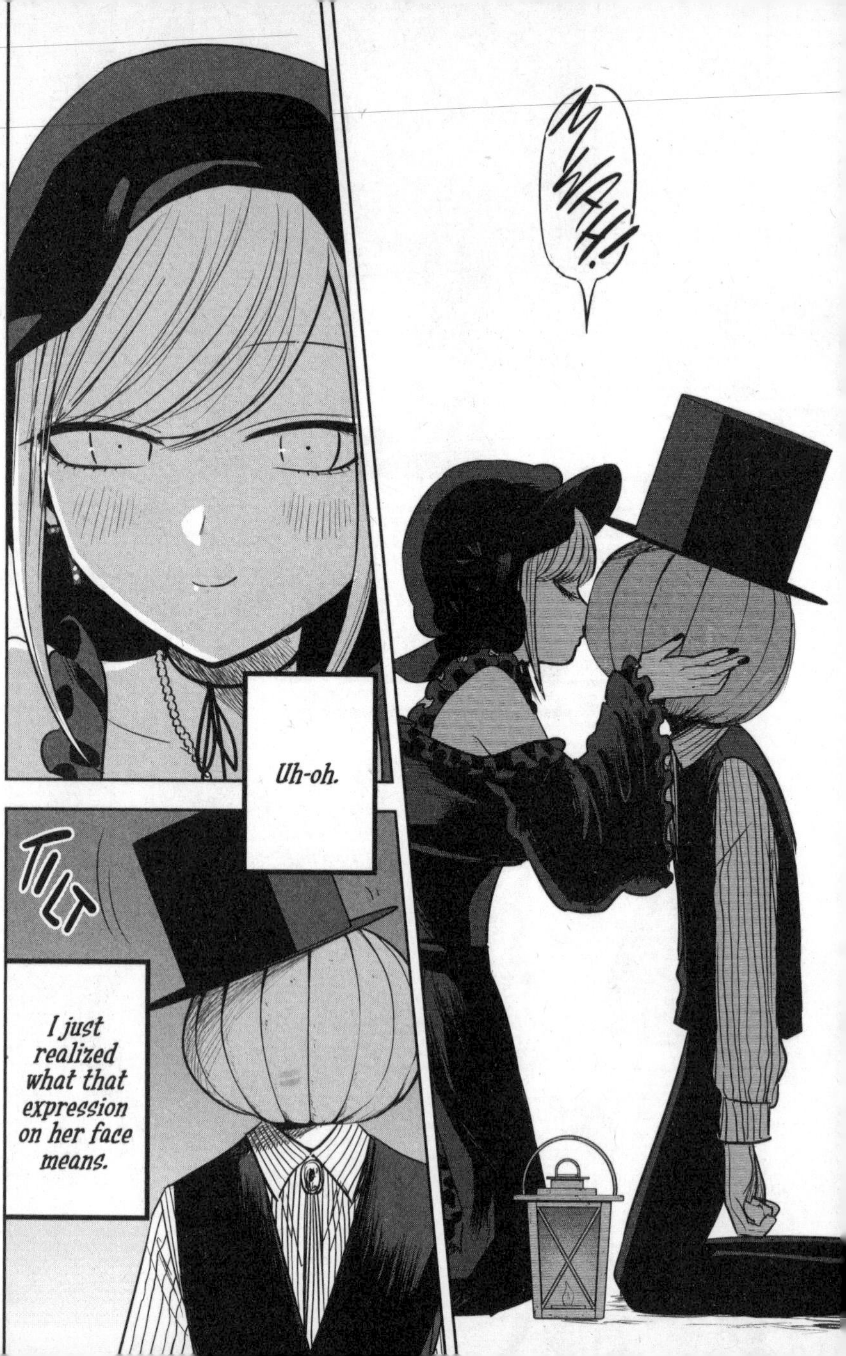
MWAH!
Uh-oh.
TILT
I just realized what that expression on her face means.

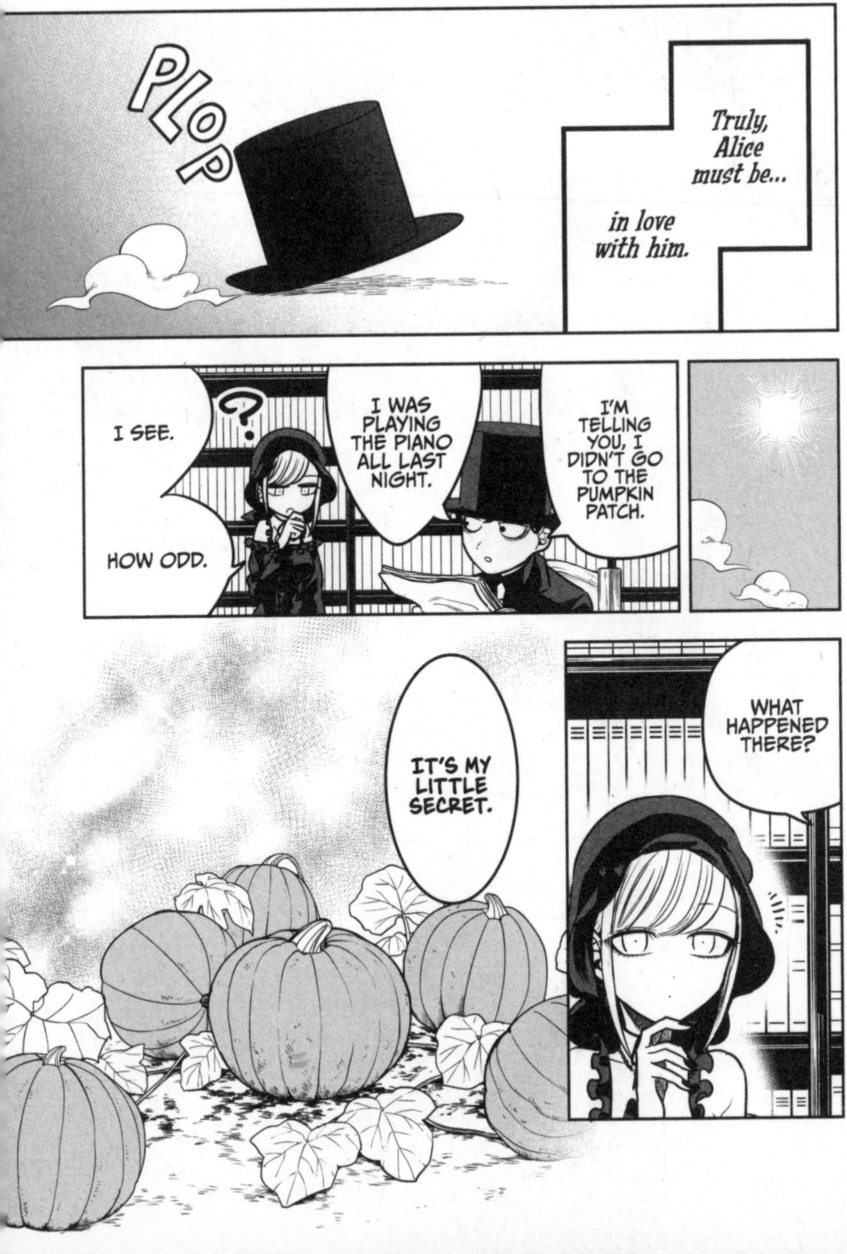
Truly, Alice must be...
in love with him.
PLOP
I'M TELLING YOU, I DIDN'T GO TO THE PUMPKIN PATCH.
I WAS PLAYING THE PIANO ALL LAST NIGHT.
I SEE.
HOW ODD.
WHAT HAPPENED THERE?
IT'S MY LITTLE SECRET.

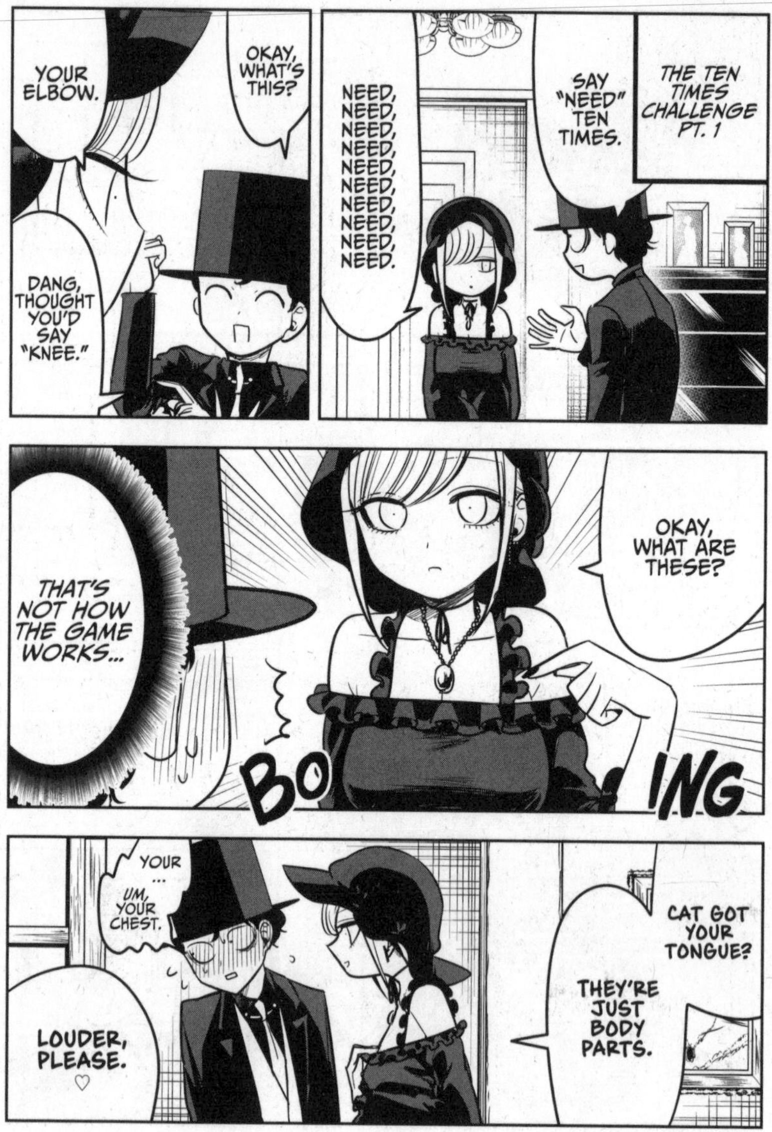
THE TEN TIMES CHALLENGE PT. 1
SAY "NEED" TEN TIMES.
NEED, NEED, NEED, NEED, NEED, NEED, NEED, NEED, NEED, NEED.
OKAY, WHAT'S THIS?
YOUR ELBOW.
DANG, THOUGHT YOU'D SAY "KNEE."
OKAY, WHAT ARE THESE?
THAT'S NOT HOW THE GAME WORKS...
BO ING
CAT GOT YOUR TONGUE?
THEY'RE JUST BODY PARTS.
YOUR ... UM, YOUR CHEST.
LOUDER, PLEASE. ♡

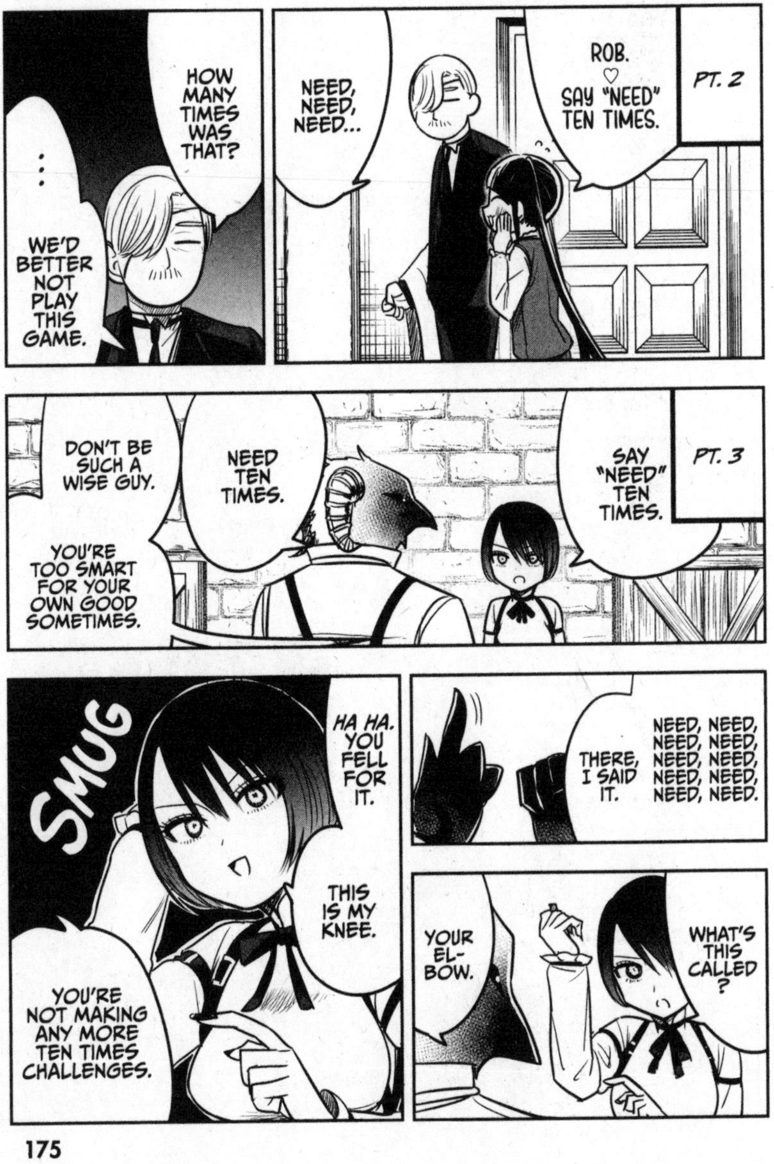
PT. 2
ROB. ♡ SAY "NEED" TEN TIMES.
NEED, NEED, NEED...
HOW MANY TIMES WAS THAT?
...
WE'D BETTER NOT PLAY THIS GAME.
PT. 3
SAY "NEED" TEN TIMES.
NEED TEN TIMES.
DON'T BE SUCH A WISE GUY.
YOU'RE TOO SMART FOR YOUR OWN GOOD SOMETIMES.
NEED, NEED, NEED, NEED, NEED, NEED, NEED, NEED, NEED, NEED.
THERE, I SAID IT.
WHAT'S THIS CALLED?
YOUR EL-BOW.
HA HA. YOU FELL FOR IT.
SMUG
THIS IS MY KNEE.
YOU'RE NOT MAKING ANY MORE TEN TIMES CHALLENGES.

THE DUKE OF DEATH AND HIS MAID

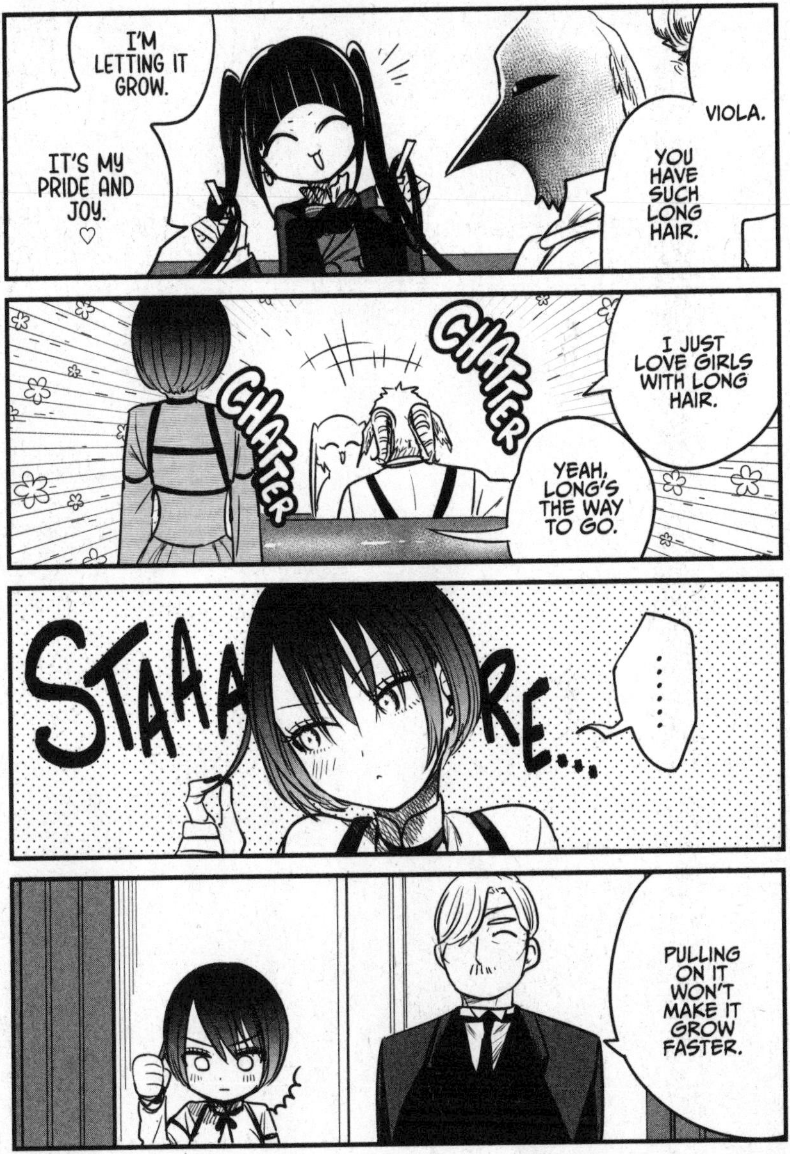

VIOLA.
YOU HAVE SUCH LONG HAIR.
I'M LETTING IT GROW.
IT'S MY PRIDE AND JOY. ♡
I JUST LOVE GIRLS WITH LONG HAIR.
CHATTER
YEAH, LONG'S THE WAY TO GO.
CHATTER
......
STAAARE...
PULLING ON IT WON'T MAKE IT GROW FASTER.

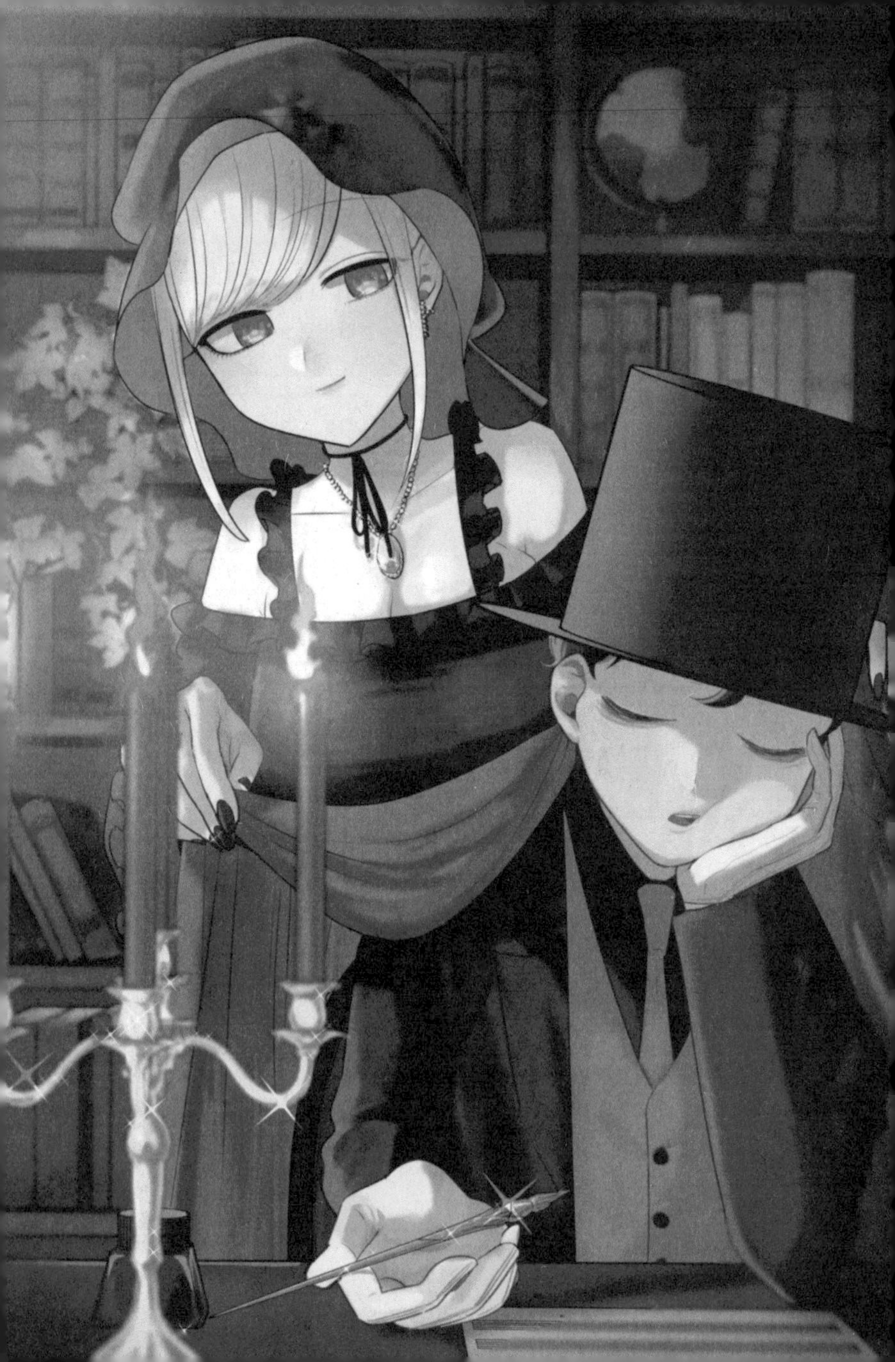

INOUE

I can curl my pinky finger
to the point where I can touch
my wrist with it. That's my
silly little party trick.

THE DUKE OF DEATH
AND HIS MAID

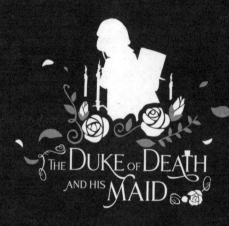

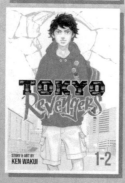

SEVEN SEAS ENTERTAINMENT PRESENTS

THE DUKE OF DEATH AND HIS MAID

story and art by INOUE   VOLUME 4

TRANSLATION
Josh Cole

ADAPTATION
Matthew Birkenhauer

LETTERING
Aila Nagamine

ORIGINAL COVER DESIGN
Yasuo Shimura (siesta)

COVER DESIGN
H. Qi

COPY EDITOR
B. Lillian Martin

EDITOR
Abby Lehrke

PRODUCTION DESIGNER
Christina McKenzie

PRODUCTION MANAGER
Lissa Pattillo

PREPRESS TECHNICIAN
Melanie Ujimori
Jules Valera

EDITOR-IN-CHIEF
Julie Davis

ASSOCIATE PUBLISHER
Adam Arnold

PUBLISHER
Jason DeAngelis

SHINIGAMI BOCCHAN TO KURO MAID Vol. 4
by INOUE
© 2018 INOUE
All rights reserved.
Original Japanese edition published by SHOGAKUKAN.
English translation rights in the United States of America, Canada, the United
Kingdom, Ireland, Australia and New Zealand arranged with SHOGAKUKAN through
Tuttle-Mori Agency, Inc.

Seven Seas press and purchase enquiries can be sent to Marketing Manager Lianne
Sentar at press@gomanga.com. Information regarding the distribution and purchase of
digital editions is available from Digital Manager CK Russell at digital@gomanga.com.

Seven Seas and the Seven Seas logo are trademarks of
Seven Seas Entertainment. All rights reserved.

ISBN: 978-1-63858-843-6
Printed in Canada
First Printing: December 2022
10 9 8 7 6 5 4 3 2 1

READING DIRECTIONS

This book reads from *right to left*,
Japanese style. If this is your first time
reading manga, you start reading from
the top right panel on each page and
take it from there. If you get lost, just
follow the numbered diagram here.
It may seem backwards at first,
but you'll get the hang of it! Have fun!!

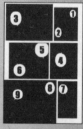

Follow us online: www.SevenSeasEntertainment.com